"When Fuller Seminary decided to launch out in our own uncharted terrain, we called on Tod Bolsinger to join our leadership team. When you read *Canoeing the Mountains*, you'll immediately understand why. Bolsinger brings a scholar's mind, a pastor's heart and a wealth of leadership and consulting experience to the task. His ability to translate the most important organizational leadership material into the day-to-day challenges of the Christian leader is without peer. His vulnerability and authenticity resonate as he shares his own leadership learning journey. This is the leadership book the church needs today."
Mark Labberton, president, Fuller Theological Seminary

"There are many books that tell us we need to change, and there are also many books that give a vision of what a new kind of church could look like. There are very few that address the difficult task of helping leaders navigate the complexities of leading that is necessary for a changing world. Tod Bolsinger's *Canoeing the Mountains* provides the right mixture of theological insight, leadership theory and relevant stories that will give the necessary principles to help leaders face unfamiliar terrain."
Dana S. Allin, synod executive, ECO: A Covenant Order of Evangelical Presbyterians

"Do not canoe another stroke or portage another step without *Canoeing the Mountains* in hand. In today's post-Christian world, we are navigating uncharted waters where our churches demand innovation at every turn. How do we lead for transformation when the world is transforming even faster? For anyone committed to and dazed by the changing realities of today's church, Tod Bolsinger offers a needed vision."
Meritt Lohr Sawyer, executive director, Paul Carlson Partnership, Evangelical Covenant Church

"How does the pastor trained in the twentieth century connect the Word of God to the society of the twenty-first century in the face of the dramatic societal changes of the last few decades? Tod Bolsinger brilliantly creates tools for the pastor who works in these uncharted areas. . . . This is an important new resource. Every pastor and leader should read it carefully."
Albert Erisman, executive in residence, Seattle Pacific University, author of *The Accidental Executive*

"While there are many books about adaptive change, the process takes years to grasp and understand. Tod's retelling of the story of Lewis and Clark provides concrete stepping stones to a fluid journey and repackages these concepts in a way that is digestible, inspiring and thought provoking. I will use this book with my own congregation as we continue to canoe the mountains of adaptive change."
Theresa Cho, copastor of St. John's Presbyterian Church, San Francisco

"We read headlines every month about some established company confronted with extinction. They were unprepared to adapt and climb. The lessons in Tod's book may be based in history but are so timely and relevant for today. Facing unpredictable and confounding unknowns defines this era of leadership. Tod's book is one I am recommending to my clients. It's a map for navigating the future that I have made part of my practice."
Rex Miller, author, futurist, principal for mindSHIFT

"Tod Bolsinger provides powerful frameworks and tools that will inspire and empower twenty-first century pastors and church leaders to maximize their impact on their congregations and in the world."
Andy Chan, vice president, innovation and career development, Wake Forest University

"In a most winsome and engaging way, Tod Bolsinger weaves together the best of current leadership research—adaptive change, systems theory, organizational transformation—with the real-life challenges of a pastor/practitioner who has spent years trying to put all this together in a congregation while still preaching Sunday by Sunday and doing funerals on Monday. . . . This is a book that you simply must read!"
Jim Singleton, associate professor of pastoral leadership and evangelism, Gordon-Conwell Theological Seminary

"Combining the mind of a scholar, the heart of a pastor and the experience of a consultant, Tod Bolsinger is the rare leader who can also teach. . . . *Canoeing the Mountains* should be required reading in seminary classrooms and leadership seminars. I know it will be for the pastors and leaders we coach."
Kevin Graham Ford, principal of TAG Consulting, author of *The Secret Sauce*

"A superb book on the need for adaptive leadership in the twenty-first-century church. . . . Bolsinger offers fresh, practical advice that integrates the best of leadership theory with the realities of church leadership, illustrated with vivid metaphors and real-world examples, resulting in a seminal book on how to navigate this new world. A must-read for everyone interested in church leadership."
Uli Chi, former board chair, Regent College Board of Governors

"*Canoeing the Mountains* is a must-read for pastors and church leaders who want to understand the precarious religious landscape in America today. . . . I am going to recommend this book not only to the hundreds of pastors in the Macedonian Ministry program, but also to church leaders across the country. *Canoeing the Mountains* gave me hope for the future of the church of Jesus Christ. I pray that it will do the same for you!"
Thomas K. Tewell, executive director, Macedonian Ministry

CANOEING

THE

MOUNTAINS

CHRISTIAN LEADERSHIP
IN UNCHARTED TERRITORY

TOD BOLSINGER

NOW WITH STUDY GUIDE

IVP Books

An imprint of InterVarsity Press
Downers Grove, Illinois

InterVarsity Press
P.O. Box 1400, Downers Grove, IL 60515-1426
ivpress.com
email@ivpress.com

InterVarsity Press® is the book-publishing division of InterVarsity Christian Fellowship/USA®, a movement of students and faculty active on campus at hundreds of universities, colleges and schools of nursing in the United States of America, and a member movement of the International Fellowship of Evangelical Students. For information about local and regional activities, visit intervarsity.org.

Published in association with Creative Trust Literary Group, 210 Jamestown Park, Suite 200, Brentwood, TN 37027, www.creativetrust.com.

Scripture quotations, unless otherwise noted, are from the New Revised Standard Version of the Bible, copyright 1989 by the Division of Christian Education of the National Council of the Churches of Christ in the USA. Used by permission. All rights reserved.

Figure 11.1 is provided by James Osterhaus. Used with permission.

While any stories in this book are true, some names and identifying information may have been changed to protect the privacy of individuals.

Cover design: Cindy Kiple
Interior design: Beth McGill
Images: © marekuliasz/iStockphoto

ISBN 978-0-8308-4147-9 (hardcover)
ISBN 978-0-8308-7387-6 (digital)

Printed in the United States of America ♾

InterVarsity Press is committed to ecological stewardship and to the conservation of natural resources in all our operations. This book was printed using sustainably sourced paper.

Library of Congress Cataloging-in-Publication Data

Names: Bolsinger, Tod E., author.
Title: Canoeing the mountains : Christian leadership in uncharted territory /
  Tod Bolsinger.
Description: Expanded Edition.. | Downers Grove : InterVarsity Press, 2018. |
  Includes bibliographical references.
Identifiers: LCCN 2018018280 (print) | LCCN 2018020407 (ebook) | ISBN
  9780830899401 (eBook) | ISBN 9780830841479 (hardcover : alk. paper)
Subjects: LCSH: Christian leadership. | Change--Religious
  aspects--Christianity.
Classification: LCC BV652.1 (ebook) | LCC BV652.1 .B65 2018 (print) | DDC
  253--dc23
LC record available at https://lccn.loc.gov/2018018280

P 26 25 24 23 22 21 20 19 18 17 16 15 14 13 12 11 10 9 8 7 6 5 4 3

Y 39 38 37 36 35 34 33 32 31 30 29 28 27 26 25 24 23 22 21 20 19 18

Dedicated to Brooks and Ali.

If I ever wonder where the "Lewis and Clark" leaders of the future

will come from, I only need look across the table on a

Sunday dinner when you both come home

from your many adventures.

Contents

Part One

UNDERSTANDING

UNCHARTED TERRITORY

The World in Front of You Is Nothing
Like the World Behind You

1

Seminary Didn't
Prepare Me for This

*If western societies have become post-Christian mission fields,
how can traditional churches become then missionary churches?*

DARRELL GUDER, "THE MISSIOLOGICAL CONTEXT"

TWO PASTORS SIT AT A BAR . . .

One night after a long day of meetings, an older pastor let out a heavy sigh. He was nearing retirement, and we were working together on a project that was supposed to reorganize our entire denomination in order to help our church better minister in a changing world. And *that* changing world weighed on him. He remembered well how not that long ago life was different. He swirled his drink and said to me, "You know, when I began my ministry in a church in Alabama, I never worried about church growth or worship attendance or evangelism. Back then, *if a man didn't come to church on Sunday, his boss asked him about it at work on Monday.*"

Sociologists and theologians refer to this recently passed period as Christendom, the seventeen-hundred-year-long era with Christianity at the privileged center of Western cultural life.[1] Christendom gave us "blue laws" and the Ten Commandments in school. It gave us "under God" in the pledge of allegiance and exhortations to Bible reading in the national newspapers. (I have a copy of the *Los Angeles Times* from December 1963 that has stories on the Warren Commission, the nine-thousand-member Hollywood Presbyterian Church and a list of daily Bible readings for the upcoming week. Can you even imagine the *Los Angeles Times* exhorting people to read their Bibles today?) It was the day when every "city father" laid out the town square with the courthouse, the library and a First Church of _____ within the center of the city.

For most of us these days are long gone. (For some of us, that is good news indeed. Did you notice the reference to "man" in my friend's statement?) When cities are now considering using eminent domain laws to replace churches with tax-revenue generating big-box stores, when Sundays are more about soccer and Starbucks than about Sabbath, when Christian student groups are getting derecognized on university campuses, when the fastest growing religious affiliation among young adults is "none," when there is no moral consensus built on Christian tradition (even among Christians), when even a funeral in a conservative beach town is more likely to be a Hawaiian style "paddle out" than a gathering in a sanctuary, then Christendom as a marker of society has clearly passed.[2]

Over the last ten years I have had one church leader after another whisper to me the same frustrated confession: "Seminary didn't train me for this. I don't know if I can do it. I just don't know . . ." A number of pastors are ready to throw in the towel. Studies show that if given a chance to do something else, most pastors would jump at it. Reportedly, upwards of fifteen hundred pastors leave the ministry *every month*.[3]

A couple of years ago I learned that three of my pastor friends around the country had resigned *on the same day*. There were no affairs, no scandals and no one was renouncing faith. But three good, experienced pastors turned in resignations and walked away. One left church ministry altogether. The details are as different as the pastors themselves, but the common thread is that they finally got worn down by trying to bring change to a church that was stuck and didn't know what to do. Their churches were stuck and declining, stuck and clinging to the past, stuck and lurching to quick fixes, trying to find an easy answer for what were clearly bigger challenges. What all three churches had in common was that they were mostly blaming the pastor for how bad it felt to be so stuck.

"If only you could preach better!"

"If only you were more pastoral and caring!"

"If only our worship was more dynamic!"

"Please, pastor, *do* something!" (That is what we pay you for, isn't it?)

And to make matters worse, the *pastors* don't know what to do either. As a seminary vice president, I am now charged with confronting this reality head-on. Our graduates were not trained for this day. When I went to seminary, we were trained in the skills that were necessary for supporting faith in Christendom. When churches functioned primarily as vendors of religious services for a Christian culture, the primary leadership toolbox was

- *teaching* (for providing Christian education)
- *liturgics* (for leading Christian services)
- *pastoral care* (for offering Christian counsel and support)

In this changing world we need to add a new set of leadership tools. And this applies equally well to Christians serving in leadership beyond the parish. The challenges of a changing world come even more rapidly in business, education and nonprofit leadership. And while this book's primary audience is congregational leaders, I have added some material specifically for Christian leaders in other contexts.

This is a guidebook for learning to lead in a world we weren't prepared for. Our guides will be none other than the first American adventurers Meriwether Lewis and William Clark.

Lewis and Clark's expedition to explore the newly acquired Louisiana Purchase was built on a completely false expectation. They believed, like everyone before them, that the unexplored west was exactly the same geography as the familiar east. This is the story of what they did when they discovered that they—and everyone else before them—had been wrong. And how instructive and inspiring that story can be to us today.

Using the story of Lewis and Clark's expedition and applying the best insights from organizational leadership and missional theology, we will learn together what it means for Christians to lead when the journey goes "off the map."

We will discuss and seek faithful responses to the following questions:

- How do we lead a congregation or an organization to be faithful to the mission God has put before us when the world has changed so radically?
- What are the tools, the mental models, the wise actions and competing commitments that require navigation?

- And mostly, what transformation does it demand of those of us who have been called to lead?

From Lewis and Clark we will learn that if we can adapt and adventure, we can thrive. That while leadership in uncharted territory requires both learning and loss, once we realize that the losses won't kill us, they can teach us. And mostly, we will learn that to thrive off the map in an exciting and rapidly changing world means learning to let go, learn as we go and keep going no matter what.

As a seminary administrator, a professor of practical theology, an ordained minister, a consultant on organizational change and an executive coach for leaders, I have written this book with three purposes in mind:

1. To reframe this moment of history for Christians in the west as an opportunity put before us by God for adventure, hope and discovery—all the while embracing the anxiety, fear and potential loss that comes from answering this call.

2. To recover the calling for the church to be a truly missional movement that demands leadership that will take up the gauntlet of Guder's charge: "If western societies have become post-Christian mission fields, how can traditional churches become then missionary churches?"[4]

3. To discover—even more than the uncharted territory around us—the capacity for leadership within us.

This book is structured around five vital lessons that every leader of a Christian congregation or organization has to learn to lead in uncharted territory:

1. *Understanding uncharted territory: The world in front of you is nothing like the world behind you.* In chapter one I share my personal encounter with the disorientation that comes from a changing world and the common experience that many Christian leaders face today. In chapter two we are introduced to Lewis and Clark and the unexpected challenges they faced. In chapter three we will learn a model for leadership in uncharted territory that will orient us for the terrain ahead.

2. *The on-the-map skill set: No one is going to follow you off the map unless they trust you on the map.* Chapter four reminds us that there is plenty of work to be done—and credibility to be won—in the everyday experiences of

administrating, teaching and caring for people. Indeed, without demonstrating technical competence *on the map*, a leader will never be given the chance to lead a true expedition *off the map*. Chapter five helps us understand that even competence is not enough without the personal congruence and character of a leader. Only when a leader is deeply trusted can he or she take people further than they imagined into the mission of God. Chapter six introduces the critical issue of the leader's responsibility to shape a healthy organizational culture. Trust is not just a one-on-one relationship between a leader and follower, but the organizational air that allows a transforming adventure to be even possible.

3. *Leading off the map: In uncharted territory, adaptation is everything.* In chapters seven to eleven we get to the heart of the book and the critical leadership capacities needed in a changing world. In these chapters we integrate the very best leadership and organizational theories from people such as Ronald Heifetz, Ed Friedman, Patrick Lencioni, John Kotter and Jim Collins with the insights and values of the Scriptures and Christian theology. Chapter seven is an in-depth study of adaptive leadership, helping us understand that adaptive challenges require *learning*, facing *loss* and negotiating the *gaps* of our values and actions. Chapter eight takes us into the realm of organizational systems thinking, and gives us a clear perspective on the underlying dynamics in every family, congregation, company or organization that deeply affects our best leadership intentions. In chapter nine we learn the process of adaptive learning and leadership that enables us to find new, innovative answers to lingering and persistent challenges. Chapter ten teaches a key leadership *principle* (the mission trumps) and the central leadership *practice* for uncharted territory: start with conviction, stay calm, stay connected and stay the course. And in chapter eleven we hit the hardest patch of all: how we stay calm when navigating *loss*.

4. *Relationships and resistance: You can't go alone, but you haven't succeeded until you've survived the sabotage.* In chapters twelve and thirteen we take up the unmistakably *relational* dynamic of adaptive leadership. From Lewis and Clark's friendship and one-of-kind (and highly unorthodox!) leadership partnership we get a lens for looking at the big bias of most

discussions of leadership: the "lonely at the top" leader. In these chapters
we go beyond the usual discussions of teams and collaboration to discuss
the *six types* of relationships and the radical kind of collaboration necessary for leading in uncharted territory. Chapter thirteen reminds us that
the necessity of relationships is also the greatest peril. We will learn, in the
words of Ed Friedman, "You have not accomplished change until you have
survived the sabotage."[5]

5. *Transformation: Everybody will be changed (especially the leader).* T. S. Eliot
   wrote that the "end of our exploring" was to "arrive where we started / And
   know the place for the first time."[6] The last two chapters and epilogue
   challenge most of our assumptions about leadership, change and growth.
   Chapter fourteen reminds us that in the same way that Lewis and Clark
   would have failed—or even died—in the wilderness without the help of
   a Native American mother, we who have been trained in a Christendom
   context will never thrive as leaders as long as the majority-world voices
   around us are silenced. Learning from those who are most at home in
   uncharted territory is one of the great opportunities that most leaders
   miss. Chapter fifteen brings home the ultimate value and gift of leading
   into uncharted territory: our own ongoing transformation. The epilogue
   reminds us that in God's church, no one is left behind. The whole body of
   Christ is going on an adventure—or at least preparing the way for God's
   people to move ahead through the leadership legacy we leave behind.

And to be sure, these were lessons that I had to learn personally—and often
the hard way.

WHEN YOU DISCOVER THAT YOU ARE THE PROBLEM

At the end of our 2006–2007 fiscal year, San Clemente Presbyterian Church
(SCPC) had a $100,000 general fund *surplus*. In twenty years of church work
I had never seen anything like it. By all common measures we were doing as
well as we could hope. We were in our tenth consecutive year of growth, we
had unified around a shared vision, and we had rebuilt our entire campus. We
were starting big initiatives to serve our community, including planting a
church, starting a community resource center and starting an additional
Spanish-language service.

REORIENTATION AND NAVIGATIONAL GUIDE FOR ORGANIZATIONS

Throughout the book, you will find a series of additional pieces to help you learn how to lead in uncharted territory. *Reorientation* lessons are one- or two-sentence bullet points that help reinforce a concept. In some select chapters the Navigational Guide for Organizations will offer glimpses that expand the conversation to include voices and perspectives of Christians in leadership of companies, mission agencies, educational institutions or other endeavors.

To begin, let's summarize the five vital lessons that make up the structure of this book:

1. The world in front of you is nothing like the world behind you.
2. No one is going to follow you off the map unless they trust you on the map.
3. In uncharted territory, adaptation is everything.
4. You can't go alone, but you haven't succeeded until you've survived the sabotage.
5. Everybody will be changed (especially the leader).

And then we began to notice something. It was subtle, but there was no mistaking that it was there. Right at the moment when we were taking concrete steps to reach out to others for the sake of the gospel, the energy in the church began to wane. We became infected with a kind of malaise, a tangible diminishing of enthusiasm. As the pastor, I was confused. How could we be doing so well and yet feel like something was so wrong?

We brought in a consulting group to take a look under the hood. They led us through an evaluative process and reported back that our scores were really strong; we were among the healthiest churches they had worked with. But they also told us there were some disturbing "early warning signs" that could be traced to an unintended consequence of the past decade's *success*.

The success of a *unified* vision had given birth to an overly *centralized* institution. The very unity, discipline and alignment needed to bring the church together to rebuild the campus around our vision were now stifling creativity, passion and energy. In an entrepreneurial culture like south Orange County, we had become too corporate. And less people were interested in being part of supporting what they saw was a growing religious institution.

When our consultant, Kevin Graham Ford, laid this out before me, I grimaced.

"So what's causing this? What's at the heart of the problem? What do we need to change?" I asked.

That's when he said the word that changed my life: "You."

I felt a little queasy.

Kevin continued,

> Tod, don't get me wrong. These people love and respect you. They appreciate your preaching and they trust you. In fact, we have never had a church talk more about a senior pastor than this church talks about you. *And that is the problem.* It's not your problem, at least not yet. Nobody thinks that you are trying to build the church around you, but that is in fact what is happening. Unconsciously, the message going out is that everybody here thinks it is *their* job to support the ministry that *you* are having here. And that model of leadership is out of date. It's a model from the past that is unsustainable in a changing world, and is slowly sapping the passion from the church.

Kevin gave me three hard options: (1) do nothing and trust that the church would bounce back, (2) resign and let the church have a new leader, or (3) I could *learn to lead differently.*

I chose option 3. I loved my church and wanted to remain their pastor, and yet I knew something needed to change. Relearning how to lead wasn't easy. And even now in my role with Fuller Seminary, I have been relearning what it means to lead ever since.

REORIENTATION

Christian Leaders: You were trained for a world that is disappearing.

My story is not unique. For the past decade I have consulted with leaders in a wide variety of contexts: once great urban churches who are now close to closing their doors, small-town congregations who are becoming older and smaller, growing immigrant congregations who are struggling with growing pains, denominational leaders facing one rapid-fire crisis after another, nonprofit boards struggling to stay afloat and find new funding, seminary leaders facing questions about whether they are even relevant anymore.

What we all have in common is that our old strategies no longer work.

LEADERSHIP FOR A CHANGING WORLD

Today's leaders are facing complex challenges that have no clear-cut solutions. These challenges are more systemic in nature and require broad, widespread learning. They can't be solved through a conference, a video series or a program. Even more complicated, these problems are very often the result of yesterday's *solutions*. They are what Ronald Heifetz calls "adaptive challenges."[7]

Adaptive challenges are the true tests of leadership. They are challenges that go beyond the technical solutions of resident experts or best practices, or even the organization's current knowledge. They arise when the world around us has changed but we continue to live on the successes of the past. They are challenges that cannot be solved through compromise or win-win scenarios, or by adding another ministry or staff person to the team. They demand that leaders make hard choices about what to preserve and to let go. They are challenges that require people to learn and to *change*, that require leaders to experience and navigate profound *loss*.

Today, I consult, coach and am on the senior leadership of a seminary dedicated to forming leaders for this changing world. But for me it all began almost ten years ago with understanding that *for our church mission to win I had to lose*. The changing world around us and even the success we had experienced had brought us to a new place where we would need a new strategy. To paraphrase Marshall Goldsmith, "What got us *here* wouldn't take us *there*."[8] So, I had to lose some of my status, power and control. I had to lose "say" over certain aspects of the mission, and mostly I had to lose my identity as the resident expert and *learn to lead all over again*.

WHAT IS LEADERSHIP, REALLY?

Let's begin by clarifying what leadership is and is not. Leadership is not *authority*. It is not the title or position that a person holds. Leadership is different from management. Leadership is not running good meetings, keeping good books, overseeing good programs and making good policies (as important as

NAVIGATIONAL GUIDE FOR ORGANIZATIONS
Disruption and Discipleship

"Because we are Christians in business and not a 'Christian business,' we need more discipleship, not less, to lead in business." The speaker was the young CEO of a Silicon Valley startup that had just received its first major funding because of his "disruptive technology." As he considered how his little idea was quickly growing into a company larger than he could imagine, he shared with a group of leaders at a dinner how he was looking for resources, relationships and mostly a lot more wisdom.

Business leaders know about disruption. Indeed, often in business the more disruptive a business plan or innovation, the more it is cherished. But because a Christian views the marketplace as a mission field in need of Christian example, witness and stewardship to reveal God's working in the world, Christians in disruptive marketplace sectors need as much discernment and discipleship as a commitment to innovation. Education, publishing, fundraising, investment banking, technology, even nonprofit or nongovernmental organizations are all marketplace sectors facing dramatic disruption.

Because the stakes of leadership are experienced tangibly and economically on a daily basis, there is an ever-present temptation to return to a sacred-secular split that separates the moral and spiritual of Sunday morning from the rough and tumble of Monday to Friday. For a Christian this is not merely a hypocritical practice but heretical thinking. The teachings of Jesus—the Lord of all—are the measure of both morals and the marketplace, both worship and the world.

The growing faith-and-work movement points to the reality that marketplace leadership requires wisdom to discern not only right from wrong but also prudent from folly, prescient from rash. For a Christian in the marketplace not only does one's company depend on the ability to respond to a changing world, but so do the livelihoods of one's employees and stockholders. In addition, Christians in the marketplace often need to make moral decisions about a technology or business practice when there is no previous experience. They must weigh the possibilities for economic growth for the company with the risks to the company or how it might affect the common good.

This discernment requires ongoing discipleship. Christians who provide leadership to businesses need just as much spiritual and biblical understanding of the priorities of the kingdom of God as they do the economics of market forces. Christians offering leadership in the marketplace, higher education, nonprofits or other sectors have to keep growing in our faith as much as we need to grow professionally. We can't lead a Christian business and organization to further the mission of Jesus (seven days a week!) unless the Christian servant-leaders become more like Jesus (every day)!

those are!). Management is a kind of stewardship. Management cares for what *is*. Leadership is focused on what *can be or what must be*. Management is about keeping promises to a constituency; leadership is about an organization fulfilling its mission and realizing its *reason for being*. To that end, let me offer three leadership principles that shape my work in leadership development (mostly in church and nonprofit circles).

1. Leadership is essential. In this book *leadership* doesn't mean titles or authority. (Both are helpful but *not* essential to leadership.) Leadership is not measured by corner offices with heavy furniture, higher salaries or august job descriptions. To be authorized or to have a title does not equate to leadership. Leadership is *a way of being* in an organization, family, team, company, church, business, nation (or any other system) that, in the words of Ronald Heifetz, "[mobilizes] people to tackle tough challenges and thrive."[9]

Therefore, *leadership is always about personal and corporate transformation.* But because we are hard-wired to resist change, every living system requires someone in it to *live into and lead the transformation necessary to take us into the future* we are resisting. The person who takes personal responsibility to live into the new future in a transformative way, in relationship to the others in the system, is the leader. If someone is not functioning as a leader, the system will always default to the status quo.

2. Leadership is expressed in behaviors. Leaders act. Leaders function. While speaking is indeed a form of behavior, and many leaders are known for their words in times of crisis, leadership is mostly expressed in *actions, relationships* and *responsibility*. Ed Friedman said, "The leader in the system is the one who is not blaming anyone."[10] Note: Every one of those words was chosen deliberately. Leaders are "in the system." That is, they have stayed *in* relationship with those they are called to lead. You can't lead from outside the system. (You can be a prophet or critic or consultant or supporter, but not a leader.) At the same time, leaders are *not blaming anyone* (or, for that matter, any circumstance) for the challenges they face but are solely focusing on personal responsibility, looking to what they can *do*—how they can *act*—differently. That *doing* is not just impulsive reacting but thoughtful, reflective responding. Perhaps the single most transformative moment of all is when a leader says, "I don't know what to do," and then goes about the hard work of leading the *learning* that will result in a new faithful action.

3. Leadership is developed. I am firmly in the "leaders are made, not born" school, convinced that leadership is a skill that can be taught.[11] Just as some have more aptitude for a skill than others, some have more natural abilities and talents that lend themselves to particular leadership in particular circumstances. *But any person who is willing to take personal responsibility, convene a group to work on a tough problem and persist in the face of resistance is a leader.* At the same time, the common inference when people want to learn to be leaders is that it is mostly head knowledge. If we read books and can repeat phrases (e.g., "adaptive challenges"), we think we have learned leadership (which is pretty much like learning to fly a plane from watching a video). But, and this is critical, *leadership is learned in the doing and by reflecting on the doing.* (John Dewey reportedly wrote: "We don't learn from experience, we learn by reflecting on experience.")[12] At the same time, even reflection is not enough. Leadership requires developing what Friedman calls "self-regulation." Because our brains don't process information and learn well when we are highly anxious, leaders must develop emotional maturity and the ability to persist in complex emotional systems without either distancing or taking resistance personally. Or as the good folks at the Lombard Mennonite Peace Center like to say, leaders must be able to "stay calm, stay connected, and stay the course."[13]

If we read these truths *backward* we get a dose of harsh reality. Since we are not *developing* leaders, there is a lack of leadership in *action*. Without essential leadership behaviors, most organizations are not growing, not transforming and certainly not facing their toughest challenges or thriving.

The culture is changing, the world is changing rapidly, and churches are facing change on an unprecedented scale. Churches and church leaders are becoming increasingly irrelevant, even marginalized. Shared corporate faith is viewed with cynicism at best, downright hostility at worst. The cultural advantage we experience during the seventeen centuries of Christendom has almost completely dissipated. Seminary training for the Christendom world is inadequate to this immensely challenging—transformation-demanding— moment in history.

We have to learn to lead all over again.

But the church is also at an exciting crossroads. We are entering a new day, new terrain and a new adventure. We are not alone. The Spirit of God goes before us. The mission of Christ will not fail. A day will come when the "kingdom of the world will become the kingdom of our Lord and of his Messiah, and he will reign forever and ever" (Revelation 11:15). The next steps are going to be demanding. More than anything, this moment requires those of us in positions of authority (and even most of us who are not) to embrace an *adventure-or-die* mindset, and find the courage and develop the capacity for a new day. We are heading into uncharted territory and are given the charge to lead a mission where the future is nothing like the past.

2

Adventure or Die

To Captain Meriwether Lewis.
The object of your mission is to explore the Missouri River, & such
principal stream of it, as by its course and communication with
the waters of the Pacific Ocean . . . may offer the most
direct and practicable water communication across
this continent for the purposes of commerce.

THOMAS JEFFERSON,
LETTER TO MERIWETHER LEWIS

Conceptually stuck systems cannot become unstuck
simply by trying harder. For a fundamental reorientation to occur,
that spirit of adventure which optimizes serendipity and which enables
new perceptions beyond the control of our thinking
processes must happen first.

ED FRIEDMAN, *A FAILURE OF NERVE*

HE DIPPED HIS HANDS INTO the icy water and took a long cool drink.

Fifteen months of hard travel, a seemingly endless string of days of back-breaking upstream slogging had led to this moment. Meriwether Lewis recalled all that he had endured: Nervous nights in a strange land. Mosquitoes galore. A dark, cold winter. Grizzly bears. A month-long portage around an immense waterfall. The death of a companion.

But he was here.

Lewis and a small scouting party had gone ahead of the rest of the Corps of Discovery to try to make contact with the Shoshone tribe. They had followed a small trail up a creek and now were at the spring itself. This little trickle was the source of the mighty Missouri River. This water would flow all the way to the Gulf of Mexico. They had found what no person of European descent had before them. And the most challenging obstacle on their journey from what was then the United States to the Pacific Ocean was now behind them.

Or so he thought.

For over three hundred years explorers of at least four sovereign nations had been looking for a water route that would connect the Pacific Ocean to the Mississippi River. And everyone *just knew* it was out there somewhere. It was a broadly believed, persistent assumption about the way the world was arranged. This assumption not only inspired the Lewis and Clark journey but fueled a frenetic race for profits and power. President Thomas Jefferson had indeed commissioned Lewis and Clark and the Corps of Discovery for just this moment, declaring that they should find the cherished water route that everyone believed existed and would insure the young nation's prosperity: "The most direct & practicable water communication across this continent, for the purposes of commerce."[1]

Finding the water route had been the key to national sovereignty and financial stability for the French, who had been in this new world for centuries, the British, who were mostly in what is now Canada, the Spanish, who controlled the southwest corner of the continent, and the Americans, who had recently purchased the Louisiana Territory from Napoleon Bonaparte. Whoever discovered and made claim to the water route would own the trade route and control the resources of this great continent. It would be like owning the Internet today. This discovery was deemed so vital to national interest that Spain sent two different war parties to intercept and kill the Corps of Discovery.

For Meriwether Lewis, slaking his thirst from that little stream meant that he was about to realize the dream of centuries of pioneers, to fulfill the ambitions of his president and to enter into the pantheon of explorers. His name and his Corps would be remembered as the discoverers of the highly prized Northwest Passage. Lewis believed that he would walk up the hill, look down a gentle slope that would take his men a half day to cross with their canoes on their backs, and then they would see the Columbia River. After fifteen months of going upstream they looked forward to letting the current swiftly whisk them to the Pacific Ocean. They would crest the hill, find the stream and coast to the finish line.

They could not have been more disappointed.

What Lewis actually discovered was that three hundred years of experts had all been completely and utterly wrong. In front of him was not a gentle slope down to a navigable river running to the Pacific Ocean but the Rocky Mountains. Stretching out for miles and miles as far as the eyes could see was one set of peaks after another.

> The road took us to the most distant fountain of the waters of the mighty Missouri in surch of which we have spent so many toilsome days and [restless] nights. thus far I had accomplished one of those great objects on which my mind has been unalterably fixed for many years, judge then of the pleasure I felt in [allaying] my thirst with this pure and ice-cold water. . . . here I halted a few minutes and rested myself. two miles below McNeal had exultingly stood with a foot on each side of this rivulet and thanked his god that he had lived to bestride the mighty & heretofore deemed endless Missouri. after refreshing ourselves we proceeded on to the top of the dividing ridge from which I discovered immence ranges of high mountains still to the West of us with their tops partially covered with snow.[2]

There was no Northwest Passage. No navigable river. No water route. The driving assumption of the brightest, most adventurous entrepreneurial and creative leaders regarding this new world had been absolutely mistaken.

Even more, Lewis's Corps of Discovery had discovered that the entire mental model regarding the continent was wrong as well. For the second assumption at work in the minds of the explorers of the day was that the geography west of the Continental Divide was the same as the geography east of it. All had assumed that in the same way the land rose gently over thousands of miles to a peak, it would also descend gently to the Pacific Ocean. In the same way they had been able to take a keelboat and canoes up a river, they'd be able to drift downriver to the ocean.

To be sure, the Mandans had told Lewis and Clark that the mountains ahead needed to be crossed. But when they thought of mountains, they pictured the rounded tree-topped bluffs of the Appalachians. Even seeing the peaks looming in front of them for miles didn't compute.[3] For no American had ever seen mountains like these. In the words of Corps sergeant John Ordway, "the mountains continue as far as our eyes could extend. They extend much further than we expected."[4] Or as another said, they were "the most terrible mountains I ever beheld."[5]

And at that moment everything that Meriwether Lewis assumed about his journey changed. He was planning on exploring the new world by boat. He was a river explorer. They planned on *rowing*, and they thought the hardest part was behind them. But in truth everything they had accomplished was only a prelude to what was in front of them.

Lewis and Clark and the Corps of Discovery were about to go off the map and into uncharted territory. They would have to change plans, give up expectations, even reframe their entire mission. What lay before them was nothing like what was behind them. There were no experts, no maps, no "best practices" and no sure guides who could lead them safely and successfully.

The true adventure—the real discovery—was just beginning.

The story of the Corps of Discovery is the driving metaphor for our present moment in history. In every field, in every business, every organization, leaders are rapidly coming to the awareness that the world in front of us is radically different from everything behind us. In the words of futurist and Distinguished Fellow of the Institute for the Future, Bob Johansen, after centuries of stability and slow, incremental change, in less than a generation our world has become VUCA: *volatile, uncertain, complex* and *ambiguous*.[6] This VUCA world will only become more so in the days ahead and *will require all leaders to learn new skills*. What we have learned in our schools, through our experiences, from our mentors and by common sense will only take us so far. We now have to use every bit of what we know and become true learners who are ready to adapt to whatever comes before us.

Perhaps nowhere is this more evident than in the arena where I spend my life: the church. We too—maybe even more so than other entities—have entered uncharted territory. Just as Lewis and Clark functioned under a set of geographical assumptions, leaders of the church in the West today have been operating under a set of philosophical, theological and ecclesiological assumptions.

Like Meriwether Lewis sitting on the crest of Lemhi Pass and looking at a landscape he couldn't have imagined, Christian leaders today are sitting in meetings, reading reports and conversing with colleagues about a brutal truth: *All that we have assumed about leading Christian organizations, all that we have been trained for, is out of date.* We have left the map, we are in uncharted territory, and it is different than we expected. We are experienced river rafters who must learn to be mountaineers. And some of us face "the most terrible mountain we have ever beheld."

HOW DO WE KEEP OUR CHURCHES FROM DYING?

The question was asked not once or twice, but in one form or another by over fifty people gathered in the room that day. I had just finished three presentations to a group of Methodist Christian educators and pastors in Portland, Maine. Now I was doing an additional workshop to answer questions and engage in further discussion on my topic. My topic had had nothing to do with church growth or congregational renewal. I was talking about Christian community and spiritual formation, sharing about my doctoral research and the necessity of healthy Christian communities for personal, individual spiritual transformation. The audience comprised Christian educators and ministers who were running Sunday schools, leading adult education classes or offering workshops and retreats for personal spiritual growth.

But that's not what they wanted to talk about.

The statistics of the Western church's steady decline are well known.[7] But most of us have been unprepared for how accelerated and disorienting that pace has become through the rapid and demonstrable marginalization of the church in Western society. Most churches (with a few obvious exceptions) are dying.[8] Extracurricular activities from music lessons to sports participation are considered by most parents to be more effective at forming good character in our children (and getting them accepted to good colleges!) than the church. Spirituality has become wildly popular but so deeply individualistic that the fastest-growing "religious affiliations" among those under thirty are "none" and "spiritual-not-religious."[9] As pastors, we were trained to teach those who come on their own, to care for those who call for help, to lead those who volunteer and to administer the resources of those who willingly give and participate. Now we are called on to minister to a passing parade of people who treat us like we are but one option in their personal salad bar of self-fulfillment. To do so will take a significant shift in thinking about pastoral leadership.

But before we get to that, let's first take a good look at how the world—especially the church world—came to be in this place.

FAREWELL TO CHRISTENDOM

After forty years as a missionary and bishop in India, Lesslie Newbigin retired and returned home to Great Britain in the 1970s. What he found in his beloved homeland was a more difficult mission field than he left behind. He wrote, "England is a pagan society and the development of a truly missionary encounter with this very tough form of paganism is the greatest intellectual and practical task facing the Church."[10]

In that one sentence Newbigin challenged the mental model of how the Christians in the West had seen their hometowns and resident cultures for what is now seventeen hundred years. No matter how many times English men and women sang "God Save the Queen," no matter how beautiful the Christopher Wren cathedrals, no matter the presence of a state-sponsored church where bishops hold seats in the House of Lords, England—and for that matter most of Europe—had become a "pagan society." Newbigin foresaw that the West was quickly becoming a mission field, and the church needed to "develop a truly missionary encounter" with their friends and neighbors.

During the last decade of the last century, Darrell Guder and his colleagues in the Gospel and Our Culture Network used the term *missional* to differentiate certain congregations from those that were primarily organized around the maintenance of Christendom culture and faith practices. Missional churches are those that understand "the church as fundamentally and comprehensively defined by its calling and sending, its purpose to serve God's healing purposes *for* all the world as God's witnessing people *to* all the world."[11] For Guder the church is sent into the world as the rightful and faithful continuation of Jesus' own sending by God ("As the Father sent me, so I send you" [John 20:2]) and so each *congregation* is a "witnessing community" to its very locale; each particular congregation has itself a unique and *apostolic* mission to fulfill.

> The apostolic mission was not merely the saving of souls and their collecting into communities of the saved. The apostolic strategy, whose message was the event of salvation accomplished in Jesus Christ and whose method was defined by the earthly ministry of Jesus, was the formation of witnessing

communities whose purpose was to continue the witness that brought them into existence.[12]

Christopher Wright has reminded us that the sending of the church as the apostle to the world goes to God's very purposes: "It is not so much that God has a mission for his church in the world, but that God has a church for his mission in the world."[13] Further, "missions" is no longer one of a number of activities requiring patronage and participation that a church provides to Christian constituents (alongside worship, education, care, hospitality and outreach), but in the words of Alan Hirsch, the mission or "sentness" of a congregation is its "true and authentic organizing principle":

> Missional church is a community of God's people that defines itself, and orga-
> nizes its life around, its real purpose of being an agent of God's mission to the
> world. In other words, the church's true and authentic organizing principle is
> mission. When the church is in mission, it is the true church.[14]

This missional frame for the church is even more critical when we consider the speed and breadth of change in our world. The rise of the digital age, the default emphasis on individualism and the shifts in media, philosophy, science and religion[15] have all led to the now widespread agreement that we are amidst an epochal change.[16] There is certainly a call for the church to recapture a robust apostolic calling and the constituent practices needed for missional congregations. Fortunately, this early discussion and observation has given rise to such a wealth of resources exploring the specific practices of the missional church that I have no need to go into them here. But chief among the topics is the acknowledgment that leadership—and especially leadership development—must be dramatically different than it was during Christendom. Seminaries that produced pastors to be the resident expert in biblical studies, theology and church history; the resident professional for teaching, counseling and pastoral care; and the local manager of the church business and bureaucracy are reconsidering both the demands of the current curricular expectations and the challenges of the changing world around us.

Darrell Guder observes,

> If, like Lesslie Newbigin, we are challenged to recognize that our own context
> has become, within an astonishingly short time, a post-Christian mission field,
> posing enormous challenges to the received forms and attitudes of Western

Christendom, then that inward-oriented, church-maintaining approach to theological education will not work. Education for maintenance is not the same thing as education for mission.[17]

It is worth pausing to acknowledge that a number of church leaders have embraced this missional reality wholeheartedly. Fortunately, there are experts today who are faithful, courageous, thoughtful and articulate. Seminars abound and seminaries now rightly offer degrees in missional theology and missional leadership. I personally have read widely, benefited greatly and am deeply indebted to them for their work. And like me a number of pastors have signed up for training programs, enrolled in cohort groups, and brought consultants and speakers to their congregations to inspire and exhort. But sadly, so little has really changed. While I am indebted to the missional thinkers of our day, it's become apparent *a missional mind shift alone doesn't lend itself to the capacity building that actually brings change.*

But if we are convinced that a change is necessary, how do we bring it without alienating the whole church? How do we face the losses and fears in our congregations, the opposition and resistance in our leaders, and the anxieties and insecurities in ourselves to truly lead the church through this adventure-or-die moment? How do we develop leaders for mission in this rapidly changing, uncharted-territory world?

A CHURCH WITHOUT EXPERTS

We are in uncharted terrain trying to lead dying churches into a post-Christian culture that now considers the church an optional, out of touch and irrelevant relic of the past. What do you do? If you are like me, indeed, like most people, what you do is default to what you know. *You do* again, *what you have always done* before.

In the movie *Moneyball*, Brad Pitt plays Billy Beane, the general manager of the Oakland Athletics baseball team. Oakland is a small-market team that doesn't have the revenue to compete with the major-market teams like New York, Los Angeles and Boston. His best players keep leaving to make more money for those teams. His owner can't give him any more money, and now he has to replace three star players. He gathers his staff together to explore what they can do about this problem. What does this highly trained, well-paid, experienced group of expert baseball minds do? They use the same thinking, the same approach, the same strategy they always use—which is not working.

Steve Yamaguchi, the dean of students at Fuller Theological Seminary, says that when his spiritual director took a flying lesson, he asked the instructor why they use flight simulators so much. The instructor said, "In the moment of crisis, you will not rise to the occasion; you will default to your training."

That was the problem of Billy Beane's scouting staff and of most church leaders today. We pastors are well trained. We have lots of education and experience, and have had generations of success. Indeed, most of our congregations are filled with people who were blessed by what *once* worked. And so, we default back to those things.

For most of us in ministry, our defaults that once worked so well are not working, and we become discouraged. So, what do we do? *We talk longer*—we preach more. *We try harder*—we go into our bag of tricks and bring out our best programs.[18] *We give a personal touch*—we hope that caring for stakeholders will inspire them to change.

We preachers are such good talkers. In fact, Morgan Murray, the senior pastor at Walnut Creek Presbyterian Church in California, likes to say, "We Presbyterians are so good at talking about problems that after awhile we think that we have actually done something."[19] And when we roll up our sleeves and dedicate ourselves to doing something, we usually do something we have already done before. We hope and pray *this time* it will work. We'll put in enough effort or preach with enough passion or give it enough of our personal attention that *this* time it will be different. So, when talking longer or trying harder doesn't work, what next? Mostly, we turn to tricks and tweaks. We use PowerPoint or Twitter. We add an electric guitar or an accordion. If we have the money, we buy new stuff.

Congregational systems guru Ed Friedman writes, "When any . . . system is imaginatively gridlocked, it cannot get free simply through more thinking about the problem. Conceptually stuck systems *cannot* be unstuck simply by trying harder."[20] Friedman clarifies the challenge in front of us: We are "imaginatively gridlocked." We can't see our way to a new way of being, a new response. We are growing more anxious about the decline of the church and the demise of whole religious structures. We don't know what to do. So we keep trying harder; we keep trying our old tricks. But, of course, it doesn't work.

In *Moneyball*, an exasperated Billy Beane looks at his manager and tries to urge him to think differently. "It's adapt or die!" he says.

Adapt or die.

So what do we do to keep our churches from dying? What kind of adaptation is necessary? And how will we find the solutions if we are "imaginatively grid-locked"? Ed Friedman continues: "Conceptually stuck systems cannot become unstuck simply by trying harder. For a fundamental reorientation to occur, that spirit of adventure which optimizes serendipity and which enables new percep-tions beyond the control of our thinking processes must happen first."[21]

What is needed? "A spirit of adventure," where there are new, unexpected discoveries (serendipities) and ultimately "new perceptions." To be sure, this is an adapt-or-die moment. This is a moment when most of our backs are against the wall, and we are unsure if the church will survive to the next gen-eration. *The answer is not to try harder but to start a new adventure:* to look over Lemhi Pass and let the assumptions of the past go. To see not the absence of a water route but the discovery of a new, uncharted land beckoning us forward—yes, in the face of the uncertainties, fears and potential losses—to learn and to be transformed.

What is needed? *An adventure that requires adaptive capacity.*

The tests we face are not technical problems that can be solved with current understanding but adaptive challenges that are more systemic in nature. They are part of the very context and culture of the congregation and the changing world around it. They are usually expressed in the conflict of competing values within the church itself.

Adaptive challenges are never solved through a quick fix. If talking, trying or tricks work, they would have worked already. They are only going to be solved through new *insight* into the context, the values and the systemic issues at play in the congregation and within the leaders themselves. In other words, before we can *solve* any problem, we need to learn to *see* new possibilities. And, ironically, because the solution will be an adaptation of the core values, identity and theology of the congregation itself, seeing those possibilities de-pends on first seeing ourselves and our congregations as we really are.

Once we understand that, perhaps the most terrifying task of leadership begins. It is an enormous risk that requires the nerve to stand in front of a group of people and say out loud three words: *I don't know.* Literally, "I don't know what to do, and maybe, just maybe, *no one* knows what to do." We need to clearly *see* that what we know to do doesn't work. We need to have the clear-eyed humility to take an honest assessment and recognize that this challenge is beyond our talking, trying or bag of pastoral tricks.

> ### *REORIENTATION*
>
> If you can adapt and adventure, you can thrive. But you must let go, learn as you go and keep going no matter what.

Eventually we will start a discipline of looking at our problems differently, acknowledging each time anew that this is not a situation that calls for a new tweak or new technique; this is an opportunity for adventure, exploration and transformation. This is a moment when our congregation can take on new life, begin a new season of faithful expression. We can start imagining different possibilities. And we can learn new ways of leading.

BACK TO THE PASS

As he stepped off the map into uncharted territory, Meriwether Lewis discovered that what was in front of him was nothing like what was behind him, and that what had brought him to this point in the journey would take him no farther. Lewis faced a daunting decision: What would he do now? Lewis and Clark and their Corps of Discovery were looking for a water route, but now they had run out of water. *How do you canoe over mountains?*

You don't. If you want to continue forward, you change. You adapt. Meriwether Lewis looked at the miles and miles of snow-covered peaks and knew that to continue his journey he would have to change his entire approach. The same is true for all who are called to lead beyond the boundaries of what is known. We go through a personal transformation of identity and mission intention. We go from being river rats to mountain climbers. We keep on course with the same goal, but change absolutely everything required to make it through this uncharted territory. We ditch the canoes, ask for help, find horses and cross the mountains. And when the time comes, we make new boats out of burnt trees.

You let go, you learn as you go and you keep going, no matter what.

Ultimately, this book is about the kind of leadership necessary for the local church to take the Christian mission into the uncharted territory of a post-

Christendom world. It is about the kind of leadership needed when the world has so dramatically changed that we really don't know what to do next. This is the leadership moment of the church today. We are canoers who have run out of water. There is no route in front of us, no map, no quick fix or easy answer.

But . . . this is good news.

This is a divine moment. This is an opportunity to express even more clearly what it means to follow and serve the God who is King of the entire world. The church at its best has always been a Corps of Discovery. It has always been a small band of people willingly heading into uncharted territory with a mission worthy of our utmost dedication.

3

A Leadership Model for Uncharted Territory

Do not be conformed to this world, but be transformed.

ROMANS 12:2

*Leadership is energizing a community of people
toward their own transformation in order to accomplish a
shared mission in the face of a changing world.*

TOD BOLSINGER

THE LAST THING YOU WANT TO HEAR FROM GOD BEFORE PREACHING

It was the still, small voice. Over a lot of years and through a lot of mistakes I have come to recognize it as the nudge of God in my life. It's not audible as much as an impression, but I have learned to listen very closely.

We were in a worship service on a Sunday evening, one of a long line of experiments trying to reach out to the young adult population that has been leaving churches in droves. It was a different kind of service with different leaders and a different format. I really liked it and wondered if we were onto something. I was energized to speak that evening, glad that I could be expositing Scripture in a different format. I was proud of my team for being so creative and was privileged to be a part. But right before I walked up to the platform, in the quiet moment of some silent prayer, this impression was imprinted on my heart: *Your people need you to lead them even more than preach to them.*

That was certainly an odd word right before I got up to *preach*. But there it was, and it so resonated with me that I didn't doubt it for a second. I don't remember what *I* said that night, but I do remember what I heard *God* say. It has been shaping my ministry ever since.

Think about the best leaders of the last two centuries. Who would you put on that list? Abraham Lincoln, Winston Churchill, Martin Luther King Jr.? (Yes, there are others.) What is the one characteristic they have in common? Now, think of the Christian leaders of the last two centuries? What is the one characteristic they have in common with the previous list? Indeed, for most church members, *leader* is synonymous with *pulpiteer*. When most churches are looking for a new senior pastor, they are looking first and foremost for a preacher.

In a Christendom context this made sense. Preaching and leadership were essentially synonymous. The leader was a person with authority, title or position who was given a voice and charged with offering a vision for faithfulness and mission. In a Christendom world we needed leaders to inspire and educate, to provoke

> ***REORIENTATION***
>
> In the Christendom world, speaking *was* leading. In a post-Christendom world, leading is multidimensional: apostolic, relational and adaptive.

the "mystic chords of memory" that would enable us to live consistently with "the better angels of our nature" (as Lincoln said in his First Inaugural Address). When those in authority were *speaking*, they were *leading*. More often than not, their vision was of *repentance* and *return*. In a Christendom context the leader's primary responsibility was to bring a people *back* to God, *returning* to the church, *turning back* to the values they had strayed from. Preaching *reiterated* the shared story, the shared vision of life, the shared values of a culture they had once learned and now forgotten. It reminded us of what most in our culture already knew and even mostly believed. In the words of twentieth-century rabbi and spiritual writer Abraham Joshua Heschel, "Much of what the Bible demands can be comprised in one imperative: Remember!"[1] And that leadership of voice, vision and values—that leadership or oration, articulation and remembrance—was mostly leadership enough.

But what kind of leadership do we need today in a culture that has become again a mission field? What does leadership look like in a day when the moorings of society have become disconnected from the anchors of faith? What is leadership in a world where the task isn't so much to *re*-mind as to encounter and engage, to proclaim and demonstrate a completely different world that is available and yet beyond awareness of or even interest to so many? What does leadership look like in a post-Christendom day when we have left behind rivers filled with the waters of shared Christian culture and are facing a new terrain marked by mountains to climb?

Ironically, it looks a lot like the earliest church leadership.

THE RECOVERY OF LEADERSHIP FOR AN APOSTOLIC CHURCH

In their book *The Permanent Revolution*, Alan Hirsch and Tim Catchim recover the concept that the church—literally, "the ecclesia"—is an *apostolic movement*.[2] Nurtured by a fivefold model of leadership (apostles, prophets, evangelists, shepherds and teachers) found in Ephesians 4:1-16, they demonstrate that the church's very nature is *apostolic*. That is, the church is the embodiment of the work of the original twelve disciples who became the first apostles, "sent" to the world, and equipping and being equipped for the sending. For Darrell Guder this is indeed the very purpose of the ecclesia, the apostolate, that is, "the formation of the witnessing communities whose purpose was to continue the witness that brought them into existence."[3]

This points to a reorientation that gives us a clear, reenergizing reason for being a part of the "one, holy and *apostolic* church." But most of us think that *apostolic* is a description of our founding and not our *purpose*. For the church to be apostolic is not just to claim a name or credibility, but a vocation. It is like a guy named Mr. Farmer buying land and planting crops like his ancestors once did.

To live up to their name, local churches must be continually moving out, extending themselves into the world, being the missional, witnessing community we were called into being *to be*: the manifestation of God's going into the world, crossing boundaries, proclaiming, teaching, healing, loving, serving and extending the reign of God.

In short, churches need to keep *adventuring* or they will die. We need to press on to the uncharted territory of making traditional churches missionary churches. How do we do that? Frankly, *not* with another seminar on being a missional church, *not* changing the labels on our committees or the names of our churches, *not* through rearranging organizational structures and *not* creating new denominations. Traditional churches will not become missionary churches by fiat or tweaking. There are no quick fixes and no easy currents to drift us lazily toward our collective goals. Traditional churches will only become missionary churches as those in authority (and even those without formal authority) develop capacity to lead their congregations through a long, truly transformational process that starts with the transformation of the leaders and requires a thoroughgoing change in leadership functioning.

To be sure, in the Christendom mental model under which most of us were trained, pastors weren't missionaries and churches weren't missions. (Indeed, my seminary had a separate school for that!) We were teachers, worship leaders and counselors. We were social workers, community organizers and program providers. We were mostly chaplains for a congregation within a Christendom culture. For many of us in midcareer, it's like we woke up one morning and found ourselves ministering in a crosscultural setting where we don't understand the customs, language or values. We are now in uncharted territory facing the same adventure-or-die moment. And if traditional churches are going to become missionary churches, then pastors must become truly missional leaders of missional *communities*.

COMMUNAL TRANSFORMATION FOR MISSION

At the heart of this book is the conviction that congregational leadership in a post-Christendom context is about *communal transformation for mission*. Christian community is not merely about connection, care and belonging. Spiritual transformation is not just about becoming more like Christ as an end in itself. In a post-Christendom world that has become a mission field right outside the sanctuary door, Christian community is about gathering and forming *a people*, and spiritual transformation is about both individual and corporate growth, *so that they—together—participate in Christ's mission to establish the kingdom of God "on earth as it is in heaven."*

In Romans 8:29 we read how even the doctrine of election is not focused on our salvation but transformation: "For those whom he foreknew he also predestined to be conformed to the image of his Son, in order that he might be the firstborn within a large family." But consider this: What is the purpose of God's family? What is the family business of the family of God?

In Genesis 12 Abram is called by God to follow him. He is promised the blessings of becoming the father of a great people, a large family, with descendants more numerous than the stars in the sky (Genesis 15:5). And the mission of his family would be to "bless all the families of the earth." This call, this mission and charge would be expressed in Jesus as the kingdom of God that reestablishes God's love and rule, his will and purpose, "on earth as it is in heaven." Or as Darrell Guder puts it,

> God's calling is not solely for the benefit of the called who are incorporated into the called-out people, the ecclesia. God's calling of a particular people is for God's saving purposes for the world, for Jerusalem, Judea, Samaria, and the ends of the earth. For God so loved the world, God was, in Christ, reconciling the world. And for the sake of that world, created and fallen, God's calling creates, forms, equips, commissions, and sends the church to carry out the witness for which it exists.[4]

Leadership therefore is about the transformation of a congregation so that they, *collectively*, can fulfill the mission they, *corporately*, have been given. Every spiritual practice, including preaching, is to serve that end. Preaching is one tool in the pastor's toolbox for nurturing and equipping a particular people to face the challenges to their *shared* mission. Today, preaching is *not* leadership but *serves* leadership.

I believe God was saying to me in that still, small voice—in that small, experimental worship service—to remember that in a changing world there is much more to leadership than speaking. As important as proclaiming the Word of God is (and it is very important), leadership for a people on a mission into a new, rapidly changing world requires more than proclamation, it requires new actions, new ways of functioning and therefore, most specifically, new *learning*. Leadership requires *shared, corporate learning expressed in new shared, corporate functioning. In order to act or function differently in a changing world, all true leadership will require transformation.* To that end, all true leadership will be anchored in the principles of adaptive leadership.

DON'T JUST FIX THE PROBLEM

According to Ronald Heifetz and Marty Linsky, *adaptive leadership* is not about finding the best-known or most-available fix to a problem, but instead adapting to the changing environment or circumstances so that new possibilities arise for accurately *seeing, understanding* and *facing* challenges with *new actions*. Just as an organism must adapt in order to thrive in a changing environment, so organizations need to adapt to the changing world around them without losing their core identity, their reason for being, their core values and purpose. This kind of leadership is complex and fraught with loss, fears and anxiety, causing us to feel off-balance and insecure. But it is the essence of leadership in a changing world. Because this is the capacity that is most unfamiliar to most pastoral leaders, the bulk of this book will focus on developing the resilience and problem-defining and problem-solving capabilities— amidst disequilibrium—required for equipping a congregation for the missional challenges before them.

Heifetz and Linsky make a distinction between technical problems and adaptive challenges. *Technical problems* are those where the solutions are available to and "within the repertoire" of the community. These solutions come from best practices, or are known and offered by an expert or implemented by a capable practitioner, professional or manager. For pastors, typical technical problems include preaching effective and faithful sermons; leading the people of God in worship, prayer and devotion; offering pastoral care; managing the church program, ministry and budget; counseling; and teaching the doctrines of faith.

It's important to note that these are deeply important and at times difficult tasks. They require education, experience and expertise. They are critical to the life, health and faith of a community and of individuals. They are as important to a congregation as was river navigation, hunting, military discipline, organization, negotiating with strangers, medicine and scientific methods of research were for Lewis and Clark. Heifetz and Linsky go to great lengths to emphasize that

> there is nothing trivial about solving technical problems. Medical personnel save lives every day in the emergency room through their authoritative expertise because they have the right procedures, the right norms, and the right knowledge. Through our managerial know-how, we produce an economy full of products and services, many of them crucial to our daily lives. *What makes a problem technical is not that it is trivial; but simply that its solution already lies within the organization's repertoire.*[5]

Adaptive challenges, by contrast, are those that "cannot be solved with one's existing knowledge and skills, requiring people to make a shift in their values, expectations, attitudes, or habits of behaviour."[6] These are "systemic problems with no ready answers" that arise from a changing environment and uncharted territory.[7] These are challenges leaders face when the world around them changes so rapidly that the planned strategies and approaches are rendered moot. This is when the discovery of the Rocky Mountains requires us to ditch the canoes and look for new ways forward.

Uncharted leadership therefore requires transformation of the way problems have been approached in the past since there is no map for uncharted territories. An understanding of this kind of adaptive leadership have three characteristics:

1. a *changing* environment where there is no clear answer

2. the necessity for both leaders and follower to learn, especially the leader's own ongoing *transformation*

3. the unavoidable reality that a new solution will result in *loss*

In this new post-Christendom era, the church leader will be less a grand orator or star figure who gathers individuals for inspiration and exhortation, and more a convener and equipper of people who together will be transformed as they participate in God's transforming work in the world. To that end, I offer this definition of leadership: *Leadership is energizing a community of people toward their own transformation in order to accomplish a shared mission in the face of a changing world.*

Leadership (as differentiated from management or stewardship) is about *transformation* and *mission,* about growing and going, about personal development and corporate effectiveness—simultaneously. We know we are facing a leadership challenge if it requires us to *grow* as leaders and as a people, to be transformed into something more than we have been—without losing our core identity—in order to accomplish the mission we have been called to.

So what does a transformational leader actually do? What is the combination of capacities and character necessary for a Christian leader in this changing world? Transformational leadership is a skill set that can be learned but not easily mastered. It is not a role or position, but a way of being, a way of leading that is far different than most of us have learned before.

TRANSFORMATIONAL LEADERSHIP MODEL

Leadership in uncharted territory requires the transformation of the whole organization: both leaders and followers will become vastly different people after they have ventured forth to live out the mission of God in a changing world. This transformational leadership lies at the overlapping intersection of three leadership components: *technical competence, relational congruence* and *adaptive capacity* (see fig. 3.1).

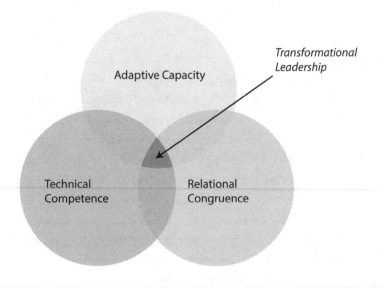

Figure 3.1. Three components of transformational leadership

These three spheres indicate the different ways that leaders function in a system in order to bring transformation. And *function* is a key word. It's an obvious but often overlooked truth: *Nothing changes until there is a change in behavior. Nothing has changed until people start acting differently.*[8] If missional, pastoral leadership is about the transformation of a congregation so they, *collectively,* can fulfill the mission they, *corporately,* have been given, the leadership in a post-Christendom context requires different ways of behaving or functioning from the old list of preaching, liturgics, pastoral care and running meetings. In this model

- *Transformational leadership begins in technical competence.* That is, leadership for transformation starts long before engaging the challenge of uncharted territory. Indeed, the men of the Corps of Discovery likely would not have followed Lewis and Clark over the unknown Rocky Mountains if Lewis and Clark hadn't demonstrated their ability on the familiar waters of the Missouri River. In the same way, before a missional community can take on the challenges of a changing world, the leadership must earn the credibility that comes from competently handling the basic management skills that serve the organization.

- *Transformational leadership is validated in relational congruence.* The credibility gained in competence must be increased through acts of demonstrated character, care and constancy. Think of it this way: If you were going to climb a difficult and potentially dangerous mountain, you would insist that your guide be an experienced professional with lots of demonstrable skills. But what would you do if you discovered your guide had a reputation as an adrenaline junkie who often takes unnecessary risks just for thrills? Would you still want him or her to be your guide? Maybe so, but you'd probably ask some very hard questions in order to discern if that guide is trustworthy. Relational congruence is a leader's ability to be the same person in every setting, every relationship, every task. The personal maturity and emotional stability to make calm, wise decisions creates the necessary health and trust in an organization that enable it to "let go, learn as you go and keep going." When leaders function with relational congruence, they strengthen the bonds, deepen the affection and create the wellspring of trust needed to go off the map.

- *Leadership becomes transformational through the integration of adaptive capacity.* Adaptive capacity is a leader's ability to help his or her community "grow, face their biggest challenges and thrive." It is the capacity to lead a process of shifting values, habits and behaviors in order to grow and discover solutions to the greatest challenges brought on by a changing world. And this is absolutely dependent on the leader's own commitment to personal transformation.

TRANSFORMATION: THE TRUE GOAL OF UNCHARTED LEADERSHIP

For Christians engaged in the post-Christendom context, *transformation for mission* is at the very center of life. While the *urgency* of transformation is made evident by the reality of our circumstances, the energy for transformation is inherent in our call and identity as followers of Jesus. We are not adapting to merely survive but to thrive! We are called to adapt to a changing world because we are called to reach that changing world. We participate in Jesus' mission to reestablish the will of God "on earth as it is in heaven," while becoming more and more "conformed to the image of his Son" (Romans 8:29) to the glory of God.

This dual vision of transformation *is* our churches' reason for being. We exist to reveal the presence and character of God in the world, being transformed as we participate in God's transforming work in the world. Leadership requires a commitment to transformation, and transformation is the goal of leadership. To put it another way: *leadership into uncharted territory requires and results in transformation of the whole organization, starting with the leaders.* Only as leaders are transformed and grow in competence, congruence and adaptive capacity do they have the ability to face the challenges of a new day, a new geography, a new set of circumstances and a rapidly changing world. God willing, as they do so, the result will be more personal and community transformation.

YOUR PEOPLE NEED YOU TO LEAD THEM EVEN MORE THAN PREACH TO THEM

For me, God's still, small voice was telling me that the skills I had depended on, the gifts and experiences I had spent years cultivating, the abilities I had honed through education and practice would be insufficient for the challenges ahead. While I would still need to teach and preach the Scriptures, offer spiritual direction and counsel, lead the church in worship and service, I also needed to lead the church in *learning*. The challenge in front of us would require a long tutorial of trial and error, of observing and interpreting and experimenting. It would require us to be changed and to attend to our own resistance to change. Personally, it would require me to embody the transformation needed and invite others to join me in it.

We closed down that evening worship service a few months later. As a strategy for helping us reach the unreached and prodigal young adults of our community, it failed. We moved on to other experiments. And many of them will likely be set aside. But that is the point. They are experiments. As such, they are more about learning and discovery than anything else. And mostly they continue to reinforce that *leadership begins with the transforming work God is doing in us before anything else.*

For Christian leaders today, this is the moment of truth. Are we willing to

- take the risks and get up the nerve to lead a big adventure?

- lead our people to face the challenge of a changing world?

- acknowledge that what is in front of us is not at all like the world where we have previously thrived?

- clarify and cling to our core convictions and *let go of everything else* that keeps us from being effective in the mission God has given us?

- let go of the tried and true default actions that have brought us this far?

- *learn a new way of leading that begins with our own transformation?*

If so, let's continue exploring what it means to become leaders who find new ways of facing the mountains ahead of us.

Part Two

THE ON-THE-MAP

SKILL SET

No One Is Going to Follow You Off
the Map Unless They Trust You On It

4

Competence and Credibility

*Capt. Lewis is brave, prudent, habituated to the woods
& familiar with Indian manners & character. He is not regularly
educated, but he possesses a great mass of accurate observation
on all the subjects of nature which present themselves.*

THOMAS JEFFERSON, LETTER TO BENJAMIN RUSH,
FEBRUARY 28, 1803

THE ADVICE OF AN ALASKAN HOMESTEADER AND DOG MUSHER

In 2008 my family and I met Jon and Karen Nierenberg while staying in their lodge outside Denali National Park in Alaska. Jon is a dog musher, homesteader and former park ranger who has literally written the book on hiking in Denali National Park.

Jon introduced us to his sled dogs. He also sent my son, Brooks, and me on a great hike to the top of a peak that was breathtaking, and one evening he showed beautiful photographs of his twenty-five years of guiding and mushing in the Alaskan wilderness.

Perhaps most touching was Jon's story about marrying Karen, and how she and her three teenagers moved from Ohio into Jon's homestead cabin without electricity, running water or indoor plumbing. Sitting there with our brood of teenagers and pre-teens, we couldn't imagine how this was even possible. A twelve-, fourteen- and sixteen-year-old moving to Alaska and learning how to walk two miles across the tundra to catch the bus to school? No electricity? No cell phones? Only a wood stove for heat?

When we asked Jon how they did it he said, "If you have someone to show you a few tricks, you can adapt to anything."

While leadership in uncharted territory may or may not require us to move our families to Alaska, Jon's advice is worth remembering. Adaptation, even adaptive leadership, begins in the nuts and bolts of surviving and thriving, in the lessons passed on by those who are a few steps down the road, in the tricks and tips of "technical competence."

Or to put it another way, unless we demonstrate that we are credible on the map, no one is going to follow us off the map.

FROM THE FRONTIER TO THE WHITE HOUSE AND BACK AGAIN

According to most accounts, Thomas Jefferson chose Meriwether Lewis as his personal secretary and leader of the most important exploratory mission of the young nation's history because of his personal relationship with Lewis. So even though Lewis was the president's personal secretary and aide-de-camp, Jefferson was well aware that Lewis's qualifications for leading Jefferson's bold expedition to explore the West and find a water route to the Pacific Ocean could come into question. Jefferson acknowledged as much to Dr. Benjamin Rush when he wrote asking for some tutelage and guidance to prepare Lewis for the journey. But for Jefferson, the young Lewis had experience that would make up for his lack of formal education: "knowledge of the Western Country, of the army and of all its interests & relations."[1] With military experience and a captain's rank, a penchant for travel and adventure, a scientifically oriented mind, experience in navigation and cartography, all the requisite skills that come from running a plantation at a young age, and the subsequent tutorial that Jefferson would provide him in botany and frontier medicine, Lewis was uniquely qualified in Jefferson's opinion. Years later, after Lewis's death, Jefferson wrote of the combination of character, skill and discernment he saw in the man he selected:

> Careful as a father of those committed to his charge, yet steady in the mainte-
> nance of order & discipline, intimate with the Indian character, customs &
> principles, habituated to the hunting life, guarded by exact observations of the
> vegetables and animals of his own country, and against losing time in the de-
> scription of objects already possessed, honest, disinterested, liberal of sound
> understanding and a fidelity to truth so scrupulous that whatever he should

report would be as certain as if seen by ourselves, with all these qualifications as if selected and implanted by nature in one body for this express purpose, I could have no hesitation in confiding the enterprize to him.[2]

In addition, Clark, who was four years older, had been Lewis's superior officer in the military, and was the younger brother of a Revolutionary War hero, brought the expedition skills, experience and especially a temperament that Lewis needed. As one scholar has noted,

> Although the journals do not indicate precisely what role each of the leaders played, it is clear that Clark was the cartographer, Lewis the field scientist; Clark the day-to-day leader of the expedition, Lewis a somewhat detached strategist-in-residence; Clark the nuts and bolts negotiator with Indians, Lewis the embodiment of President Jefferson's Indian policies; Clark the spokesman of immediate authority, Lewis the holder of final authority; Clark the man of common sense, Lewis the man of reflection; Clark the leader of logistics, Lewis alone on the shore with his gun, and his notebook and his Newfoundland dog, Seaman.[3]

Military leadership, cartography, river navigation, scientific observation, frontier medicine, administration, organization, negotiation, strategy: together, Lewis and Clark offered to Jefferson and especially the men under their charge the competence and credibility required—and demonstrated—in leadership that would eventually go beyond their known world. Uncharted leadership begins then in on-the-map technical competence.

TECHNICAL COMPETENCE

Surprisingly, transformational leadership does not *begin* with transformation but with *competence*. At the same time, many of us assume that it begins with character, that is, the personal attributes that make up a good, wise and effective leader. But in reality, the opportunity to lead usually *begins* with technical competence (see fig. 4.1). The best player on the team becomes the team captain. The expert, the high achiever, the most articulate, the best producer, the smartest, strongest, most attractive are, under most circumstances, tapped for leadership (King Saul immediately comes to mind).

Now, certainly, if technical competence is the *only* criteria for leadership, it can lead to significant problems (think Enron, the so-called Smartest Guys in

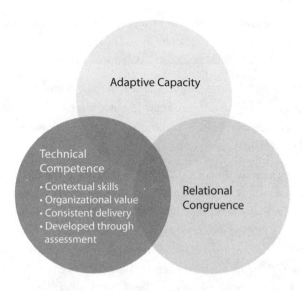

Figure 4.1. Technical competence

the Room), but before calling a community to change and grow, a leader must demonstrate the ability to serve the needs of his or her charges right where they are. Before going into uncharted territory, the leader must ably navigate the map while fulfilling the expectations he or she has been authorized to accomplish.

TECHNICAL COMPETENCE, STEWARDSHIP AND CREDIBILITY

Another way to say this is: *Stewardship precedes leadership.* Biblically, stewardship is about faithfully protecting and preserving what is most important, about growing and developing the potential of everything and everyone under one's care. It is about faithfully discharging the duties and carrying out the responsibilities that we have been authorized to do. It is the first and most basic act of being human, the first charge given in the garden to "cultivate and keep" (Genesis 2:15).

Jesus used the metaphor of the steward (manager) to describe the basic faithfulness of the disciple (Luke 16:1-15). To be sure, stewardship is not just maintenance; it is also about growth, protection and taking care of all God has delegated to us (Matthew 25:14-30), so that God will be revealed in the world. Stewardship is a response to God's "manifold grace" and is expressed in serving "one another with whatever gift" we have received and with the "strength that God supplies" (1 Peter 4:10-11).

Stewardship, therefore, is on-the-map authorization, and technical competence describes the leaders' ability to do the job they were hired to do—to navigate the known territory—*before* beginning the transformational leadership process. Before Lewis and Clark asked their men to follow them beyond the Missouri River headwaters into uncharted territory, they led them upriver with both expertise and efficiency. Before Karen and her teenagers moved to Alaska, they visited and vacationed with Jon, discerning whether this man could care for them if they became a homesteading family.

Usually, before a community of faith will even *consider* undergoing costly change, there must be a sense that leadership is doing everything within their power and their job description to be as effective as possible. Note again the word *competence*. While high achievers are often considered for leadership roles, it isn't necessary for transformational leaders to be *experts* in all technical skills. Leadership first requires "threshold competence," a demonstrable competency as stewards of the basic roles and responsibilities of their position.[4]

If a pastor is not a *good enough* preacher, if a manager is not *good enough* at meeting budgets and deadlines, if the leader of a sales team doesn't perform to *some level* of expectation, they will have no credibility for raising the issues of transformational leadership. Very often the underperforming technical leader becomes the scapegoat for the systemic issues of the organi-

> ## *REORIENTATION*
>
> Before people will follow you off the map, gain the credibility that comes from demonstrating competence on the map.

zation. And while often deeply disruptive to a faith community, changing pastors is often the default quick fix for a church. To be sure, many gifted preachers and teachers are less gifted in administration; many gifted pastoral counselors and spiritual directors are less-gifted preachers and teachers; but in order to exercise leadership, authorities or positional leaders must first demonstrate basic stewardship of at least three key areas of ministry. Again, the focus here is on *developing credibility for potential leadership that mobilizes people to grow and address their biggest challenges, not expertise for problem solving.* So to that end, let me suggest three basic tasks that leaders must exercise with technical competence before they have the credibility to go off the map into uncharted territory.

Competent stewardship of Scriptures and tradition. Ruth used to look at me with a steady gaze and smiling eyes. She was in her nineties and one of the real treasures of the church.

"Boy," she said (she was one of the few people in my congregation who could get away with calling me "Boy"), "I pray for you every day."

"Thank you, Ruth," I said with a sigh. "That means a lot to me. I can use the prayers. You know all of these changes we are making are hard on people. We have a number of folks who are uncomfortable. So please pray that God will bless what we are doing."

"Oh, I don't pray for all that. I pray for you to keep preaching the Scriptures from Genesis to Revelation. Just keep preaching the Bible and don't get off-track. That's what I pray for every day for you."

We were in the middle of a nine-year, multimillion-dollar, all-campus renovation that was at the heart of an even bigger church cultural transformation. We were going to take every building but one down to the dirt and start over. It would be costly, inconvenient and disruptive. There would be lots of excitement and quite a few grumbles at the same time. Some thought it was an unnecessary expense I was pushing through for my own ego (one pastor in town called it "Tod's Temple"); others were excited about what we were doing. But in either case, I was thrilled to have someone so respected, so deeply faithful to Christ, so clearly prayerful praying for me and my leadership.

Only she really wasn't praying for my leadership at all, she was praying for my *faithful stewardship* of what she held most dear, the Scriptures and our theological traditions. She was praying that amid all of the things that were changing, I would keep very clear on what wouldn't or shouldn't change.

There is a delicate balance here. Usually, the pastor is the resident expert on the Scriptures and theological tradition. This is the one arena of life in which we usually have more training, experience and education than most (though not all; I have had many congregants who were every bit as knowledgeable as me). Having the role of pastor also means that we are expected and authorized to stand before the congregation every week (or more) and interpret and teach the Scriptures and the traditions. This is our clear authorized role, and we are expected to be good stewards of it.

At the same time, every congregation has a history, a set of core values and beliefs, a cultural and shared DNA, a church code.[5] These shared values, or what Ori Brafman and Rod Beckstrom, authors of *The Starfish and the Spider,* call "ideology" is what gives the organization life. If shared values are not "protected and passed down" then the organization ceases to be. Indeed, as Brafman and Beckstrom write: "Values *are* the organization."[6]

In most congregations these shared values are an expression of the biblical and theological tradition that founded and sustained the church. Without asserting the validity of any particular school of biblical interpretation or the merits of any tradition, I want to stress again that before we are able to help people discover new lessons or insights, we must prove ourselves trustworthy in protecting the core of beliefs that give a congregation its identity.

Since successful adaptive change is always a healthy adaptation of the DNA of an organization, for pastors who want to lead a congregation in change the most important thing to remember is that the first step is getting clear on what will *never* change. In order to earn the credibility to lead people into *what can be*, we have to demonstrate fidelity to *what is*. In a presentation to Duke Divinity School in 2008, Ronald Heifetz put it this way:

> Most real change is not about change. It's about identifying what cultural DNA is worth conserving, is precious and essential, and that indeed makes it worth suffering the losses so that you can find a way to bring the best of your tradition and history and values into the future.[7]

In my own tradition we have a maxim that dates back to the seventeenth century: "Reformed and always reforming by the word of God."[8] This serves to remind us that all teaching—and all congregational innovation—is always measured by the rule of the Scriptures. Before there can be leadership, there must be a demonstration of faithful stewardship to the Scriptures and your own tradition.

Competent stewardship of souls and communities. Pastors are more than preachers. Christian leaders are not just trusted with the Scriptures; we are also entrusted with souls. And before we can lead our people into uncharted territory, they have to believe that we will spiritually protect and personally care for them along the way. To be truly credible we also have to be *shepherds.* We have to tend the flock and protect them, keeping watch over everyone God has entrusted to us (Acts 20:28). Indeed, most congregants prefer *shepherds* to leaders, but in the Old Testament particularly shepherd *is* the biblical metaphor for Israel's leaders.

> Then Moses said to the LORD, "O LORD, you are the God who gives breath to all creatures. Please appoint a new man as leader for the community. Give them someone who will guide them wherever they go and *will lead them into battle*, so the community of the LORD *will not be like sheep without a shepherd.*" (Numbers 27:15-17 NLT, emphasis mine)

This theme continues in the prophets, with a passionate admonition that those who lead be good, fair and especially caring leaders—leaders after God's "own heart" (Ezekiel 34; Jeremiah 3), who put the well-being of the people before their own, who are trustworthy and indeed love the people they serve.

Jesus is, of course, the quintessential Shepherd, and for pastors called to shepherd the flock (1 Peter 5:2)—just as it was for Christ—that love is both intrinsic to a loving God *and* necessary for a larger purpose: *that the people of God would fulfill the mission of God to the glory of God.*

Shepherds don't just tend the sheep, protecting and caring for them, but they also lead them. Jesus, the good Shepherd, didn't heal people because he cared about them (though he clearly did!) but also to reveal the presence of the reign of God, to demonstrate the nature of the kingdom he had come to inaugurate, and to recruit and train followers in that particular manner so they should carry on his mission.

In the same way, we are to lead the people of God into the mission of God and to care for each person with the love of the tangible embrace of Christ. We are called to offer both love for people just where they are *and* to call and equip them to be part of the kingdom mission of Jesus in the world around them. But to be sure, *people need to experience the love of God as they are led into the mission of God.* If they don't feel loved, they will likely not let anyone lead them anywhere.

Competent stewardship of teams and tasks. Technical competence for the pastor is measured not only through fidelity to the Scriptures and the spiritual tending of souls and church, but also in the ability to competently *manage* the organization or institution given to our charge. Pastors of congregations need to be both personal and organizational. If they are not, they likely are not

NAVIGATIONAL GUIDE FOR ORGANIZATIONS
Of Souls and Institutions

She was the wife of a vice-chairman of a multinational corporation. He had just finished a long, good day of conversations with Christian leaders about the challenges of the global marketplace. I was their driver escorting them back to their hotel. I asked them how his work affected their marriage.

"As Christians, we all have responsibilities that we feel deeply," she explained. "I feel the responsibilities of the individuals in our lives; he feels the responsibilities for the institutions. My view of the world is 'soul by soul,' and his is necessarily 'institution by institution.' And sometimes that is a stress between us that we have to negotiate."

Of all the competing demands of leadership in every sector, perhaps the most difficult for a Christian leader is when the tough decision that will strengthen or even save the church, organization or institution creates difficulty for individuals. To be sure, these are the hardest decisions I have personally had to make as a leader. Three different times in my pastoral ministry and within the very first year at the seminary, I was part of decisions that led to painful layoffs of beloved dedicated employees. In every case there were some who thought a Christian organization should never do layoffs. ("If we are a family, how can we just let someone go?")

At the same time, we are responsible not only to those who work for the organization but also to those who give to the mission, who are shareholders for the company, who have invested time and resources in an organization that exists for more than giving employment to Christian people.

How do we navigate the stress when the needs of the many impinge on the needs of the few?

Leadership professor Scott Cormode often says to his students, "We don't have followers; we have people entrusted to our care."[a] For Cormode that trust is about both individual people and the collective work of a people. This stewardship extends to both the souls and the institution. Political scientist Hugh Heclo defines an institution as an "inheritance of valued purposes," what I would call a set of traditions and values that is greater than any one person and exists for a greater good.[b] And inheritance brings us back to stewardship, a deeply rooted biblical concept.

For the business or organization committed to good stewardship, it is not enough to care for souls; we must care for the body too. "To live in a culture that turns its back on institutions is equivalent to trying to live in a physical body without its skeleton or hoping to use a language but not its grammar."[c] We must attend to both the spirit or ethos of a place and the structures that enable it to endure. And navigating those stresses are at the very heart of Christian technical competence.

---

[a]For more information, see Scott Cormode, "Innovation and Imagination in Christian Organizations" (unpublished paper presented to the Academy of Religious Leadership, April 2015).
[b]Hugh Heclo, *On Thinking Institutionally* (St. Paul: Paradigm, 2008), 38.
[c]Ibid.

pastors. Spiritual directors, certainly. Evangelists, possibly. Prophets, maybe. Pastoring involves both persons and the communities they are part of. And this is a difficult challenge indeed!

To be a pastor requires being stewards of Scripture and souls, but also the teams and tasks that the community takes up. It is to know the people, the Scriptures *and* the organizational systems where the Word struggles to take root, grow in the souls and bear fruit in the lives of actual persons in actual towns and cities and cultures. Being a leader is the difference between Johnny Appleseed and an apple farmer. The farmer has to attend to both seeds and soil, and indeed even more than the soil. The farmer must be personally connected to the land, yes, but also to the fences, the barns, the silos and the livestock. The farmer must pay personal attention to the environment, the weather, the terrain and the seasons. The farmer must attend to the whole organic system that is the farm. In the same way, a leader can be the very best, most personally attentive, loving, caring, engaged and involved shepherd attending to the sheep, but if the farmer doesn't build a safe sheep pen, the wolves come.

For most leaders, *the organizational part is harder than the personal part.* Those of us who became pastors did so because we love people and the Word. Most of us wish that we could somehow limit our calling to knowing our people and knowing the Scriptures. But we also know better. The church *organization* needs as much pastoring as any person, and this is exactly where most of us are ill-prepared. We till the soil, we plant the seed, we water and wait for harvest—and then the fences fail, the roof caves in, the well runs dry and the backhoe needs a new battery. The bank calls our loan, the government changes its policies, the markets fluctuate and huge cultural forces seem to conspire against us. (Sounds like a church, huh?)

The root word for "organizational" is the same as for "organic." Perhaps that is a better distinction to make. With a growing dissatisfaction of impersonal organizational models, the answer isn't to create a false divide between personal and organizational. The answer is to repersonalize the organizational and to learn the ways of organic organizational pasturing, to recover again the rich biblical concepts of the church as a body that expresses a larger systemic reality of *members*, *parts* and *ligaments* that make up a larger interconnected, interrelated whole, to reconsider our organizational models around the actual descriptions of health and fruitfulness that the Scriptures teach and humans need.[9] And when we are able to do this, we gain the credibility needed to begin building our own Corps of Discovery.

FAILING OUR WAY TO GOD'S PLAN A

Any endeavor beyond the status quo is fraught with the possibilities of failure. Any new venture into the uncharted territory will undoubtedly result in lots of trial and error, mistakes and missteps along the way. When I was beginning my work establishing the division of vocation and formation at Fuller Seminary, one of my new mentors said to me, "Tod, I believe that our plan A is never God's plan A, and we only get to God's plan A when our plans A, B and C fail. So, you need to *fail* as soon as you can, so we can *learn* as quickly as possible."

Now to be sure, this man was not advocating for sloppy work or shoddy planning. He is himself an extremely capable, successful man. His business spans the globe and his philanthropy is wide reaching. He loves Jesus and wants to see the church flourish for the sake of the kingdom of God. But he wanted me to know that failure is a necessary part of learning and therefore a necessary part of leading. And if we want to make sure that we learn the lessons from our experimentations in innovation, then we need to fail with as much credibility and competence as possible. We need to make sure that when our attempts at innovation go awry it's because we have something to learn, and not because we mishandled an otherwise good idea.

Or in the indelicate words of our unofficial team motto, "We can fail, but we can't suck."

Competence gives us the credibility needed to learn from our mistakes. Without doubt, Lewis and Clark were credible leaders. The technical competence they brought with a wide variety of skills and roles, from planning to protection, from establishing military order to distributing medicinal care, from designing keelboats to recruiting the Corps, for negotiating with potentially hostile forces to maintaining *esprit de corps*, was evident every step of the way. But these skills would have been necessary on any ordinary military venture. These were not extraordinary skills in extraordinary circumstances but the authorized and expected performance of any platoon commander. Only as Lewis and Clark demonstrated their competence over the long months of arduous upstream travel and a harsh winter did they develop the credibility they would need in the minds of their men once they were in uncharted territory.

In the same way, leaders must demonstrate competence in fidelity to Scriptures and traditions, the nurture of souls and communities, and fruitfulness in tasks and teams of people running the work of the church in order to develop the credibility that will be necessary later when the harder work of adaptation and dealing with loss begins. Even more, while critical, the credibility of technical competence is not enough to lead genuine change, there must also be present a deep personal *trust*, which can only come through the *relational congruence* of a leader.

5

Preparing for the Unknown

This is an undertaking freighted with difficulties,
but my friend I do assure you that no man lives with whom
I would prefer to undertake such a trip as yourself. . . .
My friend, I join you with hand & heart.

William Clark,
Letter to Meriwether Lewis, July 24, 1803

It is possible to prepare for the future without knowing what it will be.
The primary way to prepare for the unknown is to attend to the quality
of our relationships, to how well we know and trust one another.

Margaret Wheatley,
"When Change Is Out of Control"

PREPARING FOR THE UNKNOWN

For important tasks, Jefferson preferred friends and protégés.[1] Of all the ways that Jefferson is the inspiration, the mind and the mentor behind the expedition, it is perhaps this particular and most personal of values that proved to be the most important, because without question Meriwether Lewis's best decision was to turn to a *friend* to be *his* partner.

Very soon after receiving the commission to lead the expedition, Meriwether Lewis wrote to an old army buddy, William Clark, to be his co-commander. While Clark had been Lewis's superior officer when they first met in 1795, by the time Lewis was making preparations for the expedition, Lewis had been given a captain's commission, while Clark had long been out of the military.

In accordance with military protocol, Jefferson had chosen Lewis as the sole commander. But while Lewis saw himself as a would-be Columbus, he knew he needed a partner equally capable and, even more, who he could completely trust. In a completely unexpected departure from military protocol, Lewis wrote and asked Clark to be his co-commander, partner and equal in rank, declaring, "Your situation if joined with me in this mission will in all respects be precisely such as my own."[2] Clark agreed.

Right before they were set to depart, in the midst of all the preparations, Lewis received word that the War Department had turned down Lewis's request to grant Clark a captain's commission. Clark would instead be made a lieutenant. An embarrassed and angered Lewis wrote immediately to Clark assuring him that even so, they would function as "equals in every point of view." Lewis wrote, "I think it will be best to let none of our party or any other persons know any thing about the grade." And they never did. If there was any temptation on Lewis's part to use this turn of events to take sole command, it's never once even mentioned in any of his writings. Indeed only Jefferson and a few members of the War Department knew that Captain Lewis was supposed to be in sole command of the expedition (with Lieutenant Clark as second-in-command). As far as the men of the expedition ever knew, they had co-commanders, *Captains* Lewis and Clark.[3]

Stephen Ambrose reminds us that Lewis and Clark are etched in our minds as one relational unit: "Lewisandclark." (Indeed, to this day, when their names are separated most of us don't recognize the reference. Travelers to Lewiston, Idaho, or Clark County, Kentucky, are often completely unaware of the origins of the place names.) Lewis and Clark were partners, co-commanders and "equals in all respects." In a world where most still believed in the divine right of kings, where even American presidents were from a different standing and class, in a military culture where there was a clear chain of command, and in the midst of a task that was filled with the unknown and uncertain, the only thing that Lewis and Clark counted on was they would be "Lewisandclark."[4]

This partnership forged out of friendship and Meriwether Lewis's keeping of his word to Clark created the context for building much more than a military unit—the very Corps of Discovery. From their first conversation to every

NAVIGATIONAL GUIDE FOR ORGANIZATIONS
Christian Leadership, Crosscultural Partnership

"So, even though you are an experienced manager and valued in your company, what would it be like if your company sent you to manage a new business in Africa?"

"I would need someone to teach me how to apply my experience in another context."

"Exactly. And that's my job. You are the expert manager, and I am the expert in the Christian nonprofit world. Running a Christian nonprofit like a good business is like running a good business in a different culture."

He paused and looked at his coffee. "Oh, I get it. I don't have to give up what I learned in business, I just have to apply differently. Maybe you could be of some help for me to figure this out."

Very often, experienced marketplace leaders who want to learn to lead in a specifically Christian context discover that their expertise lands awkwardly. They come across as "too corporate" or "too harsh." Or they live in reaction, assuming that the church, the school or the nonprofit organization isn't like the "real world," and they become too passive.

As both a senior leader who has brought experienced marketplace executives into the church and the academy, and as a consultant who has worked with many frustrated marketplace leaders who came to work in the nonprofit sector only to feel as if their expertise was rejected or marginalized, I am of the conviction that marketplace leaders need a translator or guide to help them navigate the unfamiliar territory with its different traditions, customs and language.

At the seminary, when we talk about translating materials from one language to another, we describe it as having two different dynamics: the literal translation and the cultural translation. And without the latter, the former fails.

In a similar way, when a marketplace leader steps into a nonprofit, church, school or mission organization, there is an ongoing need for translation. For Meriwether Lewis this was both the role of his partner William Clark and later Sacagawea (see chap. 14). Partnership is a necessity in a strange land for those of us who are trying to live out the values of Christianity in the marketplace or the skills of the marketplace in a Christian organization.

action on the expedition (and indeed, until Meriwether Lewis's tragic death), they remained solid friends.[5] Perhaps the most unexpected, challenging and delightful work of transformational leadership is when it becomes the shared work of friends.

BEYOND CREDIBILITY

If leaders are going to take on challenges beyond day-to-day technical ones, competence isn't enough. Credibility built through technical competence, while crucial, is not enough either. Especially in a congregation. The change needed for a typical traditional congregation to become a missionary congregation is radical and scary indeed. To lead into uncharted territory is to reconsider the cherished narratives and assumptions, and as Ronald Heifetz reminds us, "Refashioning narratives means refashioning loyalties."[6] To ask church members to close down a once-cherished ministry to make room for something new, to reallocate support from a beloved foreign missionary to a new local missional initiative, to experiment with new forms of worship, to restructure the staff for less ministry to church members and more projects to reach out to the unchurched, or to even reconsider their very "beliefs, habits and values" (the core of adaptive work) will require far more than agreeing that the pastor "knows what he is doing."

In addition, we need to grasp just how difficult organizational transformation can be. Even *if* we agree that we are in an adapt-or-die (even *adventure-or-die*) moment, the urgency of the situation is not enough. When given that particular choice, *90 percent choose dying*.[7] In a study of those who were faced with exactly that choice—stop drinking or you will die, stop smoking or you will die, change your diet now or you will die, the vast majority choose to risk death. In a world where we now have the technology to do heart valve bypasses and even complete heart transplants, we continually fail at getting people to change the behavior that makes these procedures necessary. As Ronald Heifetz says, "We have the technology to fix the heart, but not change it."[8]

True change of heart, true transformation, is so profoundly challenging because "the sustainability of change depends on having the people with the problem internalize the change itself."[9] This demands new ways of thinking and new ways of behaving that depend entirely on new ways of *relating*. The transformational leader cannot rely on competence and credibility alone. In an address to a Duke Divinity School Convocation, Ronald Heifetz said, "Adaptive processes don't require leadership with answers. It requires leadership that create *structures that hold people together through the very conflictive, passionate, and sometimes awful process of addressing questions for which there aren't easy answers.*"[10]

When we think of structures, we tend to think institutionally, but what Heifetz and his colleagues refer to often as a "holding environment" or "containing vessel" is far more an expression of *relationships* than a formal configuration of policies, procedures and rules. "A holding environment consists of all those ties that bind people together and enable them to maintain their collective focus on what they are trying to do. All the human sources of cohesion."[11]

One of my clients was thrust into a leadership role when her senior pastor abruptly resigned—right in the middle of a huge organizational transition process. Not only was the church in the midst of change, but now they were without their designated leader. My client, who had been one of the associate pastors, was being asked to shepherd the church through a very uncertain season. Frankly, most of the people in the pew assumed that she would be a placeholder for a few days until a "real" interim pastor could be found. To her, it didn't matter whether she was the associate pastor, the interim pastor or the senior pastor. She just did the thing she does best: she gathered her colleagues together and they started collaborating, literally "colaboring." Together they talked, prayed, planned, prayed some more and talked even more. Soon, a few days turned into a few weeks, a few weeks into a few months, and without fanfare, huge disruption or significant financial cost the church slowly moved into its future preparing for a new pastor. The anxious church calmed down and continued their organizational transition. What was this bold leadership move? Convening the team.[12] Creating a holding environment of healthy relationships that will keep the work before the people.

> ***REORIENTATION***
>
> In uncharted territory, trust is as essential as the air we breathe. If trust is lost, the journey is over.

The ability to innovate, to be creative, to consider new options, to "shift habits, beliefs or values" requires "a sturdy, trustworthy space" fashioned out of *healthy relationships.*[13] I am not advocating that church leaders compromise on essential tenets of faith, but a number of cherished beliefs or convictions *will* be challenged in a change process. Thus, along with establishing credibility the leader must build a shared corporate culture of deep *trust*. As Margaret Wheatley observes, "The primary way to prepare for the unknown is to attend to the quality of our relationships, to how well we know and trust one another."[14] Trust is vital for change leadership. Without trust there is no "travel." When trust is lost, the journey is over.

BUILDING TRUST

Trust must be added to credibility. Relationships must be healthy, life-giving and strong. The web of connectedness within the organization must be able to hold each other in the midst of all the chaos that comes from not knowing what is to come. But how is trust established in a group, a community, a team or a family? How is congregational trust increased in a world where pastors are now considered less inherently trustworthy than engineers or dentists?[15]

Through actions.

"There is only one thing that builds trust: the way people behave," say Dennis and Michelle Rea, experts in helping corporations rebuild trust after a tragedy or scandal.[16] But to be considered truly trustworthy, those actions can't be one-off events or one-time responses to a particularly critical situation; they must be a *consistent* expression of the character and values of the leader. Meriwether Lewis did not merely invite Clark to be his partner, he insisted on it even when the War Department wouldn't give Clark the necessary rank. This partnership was not in name only. They truly functioned as partners.

Psychologist, executive coach and consultant Jim Osterhaus of TAG Consulting takes it one step further: "The *irreducible minimum* in leadership is trust, and trust is based on a leader's own self-definition." Corporate trust is anchored in a leader's own *self*-definition, and that self-definition requires repeated, consistent actions. Trust comes from the *congruence* of leaders repeatedly doing what we say. Osterhaus explains his own company's corporate culture: "It may be considered by some to be a little thing, but we say that it is a value to us that we are personally present to our clients. So, that means we can't coach from airports, we can't coach from our cars. We have to be fully present to people."

When we are experienced as congruent, trust goes up; when we are incongruent—when my words don't match my actions—the trust level goes down.

According to Osterhaus, "Trust is gained like a thermostat and lost like a light switch." A leader builds trust slowly over time by constantly monitoring the conditions and actions that create the climate of trust in the room. But even one action, if perceived as incongruent, can make the levels of trust plummet into darkness.[17] In order to establish and deepen trust, the leader must add to his or her own technical competence what I call "relational congruence" (see fig. 5.1).

RELATIONAL CONGRUENCE

Relational congruence is the ability to be fundamentally the same person with the same values in every relationship, in every circumstance and especially amidst every crisis. It is the internal capacity to keep promises to God, to self and to one's relationships that consistently express one's identity and values in spiritually and emotionally healthy ways. Relational congruence is about both *constancy* and *care* at the same time. It is about both character and affection, and self-knowledge and authentic self-expression. Relational congruence is the leader's ability to cultivate strong, healthy, caring relationships; maintaining healthy boundaries; and communicating clear expectations, all

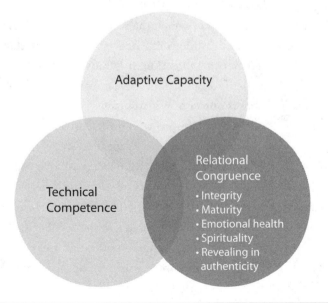

Figure 5.1. Relational congruence

while staying focused on the mission. As one of my clients, a former Army Ranger and West Point graduate said to me, "The mission first; the men always."

Relational congruence is more than consistent behavior; it is *constancy* that comes from genuine affection, warmth and indeed love for followers and colleagues. Relational congruence builds trust because it answers the two fundamental questions that every follower has for a leader: What are this person's intentions toward me? And is he or she capable of acting on those intentions?[18]

Edwin Friedman describes relational congruence using the psychological concept of *self-differentiation* developed by Murray Bowen:

> Someone who has clarity about his or her own life goals, and, therefore, someone who is less likely to become lost in the anxious emotional processes swirling about. I mean someone who can be separate while still remaining connected, and therefore can maintain a modifying, non-anxious, and sometimes challenging presence. I mean someone who can manage his or her own reactivity to the automatic reactivity of others, and therefore be able to take stands at the risk of displeasing.[19]

This rare and precious combination is the key to being a relationally congruent and ultimately a trustworthy and trust-building leader.

While relational congruence is often the result of significant amounts of crucial internal work through things like one-on-one discipleship, psychotherapy, coaching and spiritual direction, it is most powerfully developed during the early stages of the organizational transformation work itself. Indeed, Wheatley notes, "There is one core principle for developing these relationships. People must be engaged in *meaningful work together* if they are to transcend individual concerns and develop new capacities."[20]

This point should not be missed. The trust needed to bring organizational transformation in a changing context is not built sitting in a circle. It isn't built in bull sessions or ropes courses. It's not built over drinks in a bar or by telling our family histories. It's not even built in small groups or Bible studies. Those activities may create connections, strengthen affinities and even conceive friendships. But only *"meaningful work together"* develops the kinds of relationships that will endure into uncharted territory.

Even more, it's worth noting that strong social or spiritual friendships shouldn't be depended on to ignite or sustain organizational change *on their own.* Their power and loyalty may be harnessed to accomplish the work, but friendship that includes shared, meaningful work is of a different sort altogether and may come from unsuspected and unlikely pairings, trios or teams. Some existing friendships may translate well (like Lewis and Clark, for sure), but for the sake of the ministry that we have been given, we must be committed to building purpose-filled "working friendships" with those who can make change happen with us.

For the Corps of Discovery this meant that though the friendship between Lewis and Clark was important, equally important was how their partnership worked out in practice during the months of laboring together to travel upstream, the long winter in what is now North Dakota and the brutal month-long portage of the Great Falls of Montana. These were not only tasks to accomplish but tests that allowed the men to test the mettle of their leaders. As they watched and worked with the captains in a variety of challenging experiences, they saw their leaders present a competent and *unified* front.

The men of the Corps of Discovery experienced their leaders as constant and caring, and congruently so in every context.[21] There is not one documented example of Lewis and Clark breaking ranks with each other in a three-year expedition through the most dangerous and unknown territory ever explored. From the evidence we have, they had no disagreements in front of the men. There was never a hint that Lewis, who clearly had the authority to do so, *ever* pulled rank on Clark. By the time they came to the Lemhi Pass and readied themselves to go into uncharted territory, it was clear: The men now completely trusted their captains and each other. This cadre of men had become a *corps.*

For Christian leaders this means that ministry is not only the means to bring the gospel to the world, *ministry together* is how God makes a congregation into a corps that is ready to *continually* bring the gospel in new ways to a *changing* world. As missionaries who have been thrown together into unfamiliar surroundings with little more than a sense of call and commitment to each other, when we love each other and are dedicated to our mission, we change.

Of all the landmark discoveries and mental-model reorientations that resulted from Lewis and Clark's discoveries, perhaps the most overlooked is their incredibly effective model of a leadership partnership. In the face of an American mythology of the lone leader who comes and singlehandedly saves the day, Lewis and Clark stand as an alternative mental model of partnership and corps.[22] Indeed, in my experience working in business, higher education, nonprofit and church settings, I have rarely seen the level of collaboration and partnership that Lewis and Clark demonstrated. While there are churches with copastors and small businesses led by partners, the vast majority of endeavors assume the model of the sole head. Fully two hundred years after the expedition, perhaps nothing is more radical than the notion that partnership and friendship is a requirement for leading into uncharted territory. In a passage worthy of quoting at length, historian Stephen Ambrose describes the significance of the effectiveness of "Lewisandclark":

> What Lewis and Clark and the men of the Corps of Discovery had demonstrated is that there is nothing that people cannot do if they get themselves together and act as a team. Here you have thirty-two men who had become so close, so bonded, that when they heard a cough at night, they knew who instantly had a cold. They could see a man's shape in the dark and know who it was. They knew who liked salt on his meat and who didn't. They knew who was the best shot, the fastest runner, the one who could get a fire going the quickest on a rainy day. Around the campfire, they got to know about each other's parents and loved ones, and each other's hopes and dreams. They had come to love each other to the point where they would have sold their lives gladly to save a comrade. They had developed a bond, become a band of brothers, and together they were able to accomplish feats that astonish us today.
>
> It was the captains who welded the Corps of Discovery into a team. Indeed, a family. This was their greatest accomplishment. They made their divided command work as efficiently and effectively as a Roman legion or any other elite outfit in history, not one of which had risked a divided command.[23]

THE CONGRUENCE THAT CREATES A CONGREGATIONAL CORPS

Lewis and Clark used their deep friendship, built on shared, meaningful, purposeful work, to build the Corps into a family. The family then became even more effective for the sake of their mission. When they most needed it—when going off the map into the depths of the Rocky Mountains—they could rely on their deep trust in each other.[24]

For Christians who have answered the call to follow the Master who also calls us friends (John 15:15) and gives us to each other as brothers and sisters

(John 19:26-27), this relational congruence is even more critical. For the mission of Jesus entrusted to his followers (John 20:21) is expressed to the world through the love that the disciples have for each other (John 13:34-35).

But it is crucial to remember again that the goal of the expedition was *not* to build a family—it was to find a route to the Pacific Ocean. Similarly, the goal of the Christian faith is not simply to become more loving community but to *be a community of people who participate in God's mission* to heal the world by reestablishing his loving reign "on earth as it is in heaven."

A congregation becomes a corps when it develops trust in the leaders and each other. That trust is developed through technically competent and relationally congruent leaders. Relationally congruent leaders not only demonstrate constancy and care, but do so throughout the whole organization. For the pastor a missional congregation must first be a trusting and caring congregation, a congregation where there is a healthy *culture* that creates the context for a congregation to become not only a corps, but also a Corps of Discovery.

6

Eating Strategy for Breakfast

If one wishes to distinguish leadership from management or administration, one can argue that leaders create and change culture, while management and administration act within culture.

EDGAR H. SCHEIN,
ORGANIZATIONAL CULTURE AND LEADERSHIP

Leaders shape culture by default or design.

BOB HENLEY

"SO, HOW DO YOU CHANGE A CHURCH'S CULTURE?" he asked.

"Sex," I answered.

He was into his second or third tortilla chip and almost choked on the salsa. This was not the answer that he was looking for. We were not only just beginning our first lunch together as colleagues in the presbytery, but John also was only months into his new call, his first as a senior pastor. He was a young pastor with a young family the church hoped would help them reach the young families who filled the community around them. The church hired John with a lot of hoopla about how the church was going to enter a new day of creativity and innovation, but every strategy he had initiated in the first few months of ministry, every new idea he had proposed had been subtly (and sometimes not-so-subtly) sabotaged.

After telling me the story of another failed initiative to shift the emphasis of the church away from the older, long-time members to focus more on reaching out to and serving unchurched younger families, I repeated the famous phrase most often attributed to Peter Drucker, "Culture eats strategy for breakfast."[1]

What do we mean when we talk about "organizational culture," and what does it have to do with relational congruence and building the trust necessary to lead a church into uncharted territory? (And what does it have to do with sex?)

Consider this chapter one last preparatory stop before heading into uncharted territory. Like the winter that the Corps of Discovery spent with the Mandan Tribe in what is now North Dakota, this chapter is meant to help you take stock of what you have to take with you as you go off the map and into an uncertain future. Here is the key idea: *The most critical attribute a congregation must have to thrive in uncharted territory is a healthy organizational culture.* Understanding delicate and often undefined dynamics and engaging the leader's relational congruence are both necessary to cultivate a healthy culture that will sustain the mission of the organization.

ORGANIZATIONAL CULTURE

Culture, as Andy Crouch describes it, is "what we make of the world."[2] It is the combination of "the *language* we live in, the *artifacts* that we make use of, the *rituals* we engage in, our approach to *ethics*, the *institutions* we are a part of and the *narratives* we inhabit [that] have the power to shape our lives profoundly."[3] Culture is the air current that lifts the bird, the water that holds the swimming fish, the background and frame that draws the eye to the center of a picture. It is all the unnoticed, taken-for-granted and powerfully present elements that shape our lives and work.

Organizational culture, as defined by John Kotter, is the "group norms of behavior and the underlying shared values that help keep those norms in place."[4] Culture is the set of default behaviors and usually unexamined or unreflective practices that make up the organizational life and ethos of a company, organization, family or church. In short, organizational culture is "the way we do things around here."

Some cultures are formal, others informal. Some are loud, freewheeling and chaotic, while other organizational cultures are rigorous, serious and disciplined. Some are transparent and collaborative; others are polished and hierarchical. Culture is not the aspired values printed on a poster or put up on a website. Culture is the combination of *actual* values and concrete actions that shape the warp and woof of organizational life.

Kotter explains that organizational culture is usually set by the founders of the group and reinforced through success. When a value leads to a behavior that results in a desired outcome, then the values and behaviors become embedded in the group's DNA.[5] Just as a body's DNA reproduces the characteristics of that human in its offspring, the DNA of an organization is reproduced by default through the organization. Like reproduces like. The DNA of an organization, if not altered by design or default, keeps reproducing the same enduring characteristics.

The key words in Kotter's definition are *behaviors* and *values*. Actions form the organizational culture, and that culture—like the DNA of a body—keeps reproducing the same values and behaviors. Note again, it's not the *aspired* values that shape the church culture but the *actual* values that produce and are expressed in actual behaviors. It's not enough to say that "we value creativity" if every creative idea is immediately criticized. It's not enough for a church to "be committed to evangelism" if there are no adult baptisms. In the words of Dallas Willard, "to believe something is to *act* as if it is true."[6] A church can say that it values hospitality, discipleship and transparency, but these become part of the DNA of the church only when they are so resiliently present that they happen automatically, by default, because all aspects of the organizational life reflexively support and reinforce them. The *actual* behaviors of those in authority express and shape the *actual* values of the organizational culture.

This is critical for the leader who feels called to take a church or organization into uncharted territory. No matter how much power and authority you perceive resides in your title or position, no matter how eloquently you articulate the call of God and the needs of the world, no matter how well you strategize, plan and pray, the actual behaviors of the congregation—the default functioning, the organizational DNA—*dominate* in times of stress and change. Not only do we all default to our training, but we also run home to momma too. That is, in times of stress or change, if we do not deliberately and consciously pay attention to what we are doing, we *will* default and run to what is known, familiar and embedded within the organizational life. This is normal coping. This *just happens*.

For missional theologian JR Woodward this "unseen culture" is more important than strategy, vision or planning in determining a congregation's health, openness to change and missional conviction.[7] A church culture built on meeting the needs of its members will struggle with implementing changes that depend on putting those self-interested needs aside. A church that has expressed its devotion to God in the beauty and majesty of its worship will *unconsciously* resist a new informal service where people come in casual clothes carrying cups of coffee. Again, the successes of the past reinforce and remain embedded within the culture. Indeed, one of the key dictums of systems thinking (see chap. 8) is: "Today's problems are from yesterday's solutions."[8]

A church that has maintained unity through homogeneity will find it difficult to welcome those who differ in lifestyle, education, mores and social class. A congregation with a thriving ministry with young families may struggle with reaching single adults. And, especially in the missional conversation, very often the church that struggles most with mission to its neighbors has decades of success sending missionaries overseas. These mostly unconscious, often unreflective default mental models are far more powerful than any sermon, new program, revised vision or missional initiative. Numerous organizational writers have said the same thing: "After working on strategy for 20 years, I can say this: culture will trump strategy, every time. The best strategic idea means nothing in isolation. If the strategy conflicts with how a group of people already believe, behave or make decisions it will fail."[9]

ALIGNMENT TOWARD A HEALTHY CULTURE

JR Woodward writes, "While management acts within culture, leadership *creates* culture."[10] Creating a healthy culture with the capacity to experiment, innovate, take risks and adapt is one of the primary preparatory tasks of a leader. That culture creation work rests on identifying the gaps between aspired values and actual behavior, and then working with the leaders to bring every aspect of the organization into alignment with the core ideology (core values, mission, primary strategy). In chapter seven, we will see how this work of identifying the gaps is the key task for bringing adaptive change, but for now the alignment work is the initial activity for creating a healthy organizational culture. As John Kotter writes, "The idea of getting people moving in the same direction appears to be an organizational problem. But what executives need to do is not organize people but *align* them."[11] As we will see, the more aligned an organization is, the healthier it is.

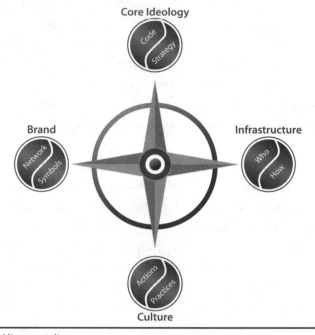

Figure 6.1. Alignment diagram

In my work with TAG Consulting, Kevin Graham Ford and I developed an alignment diagram that we use to enable our clients to see the gaps between their core ideology (core values, mission and strategy) and the actual be-haviors and ways of functioning that make up the church culture (see fig. 6.1). Before we discuss any changes in infrastructure (that is, the personnel, policies, bylaws or procedures) or branding (the public face of networks, communi-cation, alliances and publicity), we focus all our attention on bringing clarity to the core ideology and alignment expressed in how a culture functions.

As with a car's wheels, when an organizational structure is out of alignment, great effort is expended keeping things between the guardrails. It is hard to move forward when the church, family or company is lurching from one ex-treme to the other, when people are unclear about the direction, are overcom-pensating for corrections, or fearfully engage the brakes just as progress begins.

My wife, Beth, and I have consulted with a ten-year-old church that started in an elementary school multipurpose room. While the leaders talked passionately and with great pride about how "every member is a minister" and how they "all shared leadership," Beth and I soon discovered that the pastor made every important decision, personally invited and followed up every new attender, passed out fliers in the neighborhood, and drove the truck and set up every chair on Sunday mornings in order to "have church." Several times the pastor tried to delegate tasks to others, but eventually they would revert back to him. Although they are in a wealthy community, even after a decade the church has continued to sputter along on the brink of closing down. The church has good people and good theology, but the discrepancy between their stated value (every member is a minister) and their actions (including the pastor's!) demonstrates the momentum-sapping effect of a lack of alignment.

In contrast, a *healthy* culture is aligned, cohesive and clear.[12] A healthy culture is one where there is "minimal politics and confusion, high degrees of morale and productivity, and very low turnover among good employees."[13] In a healthy organizational culture, people feel free to have candid conversations, to suggest new strategies or ideas, and to take risks and experiment. There are fewer gaps between values and behavior, and more consistent actions at every level of the system, which reinforce and increase trust. If constancy is the hallmark of a trustworthy leader, then consistency is the hallmark of a trustworthy system.

For many of us an organization like this seems almost unimaginable, even (maybe especially!) in our churches. Long ago we came to expect that being part of a church community means biding our time, biting our tongues and being part of something that is at best well-meaning. But organizational health is a tangible reality that is both worth fighting for and necessary. According to Patrick Lencioni, "organizational health" is the "single greatest advantage" any company, organization or congregation can have toward accomplishing its mission, and is perhaps the single biggest differentiating quality between successful and less successful organizations.[14] And as Lencioni points out, it doesn't cost one dime. While achieving a healthy organizational culture takes time and effort, discipline and courage, the result is that when the real challenges of transformation come there will be a deep wellspring of trust and goodwill from which to draw.

So, how do we create a healthy culture or change an unhealthy one? If this is one of the primary responsibilities and results of leadership, then let me suggest three critical elements in the leader's *own* functioning for contributing to a healthy organizational culture: clarity, embodiment and love.

CLARITY

For Patrick Lencioni, organizational clarity and organizational health are virtually synonymous. After affirming the discipline of a cohesive team that creates agreements and accountability, Lencioni then advocates three more disciplines for a healthy organization: "create clarity," "overcommunicate clarity" and "reinforce clarity." As soon as an executive team builds the cohesiveness that comes from trust, they immediately start laboring for clarity of shared values, purpose, communication and behavior in every decision throughout the organization.

In *The Starfish and the Spider*, Ori Brafman and Rod Beckstrom write about decentralized "starfish" organizations of the future that run more like "networks" than "corporations." Brafman and Beckstrom highlight what they call "Rule 8" (or what I have called the "Really, Really Important Rule #8").[15] I have already mentioned it: shared values *are* the organization. If "leadership shapes culture by default or design," then whether it is a more traditional hierarchical organization or an emerging network, in a world that is now increasingly diverse, decentralized, post-Christendom and flat, this work of instilling and protecting shared values is more important than ever. Indeed, the *primary* work of technical leadership is clarifying and reinforcing shared values.

In the Scriptures we see this concept put forth by Paul in some of the strongest language of the New Testament. "If then there is any encouragement in Christ, any consolation from love, any sharing in the Spirit, any compassion and sympathy, make my joy complete: be of the same mind, having the same love, being in full accord and of one mind." What we are calling "shared values," Paul terms as the "same mind." And that same mind is more than thinking the same way; it is about common cause, common care and a shared commitment to look out for the others. Paul continues: "Do nothing from selfish ambition or conceit, but in humility regard others as better than yourselves. Let each of you look not to your own interests, but to the interests of others" (Philippians 2:1-4).

Perhaps in a previous generation where a highly regulated, centralized and authoritative structure was commonplace, some could argue that shared values could be enforced through power, position or other incentives. But today a genuine culture shift requires *voluntary* submission to shared values. No longer will church members simply accept the values of their leaders as their own. No longer will people dutifully submit their own ideals for the sake of a group. Before leaders begin any transformational work, *cultivating a healthy environment for aligned shared values to guide all decision making* must be a priority. Indeed, the values must be *truly* shared.

While this certainly includes lots of communication (what Brafman and Beckstrom call "maintaining the drumbeat of the ideology"),[16] it is also about education (teaching the values), wise collaborative discernment (determining when missional effectiveness requires change)[17] and perhaps most importantly mutual *accountability* for living out those values. Or what I like to call "embodiment."

EMBODIMENT

Can you guess this organization? There were shared values reinforced in every meeting. There were banners hung throughout the corporate offices. They were the pillars of a sixty-four-page Code of Ethics Manual that they trumpeted as the source of their wild financial success: Communication, Respect, Integrity and Excellence.

You guessed it, didn't you? *Enron*, the infamous company that became synonymous with corporate greed and unethical behavior. This much is clear to all of us: A statement of shared values, no matter how inspiring, does not make a healthy culture. Posters on the wall, seminars and training sessions, manuals and policies don't accomplish it either. What does? According to business ethicist David Burkus, who compared the corporate and ethical cultures of Enron and Zappos, "People typically do not look to written codes for clues about how to behave; they look to others."[18]

Whether in ethics or innovation, or in rule following or risk taking, organizational culture is shaped by the actions of people, especially the leaders. Note the connection that Peter Steinke makes between the behavior of leaders and the system's "direction aligned with purposes":

> Like healthy people, systems promote their health through "responsible and enlightened behavior." The people who are most in position to enhance the health of a system are precisely those who have been empowered to be responsible, namely the leaders. . . . They set a tone, invite collaboration, make deci-

sions, map a direction, establish boundaries, encourage self-expression, restrain what threatens the integrity of the whole, and keep the system's direction aligned with purposes.[19]

As we were going through our congregational assessment and revisioning at San Clemente Presbyterian Church in 2007, Kevin Graham Ford was finishing up a two-day retreat with our leaders, which clearly was going to send our church in a much more collaborative direction. The TAG Assessment had revealed that one of the largest perceived contributors to the growing sense of disconnection and disengagement among our members was that the "executive staff controls everything." As one frustrated elder said to me, "Nothing is allowed to be tried around here, Tod, until you and your Sanhedrin approve it."

He was right. In order to keep unity of purpose and direction, every program, every event and every bit of equipment required approval by the executive staff. While it helped ensure that we didn't have ministries going off in different and even sometimes competitive directions, it also meant we discovered that a number of people felt stifled.

So after two days discussing this increasing sense of disengagement, I suggested to Kevin that perhaps we should start working on realigning the organizational chart around a more collaborative model of ministry. Kevin responded, "Don't change anything in the infrastructure yet. Just start living into the new way of being. Start *functioning differently* and let's see what happens."

I had assumed that the next step of creating change within our church culture would be restructuring or reorganizing, but it wasn't. Only as we began to *act* differently would we then know what infrastructure changes were needed to reinforce the new culture.[20] John Kotter puts it this way: "How does culture change? A powerful person at the top, or a large enough group from anywhere in the organization, decides the old ways are not working, figures out a change vision, starts acting differently, and enlists others to act differently."[21]

At SCPC this meant making one small but significant change to my executive staff. We decided that for the next year, the executive team would simply approve every ministry request and then tell people to work out whatever issues came up. We didn't make a big deal of it. We just kept saying yes. Soon there was a burst of new initiatives, new leaders came to the fore, and, yes, there was a lot more mess, conflict and confusion. For someone who was trained to believe that leadership was about managing details, expectations and objectives, this was a trying season for me.[22] Friends and trusted advisers even began to ask me if I was "checking out" or "losing my passion" for the ministry. But we stayed with it, believing that increasing collaboration and expecting more personal responsibility from our church members would make us stronger. Through it all I was more engaged and passionate about what we were doing. Finally, after about a year of this creative chaos, we worked together as a larger leadership corps of about fifty people to come up with and put in place some simple rules that we used to become more self-organizing and collaborative.[23]

Creative collaboration and a more decentralized and empowering system did not come to our church because the leaders decreed it so or I gave a sermon or we reorganized our committees into teams. This new collaborative culture did not come overnight. It was a hard-won transition with lots of fits and starts, frustration and mess. Indeed, it was still incomplete even when I left my position as senior pastor in 2014. But whatever success we had in creating a new, more collaborative culture began when the executive staff changed their behaviors and embodied the new culture.

For a bunch of church professionals who had experienced success over the previous decade, it wasn't easy to change the behavior of a tightly knit group calling the shots. But change it we did, and for a most unexpected reason: we *loved* our church.

LOVE

We protect what we cherish. Love drives us to hold on to what is dear and cling to what gives us meaning and life. But it is also because of love that we are willing to change. It is a great paradox that love is not only the key to establishing and maintaining a healthy culture but is also the critical ingredient for *changing* a culture.

Which takes us back to my answer to my colleague John, who was eating chips and salsa.

How do we change the culture of a church? What if the default way of functioning is one of self-preservation? What if the behaviors of the leaders have created a culture of entitlement rather than discipleship? What if the church culture is focused on preserving American Christendom or worse? When the church's default behavior, way of functioning, its organizational DNA is now hindering the very thing that must be done to fulfill the mission God has given us, how do we change it? And if "culture eats strategy for breakfast," then how do we change the culture before we are eaten alive?

Well, how do we change *any* DNA?

Through sex. *You have to birth something new.*

Just like in biology, the elements of a new birth are a messy, mysterious combination of differences and love. When two people come together and form a bond, there is the potential for new life to emerge. In the same way, when leaders come together and create deep bonds of trust amid their differences, new life is created. Ronald Heifetz said, "You don't change by looking in the mirror; you change by encountering differences."[24] To be sure, fear of differences can keep us resolutely committed to the status quo, to rejecting what seems foreign and to circling the wagons to keep out the intruder.

My young colleague was deeply aware of the differences between himself and his new congregation. The honeymoon had ended rather abruptly, and it was clear to him that the vast majority of the mostly older, mostly traditional church congregation that talked passionately and eloquently about wanting to raise up the next generations of followers of Jesus were really not that interested in the change required to welcome the younger, unchurched families they had called him to reach. They just wanted him to settle in and minister to them. Before he knew it, he seethed in disappointment, anger and feeling a bit betrayed by both the congregation and God.

I looked at him and said it again. "You change the DNA of any living organism through birthing something new. The new birth won't be all you or all them but a new creation, a new living culture that is a combination of the past and the future you represent. But you have to communicate that you really love them, or they will never let you close enough to them to take in the different perspective, experiences and vision that you bring. Right now, they know you are disappointed in them, and they don't want to do anything but resist you. But seeing and embracing differences, if we know that we are loved and cherished just as we are, is also the way that we become open to the new possibilities. Love precedes change."

A half dozen years later my colleague and his church are moving together, extending themselves to their neighbors, welcoming new families and offering three full worship services that witness to Christ in their local community. The pastor is deeply connected to the church, and the church deeply trusts their pastor.

FROM A HEALTHY CULTURE TO ADAPTIVE CAPACITY

This chapter has been about reinforcing one final attribute before launching into uncharted territory and the transformation we desire for ourselves and our congregations. *The most critical attribute that a congregation must have if it is going to thrive in uncharted territory is a healthy organizational culture.* When leaders are perceived as technically competent, they gain credibility in the eyes of their followers. When they are perceived as relationally congruent, trust is established. When credibility and trust are mobilized to create a healthy organizational culture, then we are ready to embrace the thrilling and daunting task of entering uncharted territory. We are a corps that is ready to become the Corps of Discovery by learning together and developing adaptive capacity.

Part Three

LEADING OFF THE MAP

In Uncharted Territory
Adaptation Is Everything

- 7 -

Navigating the
"Geography of Reality"

*Those who follow Jesus embody fluidity, adaptation, and collaboration.
It's what we call the third-culture way. Adaptable to changing
circumstances. To challenging cultures. To complex crises
and problems. If there's one quality that matters most
to the fate of the church in the twenty-first
century, it's adaptability.*

DAVE GIBBONS, *THE MONKEY AND THE FISH*

*I did not despair of shortly finding a passage over the mountains
and of tasting the waters of the great Columbia this evening.*

MERIWETHER LEWIS, *THE JOURNALS OF THE
LEWIS AND CLARK EXPEDITION*, AUGUST 12, 1805

LEWIS AT LEMHI

Dayton Duncan and Ken Burns describe a defining moment in Meriwether
Lewis's life:

> He was approaching the farthest boundary of the Louisiana Territory, the Continental Divide—the spine of the Rocky Mountains beyond which the rivers flow west. No American citizen had ever been there before. This he believed

was the Northwest Passage: the goal of explorers for more than three centuries, the great prize that Thomas Jefferson had sent him to find and claim for the United States.

With each stride, Lewis was nearing what he expected to be the crowning moment of his expedition and his life. From the vantage point just ahead, all of science and geography had prepared him to see the watershed of the Columbia and beyond it, perhaps, a great plain that led down to the Pacific.

Instead there were just more mountains—"immence ranges of high mountains still to the West of us," he wrote, "with their tops partially covered with snow."

At that moment, in the daunting vista spread out at the feet of Meriwether Lewis, the dream of an easy water route across the continent—a dream stretching back to Christopher Columbus—was shattered.[1]

According to historical geographer John Logan Allen, that moment atop the Lemhi Pass was when the "geography of hope" gave way to the "geography of reality."[2] A disappointing reality it must have been. When a mental model dies, a painful paradigm shift takes place within us. It is disorienting and anxiety making. It's as if the world as we know it ceases to exist. Meriwether Lewis makes no comment about that world-rearranging moment in his journal, but Sgt. Patrick Gass describes his reaction some days later, saying that they "proceeded over the most terrible mountains I ever beheld."[3] This is exactly the moment that the church faces today with the demise of Christendom and a changing topography of faith. In this new culture a new missional mental model is needed, and a new way of leading—and learning—is necessary.

ADAPTIVE LEADERSHIP: LOSS, LEARNING AND GAPS

Adaptive leadership is about "letting go, learning as we go, and keeping going." It's about loss, learning and gaps: "Adaptive leadership consists of the learning required to address conflicts in the values people hold, or to diminish the gap between the values people stand for and the reality they face."[4]

Anybody who has ever visited London has seen the ubiquitous "Mind the Gap" signs in the underground subway system. They warn travelers to watch their steps because of the small chasm between the train and the platform. Adaptive leadership is exercised in helping our communities "mind the gap" between our aspired values and our actions, between our values and the reality we face. It is a shared realization of a group's inability to live out its own most cherished values with vibrancy and effectiveness in a changing context. Even more so, adaptive work pays attention to the deeper underlying causes that keep a group perilously perched in a state of inaction.

This mode of leading raises up and sheds light on the *competing values* that keep a group stuck in the status quo. For churches, competing values like caring for longtime members versus reaching out to the unchurched, assuring excellence in ministry programming versus increasing participation with more volunteers, giving pay raises to staff versus bringing on a new hire, assuring control and unity versus collaboration and innovation entail conflict about things of equal or near equal *value*. Because they are both valued, the competition for resources and the decisions that need to be made can put individuals and congregations into a most vulnerable moment. Like a person with one foot on the platform and one in the train, the moment of adaptation exposes the gaps within a system and forces the leadership to ask painful questions: What will we lose if we have to choose one of these values over the other? What must we be willing to let go?

Making hard decisions in the face of competing values is what every explorer confronts when they go off the map and into uncharted territory. Through their technical competence, Lewis and Clark led their men up the Missouri River. Because of their relational congruence, the men became a corps, and when they stepped off the map, they were prepared to be a Corps of Discovery requiring adaptive capacity.

ADAPTIVE CAPACITY

Adaptive capacity is defined by Heifetz, Linsky and Grashow as "the resilience of people and the capacity of systems to engage in problem-defining and problem-solving work in the midst of adaptive pressures and the resulting disequilibrium."[5]

When the world is different than we expected, we become disoriented. When the tried-and-true solutions to our problems don't work, we get stuck. When we are faced with competing values that demand a decision which will inevitably lead to loss, we can get overwhelmed. At exactly the moment when the congregation is looking to the leader to give direction, the leader's own anxiety and inner uncertainty is the highest. But this is the moment when the transformational leader goes off the map and begins to lead differently. This is when the transformational leader mobilizes a group toward *the growth they will need* in order to face the disorientation and find the capacity to reframe their *shared* identity in a new expression of their *shared* mission.

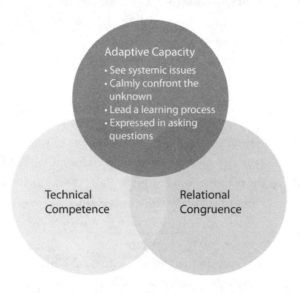

Adaptive Capacity
• See systemic issues
• Calmly confront the unknown
• Lead a learning process
• Expressed in asking questions

Technical Competence

Relational Congruence

Figure 7.1. Adaptive capacity

This *adaptive capacity* is the crucial leadership element for a changing world (see fig. 7.1). While it is grounded on the professional credibility that comes from technical competence and the trust gained through relational congruence, adaptive capacity is also its own set of skills to be mastered. These skills include the capacity to

- calmly face the unknown

- refuse quick fixes

- engage others in the learning and transformation necessary to take on the challenge that is before them

- seek new perspectives

- ask questions that reveal competing values and gaps in values and actions

- raise up the deeper issues at work in a community
- explore and confront resistance and sabotage
- learn and change without sacrificing personal or organizational fidelity
- act politically and stay connected relationally
- help the congregation make hard, often painful decisions to effectively fulfill their mission in a changing context

This capacity building is more than just some techniques to master. It's a set of deeply developed capabilities that *are the result of ongoing transformation in the life of a leader.*

SUFFERING THROUGH YOUTH SUNDAY AGAIN

When I was first called to San Clemente Presbyterian Church in 1997, the nominating committee let me know that my calling was part of a larger desire to reach out to and indeed "win back" young families who had left the church during a season of pastoral turbulence that preceded my coming. I made it clear however that we would *not* focus on getting families now rooted in new church communities to uproot again and return. Instead we would focus our efforts on reaching new families moving into our community, which was in the middle of a building boom.

Like most of the churches at that time, SCPC was segmented by age and stage, with teenagers and children rarely attending "big church" or even feeling like part of the greater church community. So our youth ministry ran like a parachurch ministry within a church. While it was great at exposing kids to the gospel, we had a serious backdoor problem with kids who came during their teenage years leaving and never returning as they entered adulthood.

Sensing an opportunity to differentiate ourselves from churches around us, we brainstormed in a staff meeting about how we could help our teens and families feel a greater sense of community with the larger church. Immediately one of the staff said, "Let's have Youth Sunday." Around the tables were nods and agreements, and the staff reminisced about previous Youth Sundays. Since I was new, they explained that about once a year the teens led the service. The youth band led worship, the teenagers dressed up in good clothes and ushered, and the youth leader picked teenagers to preach. They all talked about it with real enthusiasm. Except for two people: the business manager and the junior high director. While everyone else grew nostalgic, they both shook their heads. When I pressed them for their opinions, the business manager went first.

"That is our lowest-attendance, lowest-giving Sunday of the year. Church members feel guilty, but they hate that service. They love the kids, but they hate the music, they feel awkward for the kids up front, and most people find an excuse to be gone that day."

Ouch. I looked at the junior high director.

He said, "Yup. And the kids hate it too. They know the older folks don't like their music. They feel silly wearing shirts and ties to pass the collection plate. We have trouble getting a kid who feels capable of doing the sermon, and everybody ends up feeling awkward and patronized."

I looked back at the others, and while some still thought it was something we *should* do, they agreed it didn't help kids feel more connected. Indeed, we had been doing it and we still have the problem of teenagers not feeling part of the church community. Youth Sunday hadn't worked after all.

So, I asked, "If we knew that Youth Sunday hadn't worked to help teenagers feel more connected to the church, why did we suggest it?" After talking about it a while we came to the conclusion that we were talking about it, *because it was the only thing we knew how to do.*

Now, to be clear, I'm not criticizing Youth Sundays (or my staff). Those conversations led to a number of experiments that helped us begin new traditions that involved our youth in Sunday morning services. I'm not even criticizing my own church's Youth Sundays of the past. Indeed, that year we attempted one more Youth Sunday, and the thirteen-year-old preacher for that morning is now a young adult elder in the church. But I'm trying to point out that when we get to moments of deep disorientation, we often try to reorient around old ways of doing things. We go back to what we know how to do. *We keep canoeing even though there is no river.* At least part of the reason we do this is because we resolutely hope that the future will be like the past and that we already have the expertise needed for what is in front of us. And facing the "geography of reality" and the inner uncertainty that arises within us is extremely difficult.

As Meriwether Lewis approached the top of the Continental Divide, something within him had to be preparing for what he was about to see. Though he wrote of being sure he was about to crest the hill and find the Columbia River, ample warning signs had already suggested things weren't going to go exactly as he hoped. The Mandans told Lewis during the winter that there were mountains, not a river, ahead. The men noted in their journals that the steep grade they were slowly ascending made a navigable water route less likely. And they had recorded that they had seen the spine of the Rockies looming before them *three months* earlier.

REORIENTATION

When our old maps fail us, something within us dies.

Replacing our paradigms is both deeply painful and absolutely critical.

Even that view had raised within Lewis the thought of "difficulties which this snowy barrier would most probably throw in my way to the Pacific," including likely "sufferings and hardships."

We too are not unfamiliar with the fear of barriers, sufferings and hardships when the world as we know it is changing rapidly, though Lewis's disciplined response might be unfamiliar to most of us. Lewis immediately cast the thoughts of perceived difficulties out of his mind, writing, "I will believe it to be a good comfortable road until I am compelled to believe differently."[6]

Lewis exemplified what happens to most of us when we are confronting rapidly changing circumstances: even though the evidence is around us, *we cling to the previously held assumptions as long as possible*. Now, to his credit and as an exemplar for us, Meriwether Lewis wasted no time in casting off that assumption once the brutal facts of his situation were clear.[7] There was no water route, there were miles and miles of snowcapped mountain peaks in front of them, they had no trail to follow, food was scarce in this rugged terrain and winter was coming.

This *is* the *canoeing the mountains* moment. This was when the Corps of Discovery faced for the first time the breadth of the challenges posed by the Rocky Mountains and came to the irrefutable reality that there was no Northwest Passage, no navigable water route to the Pacific Ocean. This is the moment when they had to leave their boats, find horses and make the giant adaptive shift that comes from realizing their mental models for the terrain in front of them were wrong.

History is defined by this moment and all they *could have* done. They could have decided that they had indeed discovered the vitally important but certainly disappointing reality that the long-hoped-for Northwest Passage and its water route was a myth. They had set out defined by a myth. Imagine their thoughts as that reality set in.

They could have turned back. They could have returned to Washington, made their reports and told Thomas Jefferson that another crew more equipped to travel long distances through mountain passes should be launched on a different expedition.[8] But they didn't. At that moment, without even discussing it, Meriwether Lewis simply "proceeded on." In so doing he offers us some ways of considering our own adaptive moments and the capacities we need.

RECOMMITMENT TO CORE IDEOLOGY

First, by continuing on, they *recommitted* to their core ideology. At the core of adaptive work is clarifying what is precious, elemental—even essential—to the identity of an organization. The core ideology of any group functions as both a charter and an identity statement. *This is who we are,* we say. If we stop being about *this,* we stop being. The Corps of Discovery was a military expedition with a mission to fulfill, a charge to keep and a commander in chief who had sent them. Their captains were also men of the Enlightenment, inspired by their president and committed to learning as much as they could about this broad continent. They were a *corps.* And they were a corps *of discovery.* This was their mission and their identity. There was more to their charge than finding a water route, and there was a larger sense of purpose they needed to recover and recommit to at that moment.

Leadership author Jack Uldrich reminds us that while Thomas Jefferson had made it clear that "the object of your mission is single, the direct water communication from sea to sea formed by the bed of the Missouri & perhaps the Oregon," Lewis and Clark had an even higher purpose than finding the water route.[9] In a comparison between Alexander Mackenzie, the Scottish explorer who first made his way by land to the Pacific through what is now Canada in 1793 as a purely commercial endeavor, Uldrich notes that part of Lewis and Clark's enduring respect and fame was because they had a "passionate purpose" that went beyond personal gain borne of their Enlightenment values that permeated eighteenth-century Virginia.[10] These Jeffersonian values of education, exploration and service to others as a way to give meaning to life is most evident in Meriwether Lewis's reflection from his thirty-first birthday journal entry less than a week after he crossed over the Lemhi Pass. "I reflected that I had yet done but little, very little indeed, to further the happiness of the human race, or to advance the information of the succeeding generation . . . and resolved in the future . . . to live for mankind, as I have heretofore lived for myself."[11]

For Lewis, his commitment to the Enlightenment ideals made him even more resolved in his life and, I believe, in his mission. This was more than a commercial endeavor, and there was something even more important than Jefferson's singular object of the mission: the core values at stake kept them going beyond the map. As Uldrich writes, "Their commitment to these higher purposes, which transcended the mere worldly aspirations of power, glory, ego, or money, shines through their journals, and it is clear they affected virtually every action and decision Lewis and Clark made."[12]

For church leaders, moments of disequilibrium like Lewis and his party faced at the top of the Continental Divide certainly bring our own motivations into focus: *What are we really called to? Is it just to professional success or personal security? Is it merely to get more people in the church pews and dollars in the offering plates so our congregations can keep offering religious services to those who desire them? Is church leadership nothing more than an exercise in institutional survival?*

Or isn't there a higher purpose, a set of guiding principles, a clear compilation of core values that are more about being a community of people who exist to extend God's loving and just reign and rule in all the earth? This moment forces us to face and clarify our own core beliefs. And for each organization, this facing-the-unknown moment asks us particular questions we need to answer honestly together:

- Why do we exist as a congregation, institution or organization?

- What would be lost in our community, in our field or in our world if we ceased to be?

- What purposes and principles must we protect as central to our identity?

- What are we willing to let go of so the mission will continue?

At the heart of every leadership challenge beat deeper identity questions that demand answers. The changing terrain, the uncertainty of the future and the inner personal doubts cast us back to reflect on our deepest beliefs, our truest sense of self and vocation. When we recommit to our core ideology, we are claiming—no matter the circumstances—an identity that is larger than our success or failures.

REFRAMING STRATEGY

They *reframed* their strategy. With a recommitment to core ideology (values and mission) there is a critical moment to reframe the strategy for the mission at hand. In adaptive leadership, reframing is another way of talking about the shift in *values, expectations, attitudes* or *habits of behavior* necessary to face our most difficult challenges. It is a way of looking at the challenge before us through a different lens and in seeing it differently finding the possibilities for a new way of being and leading.[13]

Lewis and Clark reframed their mission. While it was no longer about finding the Northwest Passage or water route, it was *even more so about exploration.* Indeed, even *discovering that* there was no Northwest Passage was adding to the human knowledge of the day. In addition, they recorded hundreds of scientific discoveries, documenting species of animals and plants that were previously unrecorded. On the return trip, when there was nothing for them to gain personally, Lewis and Clark even separated for six weeks so they could explore two different areas and contribute to future explorers' greater knowledge of the West.

For church leaders facing this missional moment, the reframing of church strategy from a sanctuary-centered, membership-based, religious- and life-service provider to a local mission outpost for furthering the kingdom of God enables our congregations to discover a faithful expression of our corporate identity in a changing world. No longer will we be the center of or have a monopoly on cultural conversations regarding moral life and spiritual values. No longer do social structures support church life or give preferences to Christian tradition. But, in a more pluralistic public square, where there were many different voices and perspectives offered, we have an opportunity closer to Paul's at Mars Hill (Acts 17), engaging the philosophies of the day, or to the early Christians', whose movement gained credibility (and converts!) at least in part because of the way Christians cared for people during some of the worst epidemics.[14]

But a reframe itself is only a new way of *seeing* and describing the problem. This is as far as many missional congregations get. They change the labels on the old file folders and announce that they are now a mission and not a church. What were once called committees are now called teams, what was once a presbytery is now a mission agency, and the senior pastor is now the lead mission catalyst. A reframe, while vital, isn't enough to bring the deep, systemic changes necessary.[15]

NEW LEARNING

They *relied* on new learning. At the heart of adaptive leadership is *learning*. To put it bluntly, *if you are not learning anything new, it is not adaptive work*. It might be a good, necessary, wise, even vital strategy. But if your group is addressing a new challenge with an old solution, relying on a best practice or implementing the plan of a resident expert, then the solution is a technical one, not adaptive. Again, this is the place where so many churches' missional initiatives get stalled. We gather in large groups, we bring in consultants, we do workshops, and we create a list of missional initiatives. Very often the list of proposals sound like others we have heard: Build a gym. Bring in a rock band. Give away C. S. Lewis books. Hire a new CEO (or fire the old one). Change the name of the church. Design a cooler website.

Again, there is nothing wrong with a technical solution that works! If you can attract young families by building a gym, if you can create young adult disciples by hiring a rock band, if you can reach unbelieving skeptics by giving away copies of Lewis's *Mere Christianity*, if you can reinvigorate your church with a younger pastor (hopefully with a tattoo), then by all means do it! But if you find yourself with a high-priced rock band playing to a mostly empty gym while the tattooed younger pastor tries to organize cases of books you can't give away, then you'll need to reconsider your assumptions and look beyond a technical solution by *becoming a learning community*.

The moment Meriwether Lewis went over the Continental Divide was when the Corps of Discovery started *discovering*. As they entered the uncharted territory, they had to start learning all over again, adjusting their expectations (for one thing their trip became about a year longer than they had believed), reconsidering their strategies and forming new alliances and partnerships. At that moment their corps became a collaboration, not just between Lewis and Clark and the men, but especially with the Shoshone tribe and with the young Shoshone nursing mother who had joined their party the winter before. While we will discuss the contribution of Sacagawea in length, it's certain that without her guidance, without her people providing horses and without the presence of an older Shoshone man (Old Toby) leading them through an obscure trail through the mountains, the Corps of Discovery would have died in the mountains. But as the men learned and adapted to their surroundings, they went farther than any others of European descent had ventured.

In moments of uncertainty and disorientation, leaders own internal adaptations; that is, the work that leaders themselves have to do to clarify their own motives, identity and mission is the necessary precursor to the work that the entire community will have to do. When a leader and a people together resist the anxiety that would lead to throwing in the towel or relying on the quick fix, but instead look more deeply—recommitting to core values, reframing strategy and relying on learning—this enables them to gain the just-in-time experience necessary to keep the expedition going.

8

My Italian Grandfather
Was Killing Me

A "system" is an interconnected set of elements that is coherently
organized in a way that achieves something. If you look at
that definition closely for a minute, you can see that
a system must consist of three kinds of things:
elements, interconnections, and a
function or purpose.

DONELLA H. MEADOWS, *THINKING IN SYSTEMS*

In nature, adaptability is a highly conservative process.

RONALD HEIFETZ, LECTURE,
DUKE DIVINITY SCHOOL, OCTOBER 14, 2008

BUGGED IN THE SANCTUARY

I knew it before he opened his mouth. This guy was irked. I could see it in the way he was shifting in his seat and the way his face scrunched up like crumpled notebook paper. He sat in the back of the sanctuary. I found my attention circling back to him throughout my presentation. No surprise, as soon as I finished my presentation and asked for questions, his hand fired up. In a voice meant to carry through the cavernous space, he asked his "question."

"I don't understand what all this *business stuff* has to do with the church," he said, punching the words *business stuff* as if spitting tobacco. "We are a church, not a business. We are about saving souls, not making profits. We have the Bible; we don't need what they teach at Harvard Business School. Can you tell me what this *business stuff* has to do with us?"

I smiled. (Really!) I have answered this question a lot of times. Because I have been a pastor and a seminary professor with a PhD in practical theology from a leading evangelical seminary, most people assume that my presentation is going to be, well, more "spiritual" than it is. If they have read my other books, they come expecting me to teach about Christian community and spiritual formation. They don't expect Lewis and Clark, Ronald Heifetz, Ed Friedman and all this "B.S." (business stuff). But I have learned not to answer the question. At least not the way this kind of questioner expects. I cleared my throat, took a deep breath and gave the explanation that I have to offer almost every time I speak on adaptive leadership. It goes something like this: "This isn't business, this is biology."

If I intended my answer to uncrumple his face, I failed. But in reality, I knew for him and for many the idea of biology troubled them more than business and in fact got to the heart of the question. Business is a world many understand, even if they are not convinced that business lessons apply to the church. But most of us aren't that familiar with how God has designed all aspects of life—including corporate life, communities, families, organizations and churches—to adapt and thrive in changing environments. This is what I mean by biology, and to directly answer my troubled listener, it has everything to do with the church.

At the heart of adaptive leadership for the church is this conviction: The church is the body of Christ. It is a living organism, a vibrant *system*. And just like human bodies, human organizations thrive when they are cooperating with the wisdom of God for how that system is designed, how it grows and how it adapts to changing external environments.

You know your body has to adjust to a new time zone after a plane flight, or to new foods when you arrive in a new culture. And you know you have to learn a new language or develop the skills for navigating an outdoor market in a foreign land. That is what adaptive leadership is all about: *the way that living human systems learn and adapt to a changing environment so they can fulfill their purpose for being.*

SURVIVING THE ITALIANS

Let me offer another illustration, this time a bit more personal. My maternal grandfather was named Guido Evangelisti. I am proudly, and with great delight, of Italian heritage (my father's German surname not withstanding). I love being Italian, and I especially love Italian food. When I was a little boy, my grandmother helped raise me for a year at the Italian restaurant she and my grandfather had run for decades. It's been a joy to introduce my children to their heritage, including taking them to my grandfather's hometown outside of Lucca, Italy, for a family vacation.

But there is a sober side to being Italian. Most Italians don't live that long. My grandfather himself died at sixty, before I was born. No, I'm not referring to some shady Godfather-like violence but to heart disease. My grandfather died of a heart attack, and as I get older I realized that if I wanted to see my own grandchildren, I'd have to adapt the diet of cured meats, heavy sauces and ample amounts of pasta that I love. This didn't mean giving up Italian food but changing the way I cooked it so we could enjoy both food and life much longer than my grandfather.

My family system provides a helpful metaphor for any organizational system. Our churches and organizations are systems—organisms—with a unique life and vitality. They are not mechanistic religious production lines but bodies that need to be tended, cared for, challenged and strengthened so they can adapt to their environment. This is what adaptive leadership is all about: hanging on to the healthiest, most valuable parts of our identity in life and letting go of those things that hinder us from living and loving well.

Leadership for uncharted territory is a shared, *corporate* (see the Latin root word for "body," *corps*, in *corporate*?) learning process that enables the community to *thrive and fulfill its mission* in a new context, when the outside environment changes. Our

> ***REORIENTATION***
>
> In a Christendom world, vision was about seeing possibilities ahead and communicating excitement.
>
> In uncharted territory—where *no one* knows what's ahead—vision is about accurately seeing ourselves and defining reality.

task is leading the learning so our churches will *adapt* and *thrive* as a local expression of the larger system that is the body of Christ in the world. But in order to do that, we must first *see* the system.

LEADERSHIP VISION

Every book on leadership talks about vision. Leaders, it is assumed, are visionaries who have the unique ability to see past the horizon, to see the future coming before anyone else and prepare the organization to meet that challenge. That is surely a valuable ability. But leadership vision is often more about seeing clearly what *is* even more than what *will be*. As the former CEO and leadership author Max De Pree has famously written, "The first responsibility of a leader is to define reality."[1] And perhaps one of the most important pieces of reality that must be first defined is the reality that every organization, indeed every organism, functions within a larger system.

Seeing this *systemic nature* of all living things and seeing how one part of the system affects every other part is a crucial but often overlooked component of leadership vision. But to see the system, we must understand what systems are and how they function.

An organizational system is the composition and interaction of the people, resources, interconnections and purpose of a group. So a congregation is not just the group of people who gather on a particular Sunday, or merely those who have their names on the membership roles, but the combination of people, their relationships to each other and the mission (or purpose for being) of this congregation. This combination of elements makes up the larger system, and as any one element, relationship or the purposes changes, the system must adjust. This system definition is assumed in the working definition of leadership we are using here: *Energizing a community of people toward their own transformation in order to accomplish a shared mission in the face of a changing world.*

If a systems perspective gives us a window on the reality and dynamics of a congregation at work in this definition of leadership, then the next question understandably follows: How do we do that? What is the process or practices that energize a community for transformation and fulfilling of their mission or purpose? What are the core activities and practices of leadership in uncharted territory?

To understand that, we need to do a bit more unpacking of this key concept: Because the church is the *body* of Christ, in order to lead it a leader must be able to *see and lead the church as a living system.*

THE SYSTEM, THE CODE AND THREE QUESTIONS TO CONSIDER

"A system is a set of things—people, cells, molecules, or whatever—interconnected in such a way that they produce their own pattern of behavior over time."[2] To understand the church as a system is to understand that all living things comprise both their parts (cells, molecules, persons) and the relationships between them. The church is not a collective but a communion. A local congregation is not just a collection of individual people but *also* the love, commitment, values and mission they share. A healthy church, like any healthy living thing, is always defined by the nature, quality and behaviors of the relationships. As Wendell Berry said in a classic address titled "Health Is Membership," "I believe that the community—in the fullest sense: a place and all its creatures—is the smallest unit of health and that to speak of the health of an isolated individual is a contradiction in terms."[3] Indeed, even the Trinity is best understood as a relationship of distinct persons who share one essence.[4]

For rabbi, organizational systems teacher and psychologist Ed Friedman then, all congregational life and change is an "emotional field," a system where the relationship between the parts as they are fulfilling their purpose is even more important than the parts itself.[5] Or as an old Sufi teaching story puts it, "You think that because you understand 'one' that you must therefore understand 'two' because one and one make two. But you forget that you must also understand 'and.'"[6] Understanding living systems as a function of elements, relationships and purpose (all at the same time) enables us to understand even more clearly the work that is before us in leading transformation, and the importance of continually looking beneath the surface to the inherent parts, interactions and goals of the organization.

DNA

In chapter six I introduced the concept of organizational DNA. One of the most helpful metaphors for thinking about and then developing adaptive capacity is to think of our churches as a body with particular and unique traits that must be honored in any change process. In biology, DNA "contains the genetic information that allows all modern living things to function, grow and reproduce."[7] In human bodies our DNA is code that makes each of us unique, helps us to survive and thrive, and is what we pass on to offspring in reproduction. In organizational systems thinking the DNA of a group is a way of describing the essential and unique attributes—the "defining essence" or code of that group.[8] When describing a church's DNA, we are talking about the particular pieces that make up the church's identity and mission—the critical, essential elements that make a congregation who they are. It includes elements like core values, essential theological beliefs, defining strategy and mission priorities. Code is neither healthy nor unhealthy in itself, but the culture that comes from a church's code can be either positive or destructive. "Healthy growth is the result of a church's congruence with its code; poor health is caused by incongruence," writes Kevin Graham Ford.[9] When the elements, interconnection and purpose of a system align, the system is healthy; when they do not, the system becomes dysfunctional.

For a church this means that when the members, the relationships and the mission of the church are aligned and working symbiotically toward a shared purpose, the church functions well. People are both loved (relationship) and challenged (purpose). There is both a commitment to depth and authenticity (relationship) and space to welcome new people (purpose). There is an ability to accept people as they are (relationship) and to be continually transformed into the likeness of Christ (purpose). There is a deep desire to enjoy life together (relationships) and use our resources and energy to serve others (purpose).

Relationship and purpose are expressed in as wide a variety of ways as the diversity of the people (the elements) that make up the system. In the same way that love in one family may be expressed in big hugs and in another through home-cooked meals, in one church mission may be expressed in door-to-door evangelism and in another through starting a tutoring program. In other words, in the same way that each person is different with a unique DNA, each congregation has its own organizational DNA that affects its relationships and purpose. As Kevin Graham Ford explains, different people connect to the code of different churches: "Code is like a magnet in that it attracts people who resonate with it and are eager to be part of a similarly committed community."[10]

A few years ago a famous megachurch launched a new service in our town with a video feed of their superstar pastor. "So how did you think that new multisite megachurch was going to impact your church?" a pastor colleague from a different congregation asked me. "About the same as if a new Greek Orthodox church was planted in our town," I said.

In the same way that there are people who will connect to and be more at home in a Greek Orthodox church than at San Clemente Presbyterian Church, I believed there would be people who would connect to and be more at home with a video service in a high school gym than in our multigenerational, sanctuary communion service.

The megachurch had done its homework. They knew from their own records that a few hundred people from San Clemente drove up to forty-five minutes to attend their services. So, when they launched a new video-feed service, they weren't stealing sheep but serving their own members. These were people who wouldn't be going to our church anyway, because for one reason or another they didn't connect to the code of our church. At the same time, if we tried to become more like the megachurch or the Greek Orthodox Church to attract the people who would more naturally fit in those churches, we could potentially bring division and disruption to our church instead of growth.

This whole discussion about DNA, code and systems thinking is a way to understand the nature of the challenge we face in adaptive leadership. In the following sections I will describe in detail what those processes and principles entail, and consider the personal requirements for leaders to do this larger organizational learning, but *the core questions and the potential new solutions are always systemic issues that require the body to adapt in a way consistent to its DNA or code.* Just as human bodies adapt to a changing environment without losing their humanness, corporate bodies are also deeply protective of their essence or identity. Kevin Graham Ford explains:

> Your members will resist any change that is in conflict with the church's code. But they will also resist change if they don't perceive that leaders are intentionally preserving the church's code. By discovering and preserving your church's code, you will give your members a sense of safety so that they will be more open to change. In other words, they resonate with the church's code at a subconscious level. People will be more open to change if they know that you understand and value who they are—even if they are not conscious of their own connection to the code.[11]

Because every church has a different DNA code, Ronald Heifetz suggests that at the heart of any adaptive work are three key questions church leaders need to wrestle with together:[12]

- *What DNA is essential and must be preserved?* What, in the words of Jim Collins and Jerry Porras, "must never change"? What are the key elements of our theology, tradition, ministry practices and organizational culture that must be maintained at all costs because to lose them would be to lose our identity? Just as we discussed in chapter seven, for Lewis and Clark, *water route* was not as essential as *discovery*, and for churches, before we consider changing or adapting anything, we must first determine what is truly sacred.

- *What DNA can be discarded?* What elements of our church life, while important to us, are not essential? What can we stop doing or let die so we can free resources and energy for new forms of ministry? What do we need to celebrate for the impact it made in another day or circumstance that has outlived its usefulness? Or what do we need to set aside because there is no energy for or interest in it any longer? As we will discuss at length, this is the critical issue. "People don't resist change, per se. They resist loss," Heifetz and Linsky remind us.[13]

- *What DNA needs to be created through experimentation?* What essential part of the church's identity and mission needs to be adapted to a new day, environment or opportunity? How can the church keep doing the things it is called to do, but in a way that resonates, connects, serves and challenges people who wouldn't otherwise pay it any attention? What potential healthy partners will create the possibilities of birthing something new?

The answers to these questions are neither easy nor clear. Even the most cursory discussion reveals how what one person considers essential, another person considers expendable; and even more, what can be adapted or changed and what must remain the same. (Just think of the list of recent conflicts in most churches: worship style, polity and sexual ethics. Are these *essential, expendable* or able to be *adapted*?)

The conflict generated by these discussions can quickly cause leaders to avoid them if possible. Add to that the understandable desire to quickly find win-win solutions to problems and before we know it we are back to our old defaults, using strategies that have already proven themselves to be inadequate. We are canoeing without rivers once again.

But pausing to think about a church in light of its system or DNA gives us a frame for considering the challenges we face and at the same time, acknowledge a tension in all adaptive work:

1. *To learn and adapt we need new, creative experiments in relationships and purposes.* Although the old solutions may have been good and effective once, the old solutions are inadequate.

2. *When we are experimenting with new solutions within a living system, we are doing so with something that has a history, is alive and precious, and must be handled with care.*

Let's turn our attention to a process that will help us *carefully* work toward creative experiments.

9

Don't Just Do Something,
Stand There . . . Then Do Something

We need 100,000 people in 100,000 garages trying 100,000
things—in the hope that five of them break through.

THOMAS FRIEDMAN, *HOT, FLAT, AND CROWDED*

SURVIVING BEARS AND BRAINS

One of my early leadership coaches, Kirk Kirlin, taught me, "When what you are doing isn't working, there are two things you cannot do: (1) Do what you have already done, (2) Do nothing."[1] In other words, when we meet those moments of disequilibrium that arise within us because we are in an unfamiliar, anxiety-producing situation, we have to resist the temptation to fight, flee or freeze. We have to deliberately resist our default reaction to repeat what we have already done, hoping that this time it will have a different result (the oft-quoted definition of *insanity*), questioning our own tenacious clinging to previous training, a re-active mindset and quick-fix tactics. At those moments the tendency is to double down at doing what we have always done and resist the new information that tells us that the circumstances are different and that more drastic change is necessary.

In his *Everyday Survival: Why Smart People Do Stupid Things*, Laurence Gonzales writes that the key to surviving in a world filled with unknowns is keeping a constant posture of "curiosity, awareness, and attention." But, says Gonzales, we are not naturally inclined toward these characteristics.

Partly, says Gonzales, our brains work this way. We take experiences from our past and learn lessons—often the wrong lessons—from them. Specifically, we expect that whatever has been in the past will be the same in the future. That leads us to ignore "real information coming to us from our environment."[2]

When I was in Alaska, my friend Charlie and I went hiking with Laura, a transplanted Alaskan with lots of wilderness experience. Laura was sharing stories about encounters with grizzlies, and we were in rapt attention. She told stories and taught us good lessons. But probably the most important lesson I learned from her was the look on her face after I told her a story about a previous bear encounter in the wild. I was trail running in Mammoth Lakes, California, and made every possible mistake of judgment when I encountered a black bear. Although I know cognitively what you are supposed to do (stay calm, speak in a loud deliberate voice, wave your arms and hold your ground), I literally panicked and ran down the hill as fast as I could go, muttering to myself hopefully. "Bears don't run well down hill; they don't run well down hill," I mumbled through heavy breath and racing heart.

The bear didn't chase me. I made it back to my cabin out of breath, exhilarated and embarrassed at my own behavior.

Usually when I tell that story, I get a big laugh. The image of big, bad, experienced hiker Tod running down a hill like a shrieking kindergartner tends to get people laughing along with me at the irony and frailty of my own bravado.

But Laura didn't laugh. She just looked at me and said, "Jeez. You are really lucky. If you do that up here, a bear will kill you." Her words chilled and sobered me. I realized that because I had one encounter with a bear and acted improperly—*and got away with it*—I was more likely to do it again. To my own potentially fatal peril.

Even with all my experience with bears and wilderness, perhaps the most important thing I could learn was that *I was in a truly different place*. Most of my experience was invalid, and most of my so-called expertise was irrelevant. Indeed, my past experience, especially my past "success" could end up leading to my downfall.

In the same way, most of us trying to bring change in a post-Christendom world are attempting to use lessons we learned in one situation that are keeping us from adapting to a new spiritual terrain. But perhaps a humble stance of curiosity, awareness and attention, as well as a healthy skepticism at our own success, may indeed be the first lessons we need to learn, especially when our egos are on the line.

DECLINING ATTENDANCE AND AN ANXIOUS, ADAPTIVE MOMENT

There is nothing that freaks out a pastor like declining attendance numbers. While most of us try hard not to show it, when the Sunday morning crowds thin out, we take it personally. When we look at the attendance reports and see the decrease, it is tempting to make excuses, blame other factors or just deny it entirely.[3] If we do acknowledge the decline, we want to jump right in and turn it around. There is nothing that screams for a quick fix like less people in the pew (unless it's decreased giving too).

In the fall of 2012 we noticed that our worship attendance at SCPC had taken a dip. Nothing too serious, but it was certainly out of the ordinary for a congregation that had had enjoyed a fifteen-year season of slow, steady increase. After looking back at the data, the Session (elder board) and pastors decided to have a conversation about what could be causing this uncharacteristic ebb.

Immediately, in the brainstorming session, elders and staff started suggesting strategies for dealing with decline.

- We should offer a more practical sermon series. The one you are doing now is pretty heady.

- We should get the kids more involved, let's put together a new kid's choir.

- We could do some better marketing.

And so on. We did what most people do when faced with an anxiety-producing problem: *we try to fix it as quickly as possible.*

But soon, a few other elders started questioning the wisdom of all of this. "We really don't know *why* this is happening, right?" one said. Others suggested that it was fallout from widely publicized denominational struggles. Someone else wondered if it was because my increased travel schedule had me out of the pulpit more often than in the past. Still others asked if there were more youth sports events on Sunday this year. Most of us just scratched our heads. We knew *that* something was different; we just didn't know *what*.

Finally, one other elder spoke up. "Won't this just fix itself? By December we'll get back the crowds, and we'll still end the year with a growth in attendance. Why are we even worrying about it now?"

A few echoed that sentiment. After a few minutes of this freewheeling conversation, I called a time-out and suggested that instead of either jumping to solutions or trying to guess at causes (or ignoring it all together), we practice a *process* of adaptive inquiry and experiment that would help us use this season and learn from it. The elders agreed, and that led us to a two-month-long conversation.

IT'S ALL ABOUT THE PROCESS

The first component of developing adaptive capacity is to realize that it's a *process* of learning and adapting to fulfill a missional purpose, not to fix the immediate issues. For Heifetz, adaptive leadership tries to look behind what might be a symptom to bring health and growth to the larger system. In this way, adaptive leadership is different from what I call "directional leadership." Directional leadership offers direction and advice based on experience and expertise, while adaptive leadership functions in an arena where there is little experience and often no expertise.

Adaptive leadership, again, is about *leading the learning process* of a group who must develop new beliefs, habits or values, or shift their current ones in order to find new solutions that are consistent with their purpose for being. At the heart of this work is a three-step process of "observations, interpretations and interventions."[4] Heifetz, Linsky and Grashow describe it this way:

> Adaptive leadership is an iterative process involving three key activities: (1) observing events and patterns around you; (2) interpreting what you are observing (developing multiple hypotheses about what is really going on); and (3) designing interventions based on the observations and interpretations to address the adaptive challenge you have identified.[5]

When in uncharted territory, this adaptive *process* leadership (as opposed to directional leadership) counteracts the quick-fix mentality that is so natural and offers a structure for learning new interventions or experiments. When my elders and I found ourselves swirling in this new circumstance of declining attendance, I eventually recognized that we were facing a potential adaptive challenge that would lend itself well to this process. The first step was to spend some time accurately diagnosing the problem by getting some perspective.

GETTING UP ON THE BALCONY

Just like a doctor who does not want to prescribe a medicine until she or he has done a proper diagnosis, leaders need to take the time to insure that they have clearly seen the challenge before them before attempting a new program or making a big change. Trying to get this larger, systemic perspective is what Heifetz and Linsky call "getting up on the balcony," and it begins with making observations (see fig. 9.1).

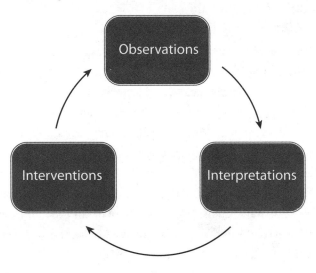

Figure 9.1. Up on the balcony

OBSERVATIONS

Observations are the data points for understanding a system. When a leadership team is on the balcony, their first task is to *get as many different observations that are as objective as possible* about the situation. In the observation stage, therefore, the group must intentionally withhold interpretations or interventions in order to gather as much data as possible. We should imagine making observations like we are doing a TV commentary on a soccer game. Our goal is simply to describe what we see: "The goalkeeper got the ball, kicked it to a midfielder, who passed it to a forward, who shot and scored."

For any human being, of course, objectivity is very hard to achieve. Indeed, Heifetz and Linsky acknowledge that observations are inherently *subjective*, especially when it comes to our own part in the system.[6] So, the first principle for good observations is to get as many of them as possible from as broad a perspective as possible. (Note that all three parts of the observations-interpretations-interventions process are *plural*.) This broad collection of observations functions like an overhead wide-angle lens on a camera that offers us a bird's-eye view of what is happening on the field below.

The National Football League uses a video system called "All-22" for all professional football games. It's a video system that records the entire game from overhead so that all twenty-two offensive and defensive players on the field are in view in any one play (or shot). It is standard for coaching and strategizing practices. Teams use it to take snapshots throughout the game and even fax pictures to the sidelines so coaches and players can get a broader perspective of what they can't see while on the field. The All-22 shows so much information that until 2012 the NFL would not release it to the public. They feared it would make Monday morning quarterbacks even more critical of players, coaches and referees, because with this perspective you can see everything going on in a play, including all the mistakes.[7]

At the same time, however, seeing from the balcony, while giving us one set of observations, doesn't give us everything we need. So, to get accurate observations, we must, as Heifetz and his colleagues say, "Look from the balcony and listen on the floor."[8] While we try to get distance and perspective to see what is going on, we can only understand it fully if we also know the dynamics on the field. From the balcony, a quarterback who looks like he missed seeing an open receiver may be running a play that calls for that receiver to be nothing but a decoy. The quarterback's "mistake" may actually be part of the play.

In autumn 2012, when our attendance did not come back from the usual summer slump, we decided to resist the temptation to either deny

> ***REORIENTATION***
>
> Leadership in the past meant coming up with solutions.
> Today it is learning how to ask new questions that we have been too scared, too busy or too proud to ask.

the problem or default to previous strategies, and instead made a plan to get as much perspective as possible. We decided to interview a cross-section of people we hadn't seen in worship in at least three months, asking every elder, deacon and staff person to identify three people they knew well who they also hadn't seen in church since the following spring. They asked their friends three questions:

1. When were you most excited or felt the sense of deepest connection to

our church? What was happening during that time in your life and in the
life of our church?

2. What has changed in your life or in the church since then that may have
   affected your sense of connection or excitement about our church?

3. What is one wish/hope/dream you have for the future of our church?[9]

Note that none of these questions asked why they weren't in worship, but tried
to get bigger observations to serve as data points. Each interviewer wrote
down the answers and then sent them on to one of the elders who collected
and collated the responses for presentation the following month.

To be sure, this work of looking from the balcony and listening on the floor
is both exhausting and often confusing. It's difficult to switch back and forth
between the balcony and the dance floor. It's very hard not to become defensive when you are a leader of the church being observed, and even more,
it's easy to feel like all you are doing is running up and down stairs, changing
viewpoints and taking in data without making any immediate progress. It may
be tiring work, but it is essential work if we are going to discover new ways of
looking at recurring problems. Leaders must be able to withhold interpretations and interventions long enough to be listeners who also have the vision
to see the deeper systemic realities at work in the organization.

At that meeting the elder presented the raw data with as many direct quotes
as possible (with some minor editing of any potentially sensitive names or
incidences). These were distributed to the elders, and all of us read through
the data looking for patterns, for common themes and especially for competing values that were contributing to our worship decline. But at this point
it was just observations. We were trying to gather and collate the responses as
the data for our study. After observations we moved to the second part of the
process, interpretations.

INTERPRETATIONS

Heifetz, Linsky and Grashow observe,

> The activity of interpreting might be understood as listening for the "song be-
> neath the words." The idea is to make your interpretations as accurate as pos-
> sible by considering the widest possible array of sensory information. In ad-
> dition to noticing what people are saying and doing explicitly, watch for body

language and emotion, and notice what is not being said. Ask yourself, "What underlying values and loyalties are at stake?"[10]

If the observation stage is to get as much data as possible, the interpretation stage is to hear the "song beneath the words." After gathering as many objective observations as possible, we then invite consciously *subjective* responses by looking for personal interpretations of the data. Again, the goal is to get as many divergent interpretations as possible, all the while listening for the common thread, themes—the song. While I may see a decline in worship service attendance as a reflection of people disliking my preaching, others may see it as God pruning the vine for further fruitfulness (John 15). While I may have received feedback that confirmed my bias that our music on Sunday morning is deeply ministering to people, others may hear a perspective that it is too repetitive and not creative enough. While these disparate interpretations may seem to contradict each other, the adaptive leader looks for the tune that weaves them together.

Listen to the songs beneath the words. In the interpretation stage we look for patterns we wouldn't normally notice. As we gather the interpretations, the leadership group also begins to question the interpretations themselves. Is this a recurring theme or just one perspective? Is there one loud voice that is drowning out others, or is there something we really need to hear that we have been unable to hear before? And even beyond those messages we listen for the unspoken emotion that creates energy in the speaker. Is there frustration, anger or sadness at work here? Is there an underlying enthusiasm, hope, determination? What is the tone of the tune?

Very often I ask my coaching clients to consider the question, What is the song behind the words that is keeping us all dancing? In other words, what deeper tune of the church is getting played in this circumstance? What is going on in this situation that nobody is talking about but is affecting the whole system of the church?

The song of worship decline. When we gathered as a Session to look over the data about our worship decline, a recurring theme was present. Very few of the respondents had anything negative to say about the worship services, the sermons or anything related to the Sunday morning experience. In fact, there was mostly nothing but appreciation. (Which I don't mind admitting was a bit of a relief to those of us who lead the worship and provide the sermons.) Those positive notes, however, were not enough to keep some coming back or even coming regularly at this time of their lives. (Which also gave the worship and preaching team a bit of pause. Are we not as important as we think we are?)

Because we asked them to talk more broadly about their own faith and life, a common theme appeared about *larger relational dynamics* that were unrelated to Sunday morning worship.

- We were so much more connected when the kids were in the youth program.

- Somehow, we got out of the habit of attending church when my husband retired and we started traveling more.

- We used to be really excited before [one of our former associate pastors] left to take another call.

And so on.

We experienced firsthand one of the laws of a system: *"Cause and effect are not closely related in time and space."*[11] That is, just like a hot water faucet that doesn't immediately deliver hot water, there is a time gap between the cause (turning the handle) and when we experience the effect (receiving hot water). The tendency then is to overcorrect while waiting for the effect (so, turning the water even hotter), and the solution becomes a new problem (burned hands).

Because of the gap between cause and effect, it is difficult to diagnose the true underlying causes of most problems. What we discovered by taking time to get as many observations and then sifting through the interpretations is that although we had diminishing worship attendance, *we didn't have a worship service problem but were still right in the middle of a larger challenge we had been working on for five years*. We also found that some of our other assumptions ("the church is declining because of denominational turmoil" or "People aren't coming because Tod is preaching a bit less" or "The congregation is getting tired of Tod's voice") didn't really have data to support them. Instead, we discovered a nuance to a larger issue that was completely unexpected: *Our church was not particularly good at helping people stay connected through life and church transitions*.

Most people in our church connect to the church like spokes on a wheel: everybody is connected to the whole through one or two points of contact.

When church members have children in the program, are settled in a small group or feel connected to a particular pastor or ministry, all is well. We are a stronger community of faith for people who are into a routine and rhythm of life. But when life changes, or when the church undergoes a change (like a higher amount of staff turnover that we went through in the previous five years), the ties that bind people together and to the church are loosened or detached completely. And even harder to detect is that it doesn't happen immediately but occurs over about a year's time.

When a couple enters the empty nest and no longer needs to bring their children to the youth program, or retire from work and have more discretionary free time, or when a key staff person leaves or a ministry is discontinued, then the connection to the church weakens. (Sadly, this seems to be true even with larger life events: the loss of a job, the death of a spouse, a divorce. While they call on the church in the middle of the crisis, the changing relational and personal dynamics seem to lead to more disconnection afterward.) Eventually this shows up in declining worship attendance, and, if not reconnected, the person drifts away. We discovered that we didn't need so much to attend to our worship as to our *web of connections*. We needed to focus our attention *not* on how to increase Sunday morning attendance but on how to strengthen and increase more points of connection for people, which would enable us *to better pastor people through life transitions*.[12] And the truth be told, that actually required much more work and more change in the way our pastors and leadership team worked than just trying to tweak the worship services.

Protect the minority voices. "People don't learn by staring into a mirror; people learn by encountering difference," observes Ron Heifetz.[13] The interpretation step is only productive if there is freedom to explore as many different interpretations as possible, and especially the opportunity to hear from usually ignored voices. When we at SCPC took the time to actually talk to disconnected people, we found something different from the assumptions of those who were still attending weekly worship faithfully. Those of us who were connected tended to think in terms of tweaking the sermon to make it a bit more relevant or making cosmetic changes to the services in order to be more welcoming, warmer or energetic. We talked about things that we, the committed stakeholders, wanted to see (like more practical sermons, more praise music, more kids singing in church), these are all good things and maybe even worthy of considering on their own, but would they actually help us grow our attendance? Then we talked to people who had already stopped attending our worship services and realized that none of those concerns were near the top of the factors that led them to become disconnected. If we had only listened to the committed people, we would never have gotten to the heart of the issues.

David McRaney, author of the book and the blog *You Are Not So Smart*, writes about "survivorship bias," that is, the tendency to look only at the "survivors" or "stories of success" and draw conclusions about reality.[14] McRaney discusses a group of World War II engineers who were trying to make bombers safer by studying the bullet hole patterns in the planes after returning from a mission. They knew that the planes needed more armor (and if they wanted it to fly they couldn't put armor over the entire plane), so they tried to determine where to put the additional armor. When they examined the planes, they discovered that they were shot up most on the bottom of the plane, on the wings and near the tail gunner. So, the engineers made preparations for putting more armor there. But one statistician, Abraham Wald, challenged the underlying assumption by pointing out that the planes they were studying were *the survivors*—these are the planes that were *not* shot down. In other words, Wald said, this is exactly where we should *not* put more armor—a plane *can* survive even if shot up in the bottom, wings and near the tail gunner. So they needed to look at other areas of the plane to reinforce. Through several tests they discovered that adding more armor to the ailerons, engine, stabilizers and around the pilot made the planes safer. Only listening to a different interpretation allowed them to find the right solution.

Survivorship bias is not only what makes us believe in the quick fixes offered by the diet industry or the magic of a celebrity CEO to turn around a company, but even, as one of my clients discovered, it's what makes a church leadership council believe that to attract young adults to their church they should never have a worship leader who is over thirty (true story, sadly!), or to mimic the success of the megachurch down the street (who has a completely different code). It is also what makes us eliminate voices we have marginalized because of whatever social criteria we unconsciously employ. The voices of women, ethnic minorities, laypeople, the young, the elderly, the poor, the less educated, the new members, the nonattenders—whatever the voice is that we are not hearing needs to be heard. And the beautiful irony is that when a leadership group insists on hearing as broadly as possible, a harmony of shared notes that are present but right below the surface often comes to the surface.

Raise up competing values. Any musician (and I am not) knows that harmonies in music are made up of concurrent concordant and discordant notes that sound in tension with each other and finally come to a resolution. That simultaneous tension of silence and sound, of notes that blend well and those that are related but different create the music that fills the ear and the heart. In organizational work the tensions in the music are caused by competing values that are usually unspoken but deeply powerful in any system. The final piece of the interpretation lens is to begin to raise up these values for discussion and consideration. Some common competing values dilemmas are

- Do we serve our longtime church members who pay the bills, or do we innovate to reach new people and risk angering the stakeholders?

- Do we have a mostly professional staff that provides excellence in ministry program, or do we want a strong, involved laity to use their gifts?

- Do we want a centralized organization unified around clear objectives, or do we want a more creative, collaborative system that is nimble, innovative and able to experiment with new ideas?

Note that competing values are difficult to navigate because each is *valuable.* These values serve the current church system, express what is truly treasured (not ideals or aspirations) and have been reinforced for a long time. At the same time, because the values are competing, the tension and stuckness they cause also reinforce the status quo. Eventually, the only way to move forward is for the leadership to intentionally make one of the competing values more of a priority than the other. But at this stage of the process, even raising the reality and reframing the church problem as an issue of competing values will help refocus the leaders on looking for new, adaptive interventions.

At SCPC the competing values in our worship-attendance decline were difficult to tease out. Now that we had an interpretation that reframed the problem as a *connection* issue rather than a worship issue, we could look for a different set of competing values from what was usually raised. This wasn't about styles of worship or excellence versus lay engagement, or seeker sensitive versus discipleship sermons. It was actually a more demanding set of questions about energy, resources, focus and job descriptions. The competing values in the worship decline was about the focus of our ministry: Is the priority taking the congregation deeper in discipleship (which had been my emphasis for the greater part of three years) or do we need to double down on creating a community with a stronger web of connections outside of the Sunday morning services? And what would that look like if we did? It also led us to some hard questions for our own introspection: Do we need to reconsider our strategies built around Sunday morning? And, even more daunting, if we have been working on this for the better part of five years, why haven't we made more progress?

Once we have made observations and interpretations, the next step in the adaptive learning process is experimenting with interventions (see fig. 9.1).

INTERVENTIONS

Without question the hardest part of an adaptive learning process is to keep people from jumping to interventions too early. Again, the desire for the quick fix is really strong. But by the time a group takes the time to go through observations and interpretations, another tendency takes root: *the tendency to talk a problem to death*. Once a group starts talking it's sometimes difficult for them to move to this third stage of experimenting. Again, it's important to note that even beginning to *do* something is still about the *learning*. This adaptive process is iterative. It repeats itself over and over again so that the organization can keep learning the lessons, adapting and implementing as we go. Now is the time to get right into the middle of the muddled mess and communicate loudly and clearly that we are going to use these experiments to learn as we go. At the intervention stage there are three principles that must be embraced in order to keep the system calm enough to move forward, make the adaptive shifts necessary and implement new solutions.

The eventual solution will be a healthy adaptation of the church DNA. Interventions must not violate the code of the church (see chap. 8). Be clear on what will never change before you start messing with stuff. To be a true adaptive experiment, interventions must be aligned with the church culture and reinforce the church core ideology; they must be *expressions* of the church's values, mission and primary strategy. If the leader uses the interventions as a way of getting through a personal agenda, all trust will be lost and all future experiments will be stopped before they start.

Interventions should start out modestly and playfully. The early experiments should not cost a lot of money, disrupt the organization chart, upset the center of the church life too much or be taken too seriously yet. They should instead be opportunities to try some things and see how the system reacts. In short, when intervening in the system, there needs to be a clear sense that *learning* is the goal, that we are not making any big, permanent changes yet but simply trying out some ideas to see what we will find. At SCPC the declining attendance numbers served to reinforce our sense that transforming the culture of our church would be even harder than tearing down all of our buildings and renovating the campus. Since we were already some years into the adaptive process, we decided the best place to experiment with interventions of connectedness was with our newest members. But mostly, the clearest intervention was *not* to make changes to the worship services. We resisted any notion that our declining attendance could be fixed through a change in worship, personnel, sermon styles or preaching schedules. Instead, we decided to focus our interventions where the observations and interpretations pointed: not Sunday morning worship but the rest of the week.

While we publicly discussed and even preached on the sense of disconnection still prevalent for many in our church, we didn't change anything in the worship services. We also didn't expect any of our long-term members who had strong connections to change anything. Instead we started some short-term groups, studies and gatherings aimed at connecting people during life transitions. Our family ministry started a wine and cheese night out for young parents (with childcare provided). We created more places of connection, conversation and common interest *between services* on Sunday morning. We also decided to spend one year with three of our committees (congregational care, discipleship and deacons) working together around one light-hearted theme of creating a "Plugged-In" church.

The interventions, while being modest and playful, also need to signal that more significant change is coming. These experiments will not go away if people get upset; we are not going back to the status quo. We are not going to rely on our canoes when we are facing mountains.

Innovative interventions will always be resisted. Most of us don't come to church to experiment. Even the idea of experiments raises anxiety. Most of the time the system will be inclined to shut down any experiments before they even begin. Growth, transformation and adaptation always means *loss*. Change is loss. And even experimental changes signal loud and clear that change—and loss—is coming.

The leaders of one of my church clients did a careful and lengthy study of observations and interventions that led the church to experiment with a contemporary blended worship service in their main sanctuary. They were not going to disrupt traditions of the choir and hymns, the traditional service; they merely were going to add an additional service led by a band to see what happened. (For this larger congregation, this was a modest experiment. They had the resources to add the service, and it didn't require making too many changes to existing staff responsibilities.)

When they installed some new drums in the sanctuary, a number of members of the congregation balked. The pastor assured them that they would *not* play the drums in the most traditional service. They just needed them available for the contemporary service. Still the members of the traditional service complained: they didn't even want to *look* at the drums, let alone hear them.

Wisely and calmly the leadership team pressed on with the experiment. They communicated that they were open to feedback, but that because their values, mission and strategy encouraged the formation of this service, they were going to keep going. The pastor took a lot of heat. Soon there was a growing movement *within the worship team* to have the drums removed so the older folks wouldn't be upset. The resistance was high, but the leadership team didn't waver. That was the moment when the adaptive capacity we had been developing was most needed.

10

The Mission Trumps!

Leadership is disappointing your own
people at a rate they can absorb.
RONALD HEIFETZ AND MARTY LINSKY,
LEADERSHIP ON THE LINE

Mature leadership begins with the leader's capacity to take
responsibility for his or her own emotional being and destiny.
EDWIN FRIEDMAN, *A FAILURE OF NERVE*

THE MAN SITTING ACROSS FROM ME was one of the most important people in my life. A mentor, a friend, an elder in my church, perhaps my biggest cheerleader; he had been on the search committee that called me. He was as responsible as anyone that my office had an ocean view in this church of my dreams. He is well known for a big smile and a radiant enthusiastic appearance. He's a dreamer, a visionary, a Barnabas if there ever was one. But he wasn't happy at all. The smile was gone. There was a look of sad resignation. He sighed, "Tod, just tell me. *Have you lost your passion for this ministry?*"

I shook my head, unsure if I had heard him correctly. "What?" I asked.

"Have you lost the passion for the church? You used to be such a *leader*, now it seems like you have lost the fire in the belly you used to have."

Okay. That one stung. A lot. But it wasn't the sting of truth. Not even a little bit. Yes, I was in the middle of an awkward stage of learning to lead differently than I had in the past. But I was more passionate than ever about what we were doing. What I felt was the sting of being misunderstood by someone I love. I just couldn't bear the look of *disappointment* on this dear man's face.

"Leadership is disappointing your own people at a rate they can absorb," write Heifetz and Linsky.[1] This painful truth brings us to the heart of the necessary adaptive capacity to lead transformational change in uncharted territory. Disappointing people "at a rate they can absorb" is a skill that requires nuance: Disappoint people too much and they give up on you, stop following you and may even turn on you. Don't disappoint them enough and you'll never lead them anywhere.

Leadership isn't so much skillfully helping a group accomplish what they *want* to do (that is *management*). Leadership is taking people where *they need to go and yet resist* going. Leadership, as I have defined it, is *energizing a community of people toward their own transformation in order to accomplish a shared mission in the face of a changing world.* It's about challenging, encouraging and equipping people to be *transformed* more and more into the kind of community that God can use to accomplish his plans in a particular locale. And often the very people who called us to lead them are disappointed when we do.

Transformational leadership is always a two-front battle: On one side is the challenge of a changing world, unfamiliar terrain and the test of finding new interventions that will enable the mission to move forward in a fruitful and faithful way. On the other side is the community that resists the change necessary for its survival. If adaptive leadership is "enabling a people to grow so they can face their greatest challenges and thrive," then it is crucial to acknowledge that a significant part of the greatest challenge is *internal*. Deftly handling resistance and the disappointment that comes along with it so a community of people can accomplish a goal for the greater good is the core capacity of adaptive leadership.

My friend didn't understand that the greatest challenge and most energizing passion of my professional and pastoral life were both being played out in the room. How was I going to lead a church into a more missional, collaborative future of widespread growth, discipleship and participation in mission so we can better reach our community if every action I took made my church members question my commitment? The answer was for me—and my leaders—to develop the adaptive capacity that comes from living out a core, clarifying conviction: *The mission trumps.* Always. Every time. In every conflict. Not the pastor. Not the members of the church who pay the bills. Not those who scream the loudest or who are most in pain. No. In a healthy Christian ministry, the mission wins every argument.

The *focused, shared, missional purpose* of the church or organization will trump every other competing value. It's more important than my preferences or personal desire. It's more critical than my leadership style, experience or past success. It's the grid by which we evaluate every other element in the church. It's the criterion for determining how we will spend our money, who we will hire and fire, which ministries we will start and which ones we will shut down. It's the tiebreaker in every argument and the principle by which we evaluate every decision we make. Denominational affiliation? Mission partnerships? Financial commitments? Staff decisions? Worship styles? The key question is: *Does it further our mission?* The mission trumps all.

One of my clients is the pastor of small church. Smaller churches usually don't have the resources to hire lots of staff, so their lifeblood is the service of committed laypeople volunteering their time. And in this case the pastor's key volunteer was a worship leader. Literally, they would not have worship on a Sunday morning if the worship leader didn't lead it or find a replacement. Over the years the relationship between the pastor and the lay worship leader turned into a dance of power. The pastor would articulate his desires for the worship service, but the worship leader would often balk and want to shape the service to her desires, have the band sing more songs or feature a solo. In a larger church where the pastor is the "boss" of a paid worship leader, this conflict certainly occurs, but usually the boss wins. But what does a pastor do to supervise or lead a volunteer? How does the pastor keep weekly worship planning from turning into a weekly power struggle? By having a clear, higher value that both the pastor and the worship leader agree to serve. By reframing the conversation around some shared agreements they both commit to serve, the conversation is no longer what each of them prefer, but serving the clear, shared purpose or philosophy. A mission statement serves the same purpose in a healthy organization. The one in power doesn't win every conversation: the mission trumps.

A shared mission, when it is a matter of clear conviction, offers *congrega-*

tional differentiation. It allows us to affirm the wide variety of the body of Christ and still be clear about the decisions we have to make. If the mission trumps all, then a leader must develop the clarity and conviction to live out that mission no matter the circumstance, no matter whether the challenge comes from the context or the very community we serve.

BACK TO THE DRUM SET AND THE WORSHIP WAR

The church leaders from chapter nine didn't waver on the drums. *But they didn't insist on them either.*

They quickly realized that this conflict was providing them with the opportunity to engage the larger church in discussions that would grow *their* adaptive capacity. They didn't minimize the concerns and make an executive decision. They didn't yield to the demands of powerful stakeholders in the congregation. Instead they used the discord around the drums to spark a conversation about something far more important than what kind of musical instrument to use.

Since adaptive leadership is about the capacity to "enable a people to *grow* so *they* can face their biggest challenges," the adaptive leader must stay continually focused on the *process* that will bring transformation to the community *and* address the big challenge at hand. The iterative process of observations, interpretations and interventions will enable the congregation to create new experimental interventions for addressing each particular challenge. For my client it was experimenting with a new contemporary worship service; for SCPC it has been trying alternative venues and ministries for reaching the unchurched, and experimenting with ways of building community and connection outside of worship. For each context the *interventions* that follow the *observations* and *interpretations* will be different, unique to each church and specific to each context. But make no mistake, experimenting is *necessary.*

Indeed, *experimental innovations are the key to surviving in a changing world.* After studying small companies that were able to stay in business seventy-five years or more, even as the world changed around them, Peter Senge concludes, "The key to their survival was the ability to run 'experiments in the margin,' to continually explore new business and organizational opportunities that create potential new sources of growth." Or as Ronald Heifetz told a group of ministry leaders at Duke Divinity School, "Adaptive change is built on experimentation."[2]

But experimental interventions trigger resistance—*internal resistance*. Resistance within our community and resistance within ourselves. Systems seek to secure the status quo, to experience and maintain equilibrium. Families, companies, organizations and congregations are wired for homeostasis. The emotional processes, ways of relating and being, decision making, symbols, values and other parts of the organizational culture (see chap. 6) naturally work together to *keep things the same*. The church leadership who calls a young pastor to reach young families thwarts every new initiative. The evangelistic pastor who attracts outsiders to the church is accused of not caring for the church membership. The preacher who was called to bring intellectual depth is chided that she should tell more stories and offer more practical teaching. The elder board that commits to a new vision for ministering to their neighbors will place all the plans on hold in order to attend to denominational issues that have simmered for generations. This is normal. It's natural. It's what Edwin Friedman calls "the persistence of form."[3] Or in the famous saying most often attributed to Edwards Deming, "your system is perfectly designed to get the results you are getting."

It's tempting to look longingly back at the Corps of Discovery and wish we were more like the brave adventurers who crossed the Continental Divide than the Israelites who yearned to return to Egypt mere weeks after their liberation. But in truth Lewis and Clark faced their share of internal issues within the Corps, especially early on. There were lapses of discipline, bouts of insubordination, even a trial for mutiny, which led to the expulsion of one of the men from the expedition. So, what is the leader to do when the resistance comes, when the very Corps of Discovery that you are leading into the uncharted territory of a post-Christendom world decides it would rather die than adapt? What do we do when the community that declares their commitment to venturing into uncharted territory is doing everything to remain huddled around a campfire in familiar terrain?

Here is the strategy for leading into uncharted territory. It is a maxim for the leader to live by and a goal to be developed within the larger leadership group. In this and the following three chapters we'll look at it clause by clause. It's that important. I encourage you to commit it to memory. Write it on a

Post-it note and put it on your bathroom mirror. Make it your screensaver on your computer. And say it to yourself over and over again:

Start with conviction,
stay calm,
stay connected,
and stay the course.[4]

START WITH CONVICTION

The first question about leading into uncharted territory is not about change but about what will *not* change. First we determine what is precious, what is worth keeping no matter the circumstances, what will never change, what is the core ideology of the church. Conviction is the core ideology in action. With each decision that a leader makes to either address a challenge or experiment with a new approach, this core ideology becomes either a *functioning reality* shaping the organization for better or empty words on a plaque collecting dust in the lobby.

Every conflict raises the question: *Are we clear on and committed to our mission?*

From that comes a reframed conversation about drum sets or anything else: It's not "What will make our congregation happy?" or "What will attract new people to the church?" or even "What does the pastor want?" But "Will this discussion about drums in the sanctuary further our mission?" Because the mission is what matters. The mission trumps. Even more than whether our stakeholders like it, our mission demands that we make decisions based on conviction. So, do we need the drums to fulfill our mission?

> ***REORIENTATION***
>
> There is perhaps no greater responsibility and no greater gift that leadership can give a group of people on a mission than to have the clearest, most defined mission possible.

THE CONVICTION OF THE COMMANDER'S INTENT

In the military a principle is drummed into all officers: *Everyone involved in an action needs to know the commander's intent.* The commander's intent is not just the orders of what a unit or battalion is to do, it also includes the goal or purpose of the mission. The purpose of the commander's intent is to empower subordinates to be able to achieve the goals of the mission if the circumstances change and they need to adapt.[5] If you tell a group of Marines, "Take the enemy airfield," that is a very different commander's intent than "Take the enemy airfield *so we can use it ourselves.*" The commander's intent clarifies the goal so that all strategies and tactics (Should we blow up the air traffic control room or not?) can be evaluated. The commander's intent is another way of describing the clear purpose and desired end state of a mission. This statement is usually brief and exceedingly clear, easily communicated to any decision maker in the change of command. There is perhaps no greater responsibility and no greater gift leadership can give a group of people on a mission than to have the clearest, most defined mission possible.

In transformational leadership the central pivot point for any discussion is the church's own clear missional purpose. This mission statement, like the commander's intent in the military, tells anyone who needs to make a decision the purpose, goal and desired end state the church is committed to achieving. It's not a motto or a marketing statement. It's not a wish or a vision. It is more than an expedient target ("we need to grow our budget a bit") or an idealistic dream ("To share the gospel with everybody on earth"). It's a clear purpose and reason for being that comes out of the core values and summarizes the core ideology of the church.

The mission, when enacted and owned, becomes a conviction that holds and changes us. It is a simple, clear, almost humble statement of the reason we as a congregation believe we are occupying the bit of real estate God has given us at this moment of history.

GETTING CLEAR ON CONVICTION

Before acting on a conviction we actually have to *have* a conviction. And this takes time. It is the result of study, conversation, humility and discernment. It is formed through processes of self-observation, self-reflection and shared aspirations. Jim Collins describes this mission-statement conviction as a Hedgehog Concept made up of the intersection of three elements:

- *What are we passionate about?* What are we constantly talking about, praying about, involved in and concerned about? In the words of Jim Collins, "Nothing great can happen without beginning first with passion."

- *What do we have the potential to do better than anyone else?* Collins says that this is an awareness of self, not aspirations or hopes. It is the humble and clear perspective about the particular value we as a church, organization or ministry have to offer our community or the larger world. It is a statement of uniqueness, not arrogance; a statement of the distinctive contribution we are equipped to make in God's work in the world.

- *What will pay the bills?* What drives our economic or resource engine? What helps us continually create the resources that will keep us going? What brings us partners, money, opportunities and the talent we need to continue our work?[6]

For Collins, when leaders develop the deep understanding of how these three come together, they develop a clear, core conviction that is expressed in the core ideology, the mission statement and through the strategic priorities that will enable us to accomplish our mission and live out our values.

Having a well-thought-out, values-based conviction—an "As for me and my house" conviction (Joshua 24:15)—is not easy. Many pastors arrive at churches with a personal motto they call a mission statement. One articulate individual wrote down something flowery and inspirational. Stationary and business cards were printed; a website banner was created. Maybe T-shirts were created. But because it didn't come from the group's own clear, deep self-understanding, it's not a conviction. It's usually not even a mission statement. It's just marketing. And since it's not a conviction, it is easily set aside when it comes time to make tough decisions for the sake of the mission.

TOWARD A MISSION STATEMENT OF CONVICTION

When I work with clients in bringing transformation, I facilitate a half-day exercise based on the work of the Mulago Foundation (mulagofoundation .org), a nonprofit venture capital firm that funds projects for combating children in poverty. Mulago requires grant applicants to write a simple proposal with an eight-word mission statement.[7] The statement must be in this format: verb, target, outcome. And it can use only *eight* words. Some of the examples offered are, "Save endangered species from extinction" and "Improve African children's health." When I have done this exercise with church leaders, they chafe under the demand of limited words. But it forces a conversation that helps build the adaptive functioning: What words are most important? What are we really all about?

Some of my clients' statements include: "Support local providers serving our community's vulnerable" and "Nurture our congregation for deployment in Christ's Kingdom" and "Prepare all generations to impact lives for Christ." These are not generic statements. They are very specific to each organization. Again, the process and the conversation around it is the most important element. As we discuss, debate and decide on each word, the mission becomes a conviction.

THE LEADER'S MISSION WITHIN THE MISSION

For the leader navigating this two-front battle, he or she must have clear convictions about his or her call and purpose. To be blunt: *The leader in the system is committed to the mission when no one else is.* For the leader the mission *always* trumps. Again, this is hard. We all have our own internal competing values. It's difficult to disappoint people who are important to us, and especially to do so when there might be a personal cost to it. Even pastors worry about things like job security, putting our kids through college and not wanting to uproot our families because people in the congregation became too disappointed in us. The temptation to thwart the change process we have begun is very real. So, it takes both skill and courage to lead the transformation process that lives out the mission of the organization when people around us are disappointed. But it depends on the leader getting very clear on his or her own convictions and personal mission. The more inner congruence between our personal convictions and the missional conviction of the church, the more likely we are able to stand and work through the resistance that follows making tough decisions.

Another conversation in my office. This time it was an older couple who were new to the church. They were registered for our next new members' class, but after hearing from some concerned friends about how liberal Presbyterians are, they thought they'd ask me some questions.

They told me they had been leaders in three well-known megachurches, but after a falling-out with the pastor they had been without a church home for several months. They started listening to a Presbyterian pastor via podcast and were so impressed they decided to check out our church (even though they had never dreamt of being part of a mainline church). They loved our church. They told me they loved our emphasis on discipleship, reaching out to the unchurched, and proclaiming and demonstrating the kingdom to those who hadn't accepted the good news. Everything they heard resonated with their hearts, and they decided to join. When they told a friend what they were intending to do, he cautioned them because of what he read in the papers. So, they came to see me. I found out that the Presbyterian pastor they had heard on the podcast was Tim Keller, and I explained that he was part of a different Presbyterian denomination. They had only recently learned that there was not only the Presbyterian Church (USA), our denomination, but others they thought they'd be more comfortable joining.

I said to them, "You have heard me talk about our mission to proclaim the kingdom of God to the unchurched. Do you think the people we are trying to reach care what denomination we are in?"

They responded, "No, not at all."

"So," I said, "The mission trumps. As long as we can fulfill our mission, we are not going to spend time or energy on denominational worries. For us, it's all about the mission."

"But Tod," the wife chimed in, "the people you are trying to reach don't care about denominational labels, but people like us do. If you want people like us to join your church, you may want to consider switching denominations."

I looked them and said softly but firmly. "You are *not* our mission."

The husband blinked. I don't think he could believe what he was hearing. He had been a pretty important person in several churches. He knew that I hoped they'd join our church, and he didn't expect that response from me.

I said it again. "You are not our mission. Our mission is to be a community of disciples who proclaim and demonstrate the good news in every sector of society. We want to reach people for Jesus Christ. Our mission is not to help Christians move from one church to our church. You are not our mission. But . . . *I think God brought you here so that you would join our mission*. You have a heart for the unchurched and desire to see people come to know Christ and experience his reign and grace in their lives. All you have heard has resonated with you, and you have already begun new ministries here. No, you are not our mission, but I think God is calling you to join us in fulfilling our mission."

The husband looked at his wife. "Honey, I think we're Presbyterians."

They joined our church in the next class.

The mission trumps, and real transformation in a congregation is only going to occur when the mission (and the decisions it inspires) begins as a clear *personal* conviction of the leader. My experience is that many people become pastors or take on leadership positions for ego needs. We see the glint of admiration in the eyes of others, we hear the way they introduce us ("You know that my son is studying to be a *pastor,* don't you? Isn't that great?"), we like the sense that we are somebody special, and we take on a role we may not even have that much conviction about. We imagine ourselves with our new titles. Spiritual writer Parker Palmer was invited to apply for a college presidency. When a "clearness committee" helped him think through his motives for pursuing the job, he finally admitted, "I guess what I would like most is getting my name in the paper with the word *president* underneath it."[8]

Soon, we are like the dog that catches the car. We are dragged along by the sheer force and energy of others' opinions and affirmation. Because we are not acting out of conviction, we fold when the resistance comes.

But a clear, thought-out conviction that comes from within one's values and is consistent with one's beliefs is like a healthy spine and strong core muscles. They enable us to stand without wavering, to keep our balance, to stay grounded without having to be overly defensive or attacking. We are like a well-rooted sequoia that can withstand fires and storms. Others may get blown away or consumed, but convictions help us stand.

In one respect the clearest sign of a leader is that he or she begins whether anyone is following or not. *In one sense* followership is irrelevant. Leaders start being leaders by acting on conviction. But what makes a leader a real leader is what we do when the followers start having opinions about our convictions. When we hear the grumblings, the criticisms, the second-guesses. When we see the rolled eyes or read the disappointment on faces, that's when the leader is truly being pressed into service.

As I sat there facing the older man who was beginning to become so disappointed in me, I prayed that he wouldn't lose heart even if he thought I had. He didn't agree with our more collaborative and less pastor-centered approach because he was raised in the era of the "great man" theory of leadership. But the changes we were going through were not only the leadership team's conviction but mine also. I believe in the priesthood of all believers. I believe that the entire church—not just the pastor and paid staff—had to be committed to our mission. I was committed to change the culture of our church so that no one would feel like "Tod and the Sanhedrin" held all the power. This wasn't just my preference; it was my conviction. But it's still hard not to react when others have such strong responses. Managing those feelings both in yourself and in your church culture is the next step in developing adaptive capacity.

11

Take a Good Look into the Coffin

*Adaptive change stimulates resistance because it
challenges people's habits, beliefs, and values. It asks them to
take a loss, experience uncertainty, and even express disloyalty to
people and cultures. Because adaptive change forces people to question
and perhaps redefine aspects of their identity, it also challenges their
sense of competence. Loss, disloyalty, and feeling incompetent:
That's a lot to ask. No wonder people resist.*

RONALD HEIFETZ AND MARTY LINSKY,
LEADERSHIP ON THE LINE

BOWLING WITH THE GHOST OF UNCLE PHIL

While I was still in seminary, Uncle Phil died. He was a big, lovable grouch who taught me how to bowl and told me stories of seeing Babe Ruth play baseball. His passing inspired my brother and me to spend an afternoon in our own private wake, bowling together and then visiting the mortuary for our own private viewing. It would be the first time I had seen a corpse. My brother didn't want to go. "Let's just bowl a few games and tell some stories," he said. "Uncle Phil would like that."

He was right. Uncle Phil would not have cared if we came and saw his made-up body lying in a coffin. But I had to do it. I was in seminary and knew I was going to be a pastor. I knew that someday I would be in this position and that I needed the experience of learning to look death square in the eye so that someday I could help others through it. I also knew that if I were going to help others go through loss, I would need to be experienced at facing my own losses.

So, I looked into the coffin. It was hard, necessary preparation for the years ahead.

As a chaplain intern in a hospital I had three patients die in one day. As a young associate pastor, I buried a toddler and then ten months later his mother in the same grave. I had to lift the naked lifeless body of one of my elders who had slipped out of bed in the moment of death. I have told children that their daddy is not coming back. I have walked alongside parents who have lost children, and children who have lost parents. I watched a mother yell at her twenty-six-year-old son, "No, don't leave. I'm not ready!" as he succumbed to AIDS. I have been with families as they sang hymns to usher their grand-mother into the arms of Jesus.

In a world where we are so often insulated from death, most pastors are the resident experts of human death, loss and grief. Indeed, most pastors are (perhaps next to nurses or paramedics) more familiar with facing death than anyone in his or her congregation. We know that as painful as it is to be with the dying and the grieving, it is also the most holy privilege. And frankly, we are usually really good at it.

The same expertise pastors bring to a dying person or a grieving family is what they bring to a dying congregation and grieving church family. In the same way that we help loved ones grieve the lost, remember the past and prepare to live a new life, our job as a leader is to help our community to let go and grieve so they can find a new life, a new purpose, a renewed mission again.

START WITH CONVICTION, THEN STAY CALM

Once leaders identify a clear missional conviction for bringing change, we are eager to see it expressed in life-changing, maybe even world-changing, ways. We are ready to launch the new initiative, call people to action and lead on! To be sure, since most of us have not even been trained in the skills of *management*, adaptive *leadership* is difficult. But the real challenge of leadership is not tac-tical or strategic but *emotional*. Not only do we have to deal with the inner uncertainty that goes with leading into uncharted territory, but we also have to manage the two-front battle, which includes our own need to be liked, to gain approval from others or to be seen as a competent professional. And sometimes we get really anxious that we are never going to measure up.

The first step in adaptive change is "start with missional conviction"; the second is to "stay calm." For the leader it is critical to monitor *our own* emotional reactivity when the anxiety within the church rises. The calm leader is self-aware, committed to the mission (the mission trumps) and focuses on his or her own self in the transformation process. As Edwin Friedman reminds us, the leader's own *presence* is the most powerful tool for furthering the transformation process.[1] Nowhere is that more evident than when the resistance in the system begins to create heat for the pastor.

Technical competence *pleases* people. When we teach a good Bible study, sing a great solo, run a fine program or hit a home run, people *cheer*. Most of us who have been asked to consider leadership have big cheering sections. We are used to applause, affirmation and feeling successful. But the

> ***REORIENTATION***
>
> When dealing with managing the present, win-win solutions are the goal.
> But when leading adaptive change, win-win is usually lose-lose.

minute we accept the call to adaptive leadership that brings transformation, we should expect most of the cheering to stop.

BEYOND WIN-WIN: COMPETING VALUES

Stephen Covey wrote *The Seven Habits of Highly Effective People,* a bestselling leadership book that encouraged leaders to always look for win-win solutions to their problems. He argues that when making a policy, negotiating a deal, managing resources, making a decision, we should always look for answers that will give the most amount of positive value to all parties involved. For most of us in ministry there is nothing we'd rather do. Win-win challenges us to think beyond competition to collaboration, and for Christians this is a logical expression for fulfilling Paul's admonition, "Let each of you look not to your own interests, but to the interests of others" (Philippians 2:4). Indeed, within the realm of *management*, a win-win approach is one of the most technically competent and relationally congruent acts possible. Whether it is divvying up resources or navigating space issues, working with vendors or setting policies, every win-win solution demonstrates a kind of cool-headed and clear-hearted character that people look for in leaders.

But when we enter the realm of adaptive work—working in uncharted territory—win-win often becomes lose-lose. Transformational leadership and the adaptive change necessary requires us to go beyond win-win to make hard, oftentimes *forced* choices. When we are faced with limited resources *and* a new experiment we can't squeeze into the budget, a choice has to be made: Either the existing programs are going to lose some of their resources or the new experiment will go unfunded. When we have to decide where we allocate the time of staff people for this new venture, staff who are already managing the programs that serve our stakeholder members, where will they get the time? Something will suffer. Someone or some program will feel a sense of loss. Even when deciding what is first priority and what is second, or what is 1 and what is 1a, someone is going to lose.

Heifetz and Linsky inform us that

> people do not resist change, per se. People resist loss. You appear dangerous to people when you question their values, beliefs, or habits of a lifetime. You place yourself on the line when you tell people what they need to hear rather than what they want to hear. Although you may see with clarity and passion a promising future of progress and gain, people will see with equal passion the losses you are asking them to sustain. [2]

One of my former clients was a large church trying to adapt to a changing culture. As they sought to come up with new experiments, interventions and innovations, they also faced tightening budgets and increasingly limited resources. The executive pastor said to me,

> As a church, we haven't had to face tough choices like this, ever. For at least a generation we could solve every problem through *addition*. If we wanted to address a need, we just added a new program, a new staff member, a new line item in the budget. But now we don't have the money and personnel to do that. We can't solve our problems through addition, and we just don't have any experience of solving problems with *subtraction*.

This church leadership faced a truly adaptive challenge that caused them to develop new capacities for decision making, priority setting and dealing with the inevitable conflict and fallout that would come. They quickly had to learn how to "disappoint their own people at a rate they could absorb."

Transformational leadership, therefore, equips people to make hard choices regarding the values keeping them from the growth and transformation necessary to see in a new way and discover new interventions to address the challenges they are facing. And this is done with values that are *valuable*. Systems theory reminds us that "today's problems come from yesterday's solutions."[3] This means that the program, ministry, staff person, principle, action or activity in danger of being lost was at one time of great *value*.

It is relatively straightforward to decide between a good thing and a bad thing, a healthy behavior and an unhealthy behavior, a strategy that is working and one that is not. But when the choice is between two *valuable* ideas, plans or programs, the transformational work gets difficult, because at the heart of adaptive work there is *no* win-win.

When people begin to anticipate the reality of the losses ahead, the two-front battle of uncharted leadership becomes even more apparent. At the same time we are undergoing the adaptive shift that will help us to reframe and experiment with ways to address the challenge of a changing world *out there*, we have to attend to the resistance and sometimes even resentment among our own people who are experiencing the loss *in here*.

And these are people we love and who love us. People we consider brothers and sisters, who are the family of God for us. People with whom we have found a place of belonging, camaraderie of beliefs, a sense of shared purpose and meaning in life. The challenge of leadership is learning how to keep innovating and experimenting while attending to and caring for the disappointment of *these* particular people. This is not what most of us considered when a most-pleased people asked us to lead them! When you stand before people and tell them that in order to accomplish a mission, they have to change, adapt, give up something for the greater good, work with those they don't like or compromise on something they care about, they get *mad*. They get *really* mad. Mostly, they get mad at *you*, and this is exactly the sign that transformation is beginning to happen.

CROCKPOT LEADERSHIP

Imagine you are cooking a meal for a big, hungry family. You decide to make a stew in a Crock-Pot. You get raw meat, hard vegetables, some stock and seasoning. You put it in the Crock-Pot, and with enough time at the right temperature you get a feast. But if the temperature is too high, the meal gets burned; too low and even though a long time has gone by, all you have is hard vegetables and raw meat.

Bringing good, healthy change to an organization, family, church or business is like cooking a stew in a Crock-Pot. Every person is a like a hard, raw vegetable or a firm piece of uncooked meat. Each has its own identity, opinions and beliefs. For the pieces of food to become a meal that will feed a hungry tribe, each bit must be transformed at least a bit. Each vegetable must be softened, the meat must share its flavor, and each morsel must contribute to a healthy sauce for all to share. When the components combine, we end up with something altogether different and tastier than if we were to cook carrots separate from the beef and separate from onions and then put them all together. Without enough heat, nothing changes. Too much heat and it burns. In either case, nobody is fed.

A leader's job is to regulate the heat. The leader is like the thermostat on the Crock-Pot, keeping enough heat in the system so things begin to change, but not enough that individual parts get scorched. When we are all so calm that we are comfortable, we don't want to go anywhere. When we are camped under a tree in the shade, even staying in the wilderness seems better than heading off for the Promised Land. If the sun is scorching, it saps all motivation for moving. Like the Israelites, perhaps you've been a part of or leader in a system that got so burned by a temperature rise that you vowed never to do *that* again. But when the heat is turned up thoughtfully and insightfully, we begin to move toward the land of milk and honey we long for. In the same way that the heat of the Crock-Pot, properly regulated over a period of time, transforms inedible parts into an appetizing whole, so does regulating the heat of system change within adaptive leadership.

THE HEAT OF URGENCY

There are two forms of heat for bringing transformation: *urgency* and *anxiety*. For leadership expert John Kotter, the first step for leading organizational change is creating a sense of urgency, what he calls a "gut-level determination to move . . . now."[4] According to Kotter, 50 percent of organizational transformation endeavors that fail do so because the leaders did not create an appropriate sense of "true urgency." Kotter distinguishes between "complacency," where everyone in the system believes that everything is fine and is resistant to change, "false urgency," where people in the system are frantically working on issues that are not contributing to the mission and transformation, and "true urgency," where there is a heartfelt sense of the importance, opportunity and necessity of the challenge in front of us.

The first step in creating change, for Kotter, is helping the organization grasp the necessity of change ("there is no water route and winter is coming; we have to cross these mountains now"). At the same time, Kotter reminds leaders that another paradox of leadership is that it takes *time and patience to create true urgency*—an approach that Heifetz and Linsky call letting an issue "ripen."[5]

Instead of patiently waiting for a widespread and true urgency, most leaders settle for the *false urgency* of attending to the most urgent issue or the one that has the most people in an uproar. Whenever the urgent pushes out the important, we fall into the trap of *feeling* as if we are busy accomplishing something while we are running on a treadmill—getting exhausted but not going anywhere.[6]

When church leaders can get up on the balcony and look at the issues at work in a congregation, it's easy to see how often energy is focused on the howling wind or even a tornado: We fill our schedules mostly meeting with complaining members. We have back-to-back meetings with groups mostly committed to having meetings. There is one new cause after another, a new program to roll out, a new event to create, a new campaign, a new movement to launch. We react to the latest denominational crisis that hits the headlines. All the while the true urgency our mission requires and inspires dissipates, gets pushed under the surface or is drowned out.

A pastor who heard me speak at a conference said, "I absolutely agree with all that you said. The world around us is changing so rapidly and our church is dying. We need a new strategy and new staffing, and we need to take a good, hard look at why we are so stuck. But we won't be able to start any of that for about five years because all of our money and effort is going into leaving the denomination and taking our property with us." Denominational lines and property matters may seem more urgent than the mission of the church and the reality of a dying congregation. Issues like this one often threaten to or actually do take center stage and carry a false urgency that redirects focus and energy from the deeper issues of purpose.

True urgency, on the other hand, is centered on the passion and vision that comes from developing a clear conviction and mission. It is the urgency of seeing both the reality of the moment and the opportunity God has given. It is, ideally, the constant urgency that comes when church leaders neither shield the congregation from reality ("Our church is decreasing in membership," "We haven't had an adult baptism in five years," "We are losing the next generation") nor fail to call them to the shared mission God has put before them. When we keep our deepest purpose/mission/vision as our true urgency, it should not wax and wane; it should remain the central root of urgency around which we regulate the heat of peripheral issues.

As a consultant I strongly encourage my clients to use an assessment tool and focus groups to get honest feedback from their congregation or customers. These tools are sometimes painful for church leaders. One of my clients described it as like going to a doctor for a checkup when you know you are greatly overweight. The truth can really hurt, but it can also be the reality check needed. Sometimes that feedback is enough to raise the heat and begin the transformation process. Other times it is a tool to ripen the issues by raising questions.[7]

I also often coach my pastor clients to give a yearly "I Have a Dream" sermon in order to keep raising the urgency in the congregation.[8] It's important that the sermon is not shaming or demanding. It's not a presumptuous "God told me this to tell you" or "this should be your dream" or even "an expert told me that this should be our dream" sermon. Instead this is an honest and very personal sharing of hopes and visions. To be clear, this is *not* a prophetic "God's dream" for the church. Discerning that is the work a pastor and the church leaders do *together*. This "I Have a Dream" speech is simply the pastor articulating the power of *dreaming*. When a pastor shares his or her dream for what God *could* do in and through them, the congregation begins to realize that they too can dream, that God speaks to the whole community, that it is a sign of the movement of the Spirit when "your sons and your daughters shall prophesy, / your old men shall dream dreams, / and your young men shall see visions" (Joel 2:28). But like all prophetic ministries, it too is risky.

One of my colleagues shared the dream of his congregation being a church that ministered to their community by reaching out to their neighbors. He shared a dream of the church growing, adding staff and becoming known for a commitment to evangelism. By all measures this pastor is a fine preacher and the congregation heard the challenge. But that was also the moment when underlying anxiety began to come to the surface. Often when a leader shares a dream, the organization begins to wrestle with their untapped potential, the demands of change and the realization that they are being led forward.

Which is when the heat really starts to rise.

THE HEAT OF ANXIETY: IS THAT A LION OR NOT?

In the harsh midsummer African heat, a herd of impala finds an increasingly rare water hole. They rush to drink, crowding in, fearful of not getting enough water to sustain them. Suddenly, one impala raises his head in high alert. Immediately every other impala stops drinking and stands at attention. No impala moves, none utter a sound. But the tension is palpable, there seems to be a crackle of electricity in the air. Every impala at that moment has a life-or-death decision to make: Is that a lion or not?

If there is a lion lurking near that hole and they don't run, they become lion lunch. If there is *no* lion lurking near the hole and they *do* run, they lose their place at the watering hole and could die of thirst. If there *is* a lion and they do run, or if there is *no* lion and they don't run, they live another day. But all that matters is: Is that a lion or not? Everything in their impala being is focused on making that crucial life-and-death decision. Just like they do every day. Numerous times a day.

Part of what helps the impala make that decision is the herd energy, the animal anxiety that permeates the group and causes them to share listening, hearing and deciding together. Similarly, depending on how the system responds to anxiety is one of the key factors for facing changes in climate or challenges in terrain for a herd, a family, a church or organization.

A significant part of staying calm and regulating heat is in understanding that most often the heat that hinders organizational systems from moving toward their aspirations and goals is anxiety. Anxiety isn't a bad thing; it's a creaturely thing. It just is. We feel anxious when we are reacting to a threat, whether real or imagined. Sometimes the anxiety is a gift that tells us something bad is threatening the clan (a fire alarm sounding, the sixth sense that someone is lying to you, the motivation to lose weight when the doctor says your cholesterol is so high you won't live to see grandchildren). This is called "acute anxiety." It motivates us to do something to get ourselves or our loved ones out of danger (e.g., a lion is at the watering hole).

In his book *The Anxious Organization*, Jeffrey Miller writes, "In and of itself, anxiety is neither functional or dysfunctional. It is a state of readiness to do something or other that may or may not be appropriate in response to a threat that may or may not be accurately perceived."[9]

But the key difference between animals and humans is that with humans real or acute anxiety often becomes chronic anxiety, lingering in a family or social system even after the threat is gone. Acute anxiety is a pervasive state of being that continues even after the threat is gone. (Soldiers with post-traumatic stress who wake up on high alert even while safe at home, depression-era senior citizens who stock up on eggs or toilet paper years later, an adult who grew up in an abusive home who winces every time someone raises their voice even the smallest bit.) Chronic anxiety is present when the threats of the past continue to hold power even though the system is no longer in danger.

There are many studies about the effects of stress and anxiety in life today. We are taught stress-reducing tricks like exercise or deep breathing or taking mini-vacations while at our desks, lowering our anxiousness by thinking of our "happy place." These things are all good for our personal well-being. But in the midst of leading change, they miss the point.

For leaders the point of calming down is not to feel better; it's to make better decisions. *It's to make the best decisions for furthering the mission.* When people are too hot, they don't. The only issue is: Is there a lion or not? Is there a threat, or are we making this up? Is this true urgency or false urgency? Do we need to run, or should we stay here, get water and then calmly continue our journey?

"When I identify that I am being motivated by fear, I realize that I am not making a good decision." He was, by all accounts an affable man of devout faith. For three decades he has had his own business, had been a good neighbor and a leader in his church. He is the model of a deeply content, successful man. And yet when we sat in a circle of other business leaders, he confessed how often in his business life fear had been the motivating factor.

"It took me a long time and a lot of therapy to realize that many of my motivations were fear-based," he said. Only when he and his wife began to work on some marital issues did he come to realize that most of the challenges he faced in his business were also rooted in his deeper psychological responses to fear.

For leaders this is the point to remember about anxiety: *People who are overly or chronically anxious don't make good decisions.* When anxiety spikes we revert to more primitive ways of being. We fight, we flee, we freeze. We run from danger and leave others to face the lions alone. Or we capitulate and allow the herd to be overrun. We turn on each other instead of working together. We jump to quick fixes; we look for technical solutions to adaptive issues. Transformational leadership is built on leaders making good, wise, discerning decisions for the sake of both the health and the mission of the community—decisions that reinforce the missional conviction—and this requires leaders who are able to *stay calm*.

STAY CALM

What does it mean to stay calm? That we become a Mr. Spock-like Vulcan with no emotions and complete rationality? No. That would be impossible. To *stay calm* is to be so aware of yourself that your response to the situation *is not to the anxiety of the people around you but to the actual issue at hand.* Staying calm means so attending to our own internal anxiety in the heat of a challenging moment and the resistance around us that we are not tempted to either cool it down to escape the heat (thus aborting the change process) or to react emotionally, adding more fuel to the fire and scorching the stew we are trying to cook.

In their book *Thriving Through Ministry Conflict*, Jim Osterhaus, Joe Jurkowski and Todd Hahn outline what they call the Red Zone–Blue Zone model for looking at conflict and resistance. Osterhaus and his colleagues help us understand that the best decisions come out of the Blue Zone. Blue Zone is about serving the mission. Blue Zone decisions are marked by consistency and are focused on effectiveness. In the Blue Zone the mission trumps. But most of the time, when the heat is on, if we are not deliberately conscious to do otherwise, we will operate out of the Red Zone of high emotional reactivity based on one or more of four core issues: *survival, acceptance, competence* and *control*. Each person is different, and each person must negotiate different Red Zone issues. Red Zone issues come from our life experiences and brain wiring, they come out of the reactivity that assumes a system should focus more on how people feel than what we are called to do.[10] In the Red Zone, people expect the organization to operate like a family; they often assume family roles and replicate the unresolved issues from their family of origin. When a conflict or challenge we are facing triggers one of these issues, instead of making decisions based on what is best for the mission, we tend to make decisions based on what is best for *me*.[11]

For example, my pervasive Red Zone issue is *competence*. If I am in a heated conflict with someone and they try to take too much control, tell me they don't like me or threaten my job, it is not pleasant, but I can usually stay pretty centered. I don't get hooked by the comments and am able to remain a professional. But if I am accused of doing a poor job, missing critical information, being over my head in experience or wasting time with a misguided strategy, I can get very defensive. Before I know it, instead of keeping the conversation moving toward our goals, I am trying to demonstrate my competence. If I am unaware of it, soon the entire strategy, program or experiment will be shaped around actions in which I can demonstrate my competence even if it isn't the best approach for accomplishing our goals.

Think of how many ministry decisions have been made in order to not hurt the feelings (acceptance) or threaten (survival) or challenge (control) a leader, a group, a big giver or a significant part of the congregation. Think of how often the deciding factor was not mission but what will anger the least amount of people. Think how often a congregation decides to do something because they were scolded or guilted by their pastor into doing so? Blue Zone decisions come from the calm, cool peace of good spiritual discernment, not urgent thrashing about.

BUT IT'S COOL TO LOSE YOUR COOL, RIGHT?

Some of us may be recalling great illustrations of passionate and prophetic leaders who lose their cool. Didn't Jesus drive out the money changers? Don't the prophets rail out in condemnation? Doesn't that turn up the heat? From the 1970s movie *Network* to so much political discourse today, we assume that if change is going to come, somebody is going to have stand up and yell, "I'm mad as hell, and I'm not going to take this anymore!"

While that kind of passion is often prophetic (and prophetic action was exactly what Jesus was doing when he condemned the temple), it's not usually effective in terms of leadership. It may feel good to shout down the crowd, but it actually tends to only make things worse. Leaders have to bring along their resistant followers. A firm denouncement or a stirring call to action is the act of a prophet. But prophets become leaders when those around them follow their lead.

Most of the time when things get heated, people get scorched. The meal is ruined and most is thrown out of the Crock-Pot. The community stops following and starts fighting or fleeing. While passion has its place for inspiring the committed and prodding the hesitant (see *Braveheart* or Shakespeare's *Henry V*), far more leadership requires a calm, confident presence in the middle of a highly anxious, instinctively reactive situation that threatens to burn everyone, because calm, like anxiety, is contagious. Anxious people scurry to quick fixes and work avoidance. But when the leader stays calm enough internally to attend to and regulate the heat of chronic anxiety so that it is instead the clear blue flame of urgency and mission, then transformation can occur.

HOW DO YOU REGULATE THE HEAT?

This is the delicate work of adaptive leadership. We need our people feeling the urgency and healthy anxiety enough to overcome complacency and move. At the same time we need our people to calm down enough to get beyond technical fixes, false urgency and work-avoidance scrambling. If the system is too cool and needs more heated urgency to change, then the leader's own heat (passion, truth-telling, conviction, actions) begins to get things cooking. But when the system gets too hot and people are in danger of burning each other or bailing out of the change process, the very presence of a calm, connected leader cools the system down so people can tolerate staying on course.

Going back to the Red Zone–Blue Zone analogy, since the pastor serves as the system's thermostat, which regulates the heat, I coach my clients to pay attention to "purple." That is, pay attention to the issues that trigger *their own* anxious reactivity and thwart their ability to make and help others to make Blue Zone decisions. Once we can recognize the kind of issue that creates a Red Zone response triggered by survival, competence, acceptance or control, we can intentionally attend to it, give it to the Lord, pray for peace and clarity, and ask for God's wisdom and perspective. Even taking the time to breathe, to release and pause to respond instead of react can help the leader calm down.

In his book *Just Listen: The Secret of Getting Through to Everyone*, Mark Goulston recommends a simple process of self-talk that literally slows the brain processes down. It begins by *acknowledging* the anxious, angry or fearful feelings and breathing slowly until your heart rate comes down and you are able to hear and respond instead of lash out reactively. This process, which takes between ten seconds and two minutes, is both simple and critical in the middle of a heated discussion.[12] As the thermostat of the transformational Crock-Pot, the leader must be able to stay calm enough internally so he or she can help the leadership make the best Blue Zone decisions (see fig. 11.1).[13]

Red Zone	Blue Zone
• Emotionally charged	• Values are in conflict
• Personalized conflict	• About issues
• Unresolved issues in self	• Self-awareness is key
• Disproportionate intensity	• Proportionate intensity
• Conflict is unsolvable	• Conflict is solved
• The conflict is always about *me!*	• The conflict is always about the *mission*

Figure 11.1. Red Zone and Blue Zone

THE PARADOX OF CHANGE PROCESS

The paradox of the change process is that it is less about changing anyone else and more about *being* the leaven of transformation within the church. That is even truer when it comes to regulating the heat of transformation. Regulating the heat is a delicate art built around one crucial leadership skill: *regulating ourselves*. Remember: we don't *act* like a thermostat, we *are* the thermostat. We regulate the heat by monitoring and regulating ourselves in the middle of the stew. (Think about it: It is impossible to monitor anyone else's anxiety and anger, isn't it? It doesn't do any good to tell someone to calm down, does it? Don't believe me? Try it on your spouse or friend next time you two are in a heated argument.) Congregational systems expert Peter Steinke writes, "To lead means to have some command of our own anxiety and some capacity not to let other people's anxiety contaminate us; that is, not to allow their anxiety to affect our thinking, actions, and decisions."[14]

Trying to be perfectly calm can create its own stress and anxiety. The last thing most of us need to do is to put more pressure on ourselves to calm down when we are getting anxious. (Try to stop sweating or stammering when you are starting to feel the heat in the middle of a conflict.) So, as a leader who often gets to walk into hot kitchens (what is a church patio or narthex but a big family kitchen table?) I try to focus on a more modest goal than being perfectly calm: being *just a bit less anxious than everyone else*. All I want is for my presence to turn the anxiety thermostat down one click on the dial so we can focus on the urgency of our mission. Peter Steinke notes, "The leader's 'presence' can have a calming influence on reactive behavior. Rather than reacting to the reactivity of others, leaders with self-composure and self-awareness both exhibit and elicit a more thoughtful response."[15]

When a leader with conviction can stay calm amid the losses and reactivity of a congregation, then thoughtful, Blue Zone, "it's all about the mission" decisions are possible. But sometimes being calm is not enough. So, what do we do when the others around us choose to fight or flee because of their Red Zone issues? The opposite of what our human nature does reflexively: we draw closer.

Part Four

RELATIONSHIPS
AND RESISTANCE

You Can't Go Alone, but You
Haven't Succeeded Until You've
Survived the Sabotage

12

Gus and Hal Go to Church

No one would live in Boston without owning a winter coat.
But countless people think that they can exercise
leadership without partners.

RONALD HEIFETZ,
"THE LEADER OF THE FUTURE"

The colossal misunderstanding of our time is the assumption that
insight will work with people who are unmotivated to change. If you
want your child, spouse, client, or boss to shape up, stay connected
while changing yourself rather than trying to fix them.

EDWIN FRIEDMAN, *A FAILURE OF NERVE*

THE CHURCH AND THE WHEELCHAIR

Hal is blind. Gus is an amputee confined to a wheelchair. Alone they would each be what we sometimes call shut-ins. Octogenarians both, they don't get around very easily on their own. When they come to worship services at SCPC, Hal pushes Gus and Gus directs Hal. They make their way through the parking lot and the patio to their place together in the pew. Gus sits in his wheelchair and gives direction, Hal pushes the wheelchair and follows Gus's lead, and together they get to where they want to go. And together, and only together, they come to church. A blind man giving energy to a man who can't walk. A disabled man giving direction to a man who lacks vision. But together, they worship, take part in community and offer their gifts and inspire a whole lot of us.

NAVIGATIONAL GUIDE FOR ORGANIZATIONS
Aren't We Supposed to Be a Family?

The young woman raised her hand at the town hall meeting. "If we are Christians, aren't we supposed to be a family? How do we fire a sister in Christ?"

When I married Beth, I married into a small family business. As one of the in-laws I had no authority, but since the family business did affect my children's college funds, I often sat in meetings or listened in on conference calls making silent observations. Over the years of being part of these calls, I learned a lot about family businesses, and mostly I learned that they are very complicated.

One minute we are discussing vacation plans; the next we are arguing over an investment strategy. One minute the principals are making a hard decision about which member of the family would be in charge of a project; the next someone expresses fear that Christmas may be really uncomfortable.

Similarly, the church is an organic relational system: a people, a community, what some even consider a family. As an organizational system, that means that the churches (and other Christian organizations) often function with unexpressed expectations to meet the emotional needs of it's members. Even in the seminary where I serve today, the lines between our responsibilities as staff members and faculty members and our commitment to each other as "brothers and sisters in Christ" can get confusing. To make things even more complicated, a Christian organization is not a family that exists for itself, but it also has a mission that gives it a purpose for being and shapes its life together. In effect, Christian organizations are family businesses where each member of the family contributes to the work of the family. These challenges create a kind of role conflict that must be continually navigated.

Over the years of observing an actual family business, leading a church and being a leader in a Christian organization of higher education, I have learned that the complexity of Christian organizations as family businesses requires more communication, not less, more clarity of agreements and even more difficult conversations to name and navigate the role conflicts inherit in such a system. Church leaders and family business owners could learn a lot from comparing notes.

THE REALITY

You take on the big problem. You work hard. You learn. You listen. You consult. You think. You scribble. You problem solve. Then, the muse inspires. The bolt of lightning strikes. Clarity comes from the sky and you see the *big idea*. You frame it in what leadership authors Jim Collins and Jerry Porras call a "Big Hairy Audacious Goal."[1] You can see the future laid out before you. You write it up. You create the PowerPoint. You shape the concept into a memorable phrase. You launch the initiative. You make the announcement. It is met with wild affirmation, appreciation, applause and commendations all around. You are a star. The organization rolls out the new plan. The organization chart is rearranged. Teams, plans, goals are renamed. Objectives are set and all is good. And then . . .

Nothing. Nothing changes. At least nothing really important. Oh, a few cosmetic shifts. But mostly everything defaults back to where it was. Homeostasis rules. The "persistence of form," as Ed Friedman calls it, really is persistent. Cynicism follows. Resistance becomes more entrenched. True transformation just got that much harder.

Why is it so difficult for the *great idea* to become embedded in the culture of the institution? Why does a new missional conviction so rarely become the new way of being, the new strategy for acting, the new *normal*? Why do so many innovations get stopped before they can be tried as an experiment? This is the demoralizing frustration for so many leaders. We see ourselves as a prescient Thomas Jefferson recruiting Meriwether Lewis. Or as a vigorous President Kennedy laying out the challenge to put a man on the moon. We believe people will rally to the vision and eagerly sacrifice their personal goals for the higher good. But as we have seen, that is only partly true. Very often the same people who applaud the stirring vision resist the implementation. Leaders are lauded for their boldness and creativity, and then in the very same breath shouted down for suggesting that the change effort will require each of us to change personally. We think we can single-handedly overcome this obstacle, that our passion, commitment and conviction will win the day. But it rarely does. Hardly ever. Almost never. This is the truth. The sooner the curtain is pulled back and we see the cheap parlor trick that is really not transforming anything, the sooner we can get to real leadership.

There is a noble but deeply misguided belief that leadership requires broad shoulders and an ability to stand under pressures *alone*. Most of us give lip service to needing colleagues and being collaborative, but when the buck stops, we really do believe that it stops on one desk only. Sadly, this is far removed from the New Testament witness where, short of Jesus' own work on the cross, virtually every other expression of the ministry of the Spirit was revealed to the world in pairs or trios (or more). Jesus sent the Seventy two-by-two. Peter, James and John healed and preached. Paul and Barnabas, Paul and Silas, Paul and Silas and Timothy, Barnabas and John Mark, Priscilla and Aquila. And a host of other examples, of course.

If, as I define it, *leadership is energizing a community of people toward their own transformation in order to accomplish a shared mission in the face of a changing world*, then leadership is *always relational*. It is focused on a *community* of people who exist to accomplish a *shared* mission. So, while we *start with a missional conviction* and regulate the heat by *staying calm* and focusing on our own self-awareness and personal responsibility, organizational transformation cannot be accomplished through the efforts of one person, no matter how gifted. So, in addition to "start with conviction and stay calm" we add *stay connected*. Which leads us to the next key principle of adaptive leadership. After finding a missional conviction and regulating the heat, to bring change we must *enact relationally*.

We are all Gus and Hal going to church.

THE BIG BIAS

But somewhere along the way partnerships—even in a work that is defined by relationship of siblings (sisters and brothers)—were considered too unwieldy or unworkable, and we started imagining hierarchies, where there is one head. Today, we hear people speak of a kind of military chain of command that is necessary in the battle for the kingdom of heaven. Community and collaboration may be good for dividing up tasks in camp or when we are settled in some place. Partnership may be good for a family but not a mission, we think. On the front lines someone needs to be in charge. If we are leading into hostile or uncharted territory, it's best we follow one vision, one voice, so we think. "Lewisandclark" defied this assumption in a most startling and dramatic fashion, which we have yet to probe in depth. Two hundred-plus years after the Corps of Discovery, and the dominant model of leadership is still deeply individualistic.

It is worth noting that, even within the military itself, the complexities of a rapidly changing world—including enemies that are no longer nation-states but terrorist groups—has brought the whole sacrosanct notion of "chain of command" into question. In order to combat Al-Qaeda in Iraq in the first decade of the twenty-first century, General Stanley McChrystal had to morph the leadership structure from a traditional "command" to a "command of teams" and finally to a "team of teams." It was only as the different special forces groups, intelligence agencies and military units learned to work as partners with high degrees of trust and shared purpose that they were able to create the adaptable structure and "shared consciousness" that enabled a *team of teams* to finally succeed where a highly trained, richly resourced and exceedingly disciplined *command* did not.[2]

For my own denominational clan, this addiction to individual leadership is a contradiction to our core principles. As much as we Presbyterians live under the constitutional conviction that all leadership is shared between elders and pastors, still most of us function as if the role of elders is either to be a board of directors to the executive officer pastor, or to be a "spiritual council" that gives advice and offers prayers to the pastor as the *one* true minister of the church.

Ironically, the phrase repeated in our Book of Order to describe that actual work of pastors, begins with the clause "Together with . . ." Pastors lead the church together with the Session, the elders, the deacons and, of course, associate pastors. But of course, we don't—at least not enough to make a difference in our functioning and health.

Most of us haven't taken seriously our limitations when we carry the burden of leadership alone. Some of us are blind; some of us can't move. Most of us don't solely possess the "energy, intelligence, imagination and love" that a congregation needs.[3] Frankly, the stubbornness to think that we can lead without taking into account our limitations is much of what is burning us out, discouraging us from going even further into uncharted territory or, even worse, keeping us from seeing any of the real fruit of transformation.

THE SIX NECESSARY RELATIONSHIPS FOR LEADING INTO THE UNKNOWN

Heifetz and his colleagues use a phrase that is distasteful for most of us in the church world, encouraging us to "think politically." They want leaders to accomplish their mission by considering the larger relational dynamics and multiple constituencies to which every influencer in a system answers—thinking politically. "The key assumption behind thinking politically is that people in an organization are seeking to meet the expectations of their various constituencies. When you understand the nature of those expectations, you can mobilize people more effectively."[4] Everyone in a position of authority has a constituency (the leaders' "own people" they have to "disappoint at a rate they can absorb"). We are all tempted to short-circuit change efforts when we get pushback from those we assume are on our side.

Part of the dynamic at play here is that not only does everybody have a constituency but *everybody also wants to be a hero to their constituencies.* The elder who is choir president has a tendency to want to meet the expectations of his friends in the choir; the board member who is part of the mission committee is prone to be more committed to making the missionaries happy than balancing the overall church budget. The associate pastor gets kudos for going to bat for the programs and ministries of her department against the "powers that be."

In the seminary, our president often reminds us that our executive team must be committed to support the mission of the whole school over any individual program. As a pastor I had to work with my colleagues and elders to understand that the first commitment of church elders is to the whole church, that the Session itself is the "first team."[5] But human nature being what it is, it's more effective in a change process for a leader to think not only of *one* team but *six*. Six different teams that reflect the different kinds of relationships a leader must attend to in order to bring transformation to the whole organizational system.[6]

1. Allies. An ally is anyone who is convinced of the mission and is committed to seeing it fulfilled. In this sense, allies are *inside* the system, taking part of the change process with a stake in it and *aligned and in agreement*—at least for the moment—with the adaptive changes the leader is attempting to bring.[7] They may or may not be friends or natural allies, like those who share your values and vision for change, but can even be unlikely allies who directly benefit from the change you are trying to bring. A big mistake that many leaders make is to assume that all friends are allies. In a complex organizational system like a church, this is very often not the case. Friends are those who love you and are loyal to you as a person. When the vote is cast or the initiative has succeeded or failed, friends will still love you. Friendship is so beautiful because it is not connected to accomplishing anything except enjoying and encouraging the friendship. But because churches are about both relationship *and* mission, friends can find themselves on opposite side of change initiatives. This often creates confusion and hurt feelings. Later, we will talk more about separating role from self, but for now it's important for the leader to differentiate between friends and allies. Allies, are all about furthering the mission. Period.

Questions to consider:

- Who might be your allies?

- *Why* might they be allies? What do they stand to gain or lose from allegiance to your initiatives?

- What's their main objective in being your ally? (Support you? Support the initiative itself? Support the organization?)

- How can this ally best help you successfully implement your initiative?

2. Confidants. To be a confidant, a person must care more about *you* than they do about the mission of the organization. Therefore, healthy confidants are usually those *outside* the system who can give you honest feedback about yourself as a leader *in* the system. Being a confidant is usually most comfortable and healthy for our friends and family. Confidants are those who can help you stay aware of your own Red Zone and your own self-care. You can go to confidants without fear of losing face or being embarrassed to ask for help, encouragement and support. They listen to you, ask questions, offer perspective and prayers. Confidants are not invested in the outcome of the change initiative, because they are far more invested in you whether the change initiative succeeds or fails.

As a coach to pastors, I am almost always in the role of confidant. Even when I work with the larger church system in a visioning or strategic planning process, more than anything else my role is helping leaders further the mission by developing adaptive capacity and functioning in the Blue Zone.

- Who are your confidants?

- What perspective do they offer?

- What do they need to fully support you?

- How can they help you best?

In my experience the greatest confusion when assessing the teams involved is between allies and confidants, especially when there is a personal friendship also involved. The rules and boundaries can get very fuzzy (see fig. 12.1). One of my clients helped the Christian organization he serves find a director for an innovative new program. The new director just happened to be one of his oldest friends. At first everything went wonderfully. But over time a disagreement arose about the direction of the ministry, with my client siding with the organization against his friend. When the director was released, my client did everything in his power to help his old friend get the best severance and strongest references possible. The director, first hired and then eventually fired, at least in part because of the input of his friend, felt betrayed. Their friendship has never recovered.

Allies	Confidants
Within organization	Usually outside of organization
See your goals	See your heart
Have other (even competing) loyalties	Loyal only to you
Give you perspective	Give you encouragement
Can build alliances	Can build you up
Not friends	*Not* partners

Figure 12.1. Allies and confidants

Some would say this points to why friends shouldn't work together. I don't think that's right. I believe that all relationships need good, clear boundaries with good, clear agreements. And when friends work together, they need even clearer boundaries and clearer agreements. They need even more communication, not less. Even more understanding of their roles and the responsibilities, not less. Remember, in a healthy organization the mission trumps, even their friendship. My client and his friend hadn't clarified that once they were colleagues working together they would have to work on being good allies even more than confidants. When counting allies, don't necessarily count on your friends.

3. Opponents. Potential opponents are stakeholders who have markedly different perspectives from yours and who risk losing the most if you and your initiative go forward. Let's be clear here, if you are leading a change process, opponents are not your enemies in much the same way that allies are not necessarily your friends. Opponents are nothing more and nothing less than those who are against the particular change initiative. Knowing, respecting and staying connected to your opponents is a critical part of staying in the Blue Zone. Often healthy, respected opponents become the catalyst for finding new solutions that create more widespread support. But since adaptive change is not a win-win proposition, there will be loss; since there will be loss, those who oppose the losses will oppose you.

- Who might be your opponents?
- Why might they be opponents?
- What do they stand to lose if your initiative succeeds?
- How might you neutralize their opposition or get them on your side?
- How will your initiative be stronger through incorporating some of the ideas of your opponents?

4. Senior authorities. As I have said from the outset, leadership is not the same thing as authority. Authority is your role, your position of formal power, but leadership is a way of functioning. Very often the leader in uncharted territory is not the authorized leader but someone tasked to explore the new terrain. Remember, it wasn't Commander in Chief Jefferson who crossed the Continental Divide, but two captains. At the same time even the most senior authority is under authority to someone even more senior. A CEO has a board of directors and a senior pastor has a board or council to which he or she is accountable.

The key strategy for working with those above you in the system is, again, stay connected. Stay in relationship and close proximity with those above you. It's harder for someone to sabotage you who is in a relationship with you (see chap. 13). Edwin Friedman offers good counsel for those who are working under someone. If you have a good relationship with your superior, then, according to Friedman, it's best not to push superiors to take a stand (supporting a controversial change effort publicly and early) but instead to pass the system anxiety and challenges on to them. Help your senior authority feel the heat of urgency and anxiety that is creating the need for change. Don't shelter them from anxiety in the system, stay connected to them, even offering appropriate support as they work through *their* challenges. In this way, you build healthy alliances with your superiors for them to stay with you in your challenges.

- Who are the senior authorities most important to your program or initiative's success?

- Why are they important?

- What signals are they giving about how the organization perceives your initiative?

- What might you say or do to secure their support as your initiative is being implemented?

5. Casualties. In any transformational leadership effort there will be casualties. You can't go into uncharted territory without risk. Even Lewis and Clark had to bury one of their men along the way. If a leader is "the person in the system who is not blaming anyone," then the leader is also the one who *assumes the responsibility for these inevitable casualties.*[8] As change initiatives are being proposed, don't whitewash the losses. Acknowledge them. Help to mitigate them in any way.

Pay extra attention to those who are going to experience the change most personally and dramatically. Spend time with them, acknowledge your role in their difficulties, and find ways to help them endure the experience or get on with their lives in another way. When you take responsibility for casualties in these ways, some of them may even rise to the occasion and support the intervention despite the fact that it puts them in jeopardy. Strategically, you are also communicating to the allies of those who have become casualties: If these allies see you treating their friends humanely, they may have more positive feelings about you and your initiative. If they see you treat their friends callously, they will have one more good reason not to come onboard.

- Who will be casualties of your program or initiative?

- What will they lose?

- What new skills would help them survive the change and thrive in the organization?

- How might you help them acquire those skills?
- Which casualties will need to leave the organization?
- What can you offer in terms of permission and support to leave the organization?
- How could you help them succeed elsewhere?

6. Dissenters. In true adaptive change *there are no unanimous votes.* Someone, usually a significant number of people, will say no, no matter what. These voices of dissent are extremely important at every step of the way. The early naysayers are the canaries in the coal mine. They will help you see how opposition will take form and will raise the arguments that eventually will come to full volume. Dissenters have the uncanny capacity for asking the tough key question that you have been unwilling to face up to yourself or that others have been unwilling to raise.

At the seminary where I have joined the work of a faculty committed to a significant transformation of theological higher education, some of the dissenters are our most respected, beloved and genuinely valued faculty members.[9] And understandably so. They are the pantheon of their fields of study, and are, in many cases, the reason the school has such a great reputation (and are my personal heroes). For them, changing the institution is only going to be experienced as loss. So a significant amount of my leadership work is spending time listening to, understanding and incorporating the concerns of the dissenters into the future of the school. This is not only appropriate but a privilege. And our work is stronger because of their dissent.

In his book *Buy-In: Saving Your Good Idea from Getting Shot Down,* John Kotter encourages leaders to engage dissenters, not discourage them: "Don't scheme to keep potential opponents, even the sneakiest attackers, out of the discussion. Let them in. Let them shoot at you. Even encourage them to shoot at you!"[10] By doing so, you are giving dissenting voices a hearing, demonstrating respect for them and a confidence in your ideas (remember: the *mission* trumps, not you!). Giving dissenters a voice keeps the system open and transparent, encouraging everyone to act in the best interest of the organization by putting all cards on the table. At the same time, the dissenters are helping you raise the very competing value issues that need to be confronted.

- Who are the dissenters in your organization?
- Who are those who voice radical ideas or mention the unmentionable?
- What ideas are they bringing forth that might be valuable for your initiative?
- How might you enable their ideas to have a hearing?

Beyond the six kinds of relationships, there are also two *groups* who are necessary for every organizational transformation process.

THE GROUPS THAT GET TO THE MOON

When President Kennedy announced his "moon shot," he had far more than a good speech and a compelling vision. He was coming off a failure (the Bay of Pigs fiasco) that convinced him he needed to take a big risk on a big idea. The Russians were already ahead of him in the space race, creating a compelling sense of *urgency*. He also had at least some tepid support of the Congress. (Reportedly, on the way back to the White House after the now famous speech, Kennedy turned to speechwriter Ted Sorenson and said, "That didn't go over well, did it?")

Most importantly, he had NASA. He had a group of smart, committed, roll-up-the-sleeves-and get-it-done taskmasters who were ready to get to work.

As John Kotter and other gurus of deep organizational change tell us, transformation does not merely come from a big idea. Deep change is more than genius, inspiration and marketing. Transformation requires risk-taking born of urgency, leadership, a holding environment that will create enough stability and support in an organizational system to experiment with a big idea, and a guiding coalition or a transformation team ready to do the work of bringing the idea to reality.

- Without the Bay of Pigs, Kennedy wouldn't have been willing to take a risk.
- Without the Russians, there wouldn't have been the urgency to act.
- Without even the tepid support of Congress there wouldn't have been the resources to even try.
- But without NASA, nothing would ever have gotten off the ground.

Every architect needs both a bank to fund the project and a construction team to build it. Every visionary leader needs both a group to keep attending to the necessary work and a team to lead the transformation of the organizational culture. And while they may be one and the same in some circumstances, a great idea needs at least *two* groups of people to see it through: the *maintaining mission group* and the *transformation team*.

The maintaining mission group. The maintaining mission group has to be committed to giving safety, time, space, protection and resources to the project. At first, they don't need to actually do anything except *not* create obstacles and not sabotage the change process (a big task, in itself!). At best, they actively voice support, keep a steady hand at the wheel and monitor the inevitable anxiety. They provide cover for the transformation team, while also caring for the organization. They make sure that the community feels safe while a few are venturing forth.

In the church setting that I have mostly worked in, this is the perfect job for the Session or board. For a nonprofit this is the board of directors. In the seminary, this is the work of the board of trustees, senior faculty and administrators. They don't so much have to make it happen as buy-in *enough* to giving the transformation team *time to make it happen*. They have to understand and own the changes, but not necessarily give much personal energy to them. Or to shift the metaphor, they need to keep the wagon train moving, even while the scouts are looking for a new pass through the mountains. Eventually, this group is the most important. They will choose to institutionalize the change or not.

> ***REORIENTATION***
>
> In a Christendom world, visionary management usually comes from the board of directors. In the uncharted world of post-Christendom transformation, leadership will more likely come from a small Corps of Discovery who serve as a transformation team while the board manages the health of the organization currently.

This team protects the culture of the organization, and they can single-handedly thwart the transformation if they choose to do so.

The transformation team. The transformation team is akin to what John Kotter calls a "Guiding Coalition."[11] This group will add *effort* to the inspiration. They are going to do the work of listening, learning, attempting and, yes, failing. (Remember how many early attempts at building rockets flamed out on the launch pad?) This team needs to be innovative and persistent, cohesive and communicative. In many situations this is the staff executive team, but often it is not. Indeed, in church settings, I believe it is usually a mistake to assume that the church staff will be the transformation team. In churches the transformation team needs to be made up of both staff and lay leaders. In any organization the transformation team requires both those who have authoritative positions and those with informal influence. In short, the transformation team must be those with the most creativity, energy, credibility, personal maturity and dogged determination. They must be enthusiastic for the idea, resolute about seeing it through and willing to expend relational capital to bring genuine culture change. And perhaps most importantly, they must be volunteers. Even if leading this change is in someone's job description (as it should be in a truly transformative organization) most of those on the transformation team will be giving time, energy and effort far beyond a usual forty-hour week. Perhaps most important, this team should be ready to disband, giving up their power and influence so the organization itself will embrace and institutionalize the changes.

For most leaders I know, and especially for pastors, all of this discussion of the different relationships certainly doesn't sound like good news. While most of us are good at *personally* relating to people (praying, teaching, counseling), most of us have not been trained in *organizational relationship skills*. The ways we have been taught to lead are inadequate for this new terrain or circumstance. The skills we have honed (write sermons, visit hospitals, counseling, teach classes) we do independently, even individualistically. When we work with a committee, it is usually as a moderator, not a leader. Typically, we are more concerned about making sure the conversation is orderly than courageous or creative. So, most well-intentioned, even ambitious attempts for a Session or a pastor to bring transformation are *doomed* because of a lack of capacity more than anything else. A pastor needs to inspire like Kennedy, moderate governance like the Speaker of the House, and establish and lead innovation at NASA—all at the same time.

The good news in the midst of all this doom and failure is that our own Christian tradition is filled with examples of transformation teams who succeeded in ways far beyond their imagination. (Even Jesus had a transformation team of Twelve.) Our theology affirms that leadership is a shared task, and the church is meant to be both a safe environment for protecting the community and a group willing to lay down their lives for the vision of God's kingdom come to earth.

TAKE ACTION

For inspired ideas to take root within the culture of an institution, there must be a series of intentional actions. Pastors need to learn a new set of skills to go along with our abilities to preach, teach, counsel and moderate meetings. When leaders are willing to give up the myth of the lone individual with the inspiring idea and instead learn to build teams of shared inspired action, then the church will begin to see more dreams become reality. Let me offer some specific actions steps for doing so.

    1. Give the work back to the people who most care about it. Are you the only one losing sleep over the challenges you face? Then you need to raise the urgency with a broader coalition of people. When a group of people bring a complaint, don't jump to fix it but instead engage those who raised the complaint in the process of transformation. Find the people who are most heated about the issue and engage them in taking on the challenge. If "adaptive leadership is *the practice of mobilizing people* to tackle tough challenges and thrive," then if nobody is being mobilized, nobody is being led.[12] This is a critical moment in organizational transformation. While we absolutely need people to keep raising awareness of what is not working in our midst, we must remember that nothing changes by complaining. Only when someone steps up to convene a group to address a problem does transformation occur.

    2. Engage the mature and motivated. Let's face it, most of our work (especially for pastors) is putting out fires, dealing with the resistant, attending to the cranky and trying to appease the complainers. These are part of our work and are indeed the people to whom we are called. But when it's time to lead on, more and more of your energy must be invested in those who are motivated to grow and take responsibility for themselves. Work with the mature and motivated. Find those who are eager to take on a big challenge. Be Meriwether Lewis and find your William Clark. Go with the energetic and you'll have more energy for the others.

    3. Stay connected to your critics. From *The Godfather* we learned to "keep your friends close, but your enemies closer," but that was for self-protection.

In this case that great advice is a way to keep trying to turn enemies into friends (*not* through accommodation but through influence). This is the essence of what it means to "stay connected."

While some of us respond to threats or emotional attacks by fighting, most of us are more prone to flee. Most of us who work in organizational life, especially organizations filled with volunteers (like churches), tend to avoid conflict at all cost. The normal response to a threat for most of us is to distance, to disconnect, to grumble to ourselves or gossip to our friends, but we avoid confrontation for fear that it will turn into a bad scene or that we'll get a reputation for being a grumpy complainer. So fearing that we will stew in the searing emotions swirling around us, we check out, get busy with something else or simply drift away.

We tell ourselves that if we don't back down we'll do something in anger that we'll regret. So we do nothing instead. Face-to-face conversations become quick voicemails, phone calls turn into emails, and discussions over lunch become formal letters. After a while, because we are so afraid of the heat, thick walls of ice rise up around us, and while we may be able to see the subjects of our conflicts, we can't hear or touch them. But when we lose connection, we lose the opportunity to keep gently influencing the system for good. We need at least a light touch on the wheel to steer the car toward the destination of our convictions.

So what is a leader to do? *Stay connected*. Keep contact. Close the distance with word and touch. When someone writes me an angry email, I call them at home. When someone sends a formal letter of complaint, I invite them for coffee. When people start getting upset, I call a meeting and invite them to talk. The more heated the situation, the closer I want to get to it. Believe me, this is hard. I'm no different than anyone else.

Margaret Wheatley says,

> In order to counter the negative organizational dynamics stimulated by stress and uncertainty, we must give full attention to the quality of our relationships. Nothing else works, no new tools or technical applications, no redesigned organizational chart. The solution is each other. If we can rely on one another, we can cope with almost anything.[13]

Stay connected to those who are resisting change to keep influencing the system toward health and life. This is counterintuitive and, yes, dangerous. While we know that regulating the heat is crucial to transformation, most of us avoid heated situations because we don't want to get burned or we fear we'll be gasoline to the blaze that will torch the whole house. The purpose for staying connected is to calm the situation down. To regulate the heat so we can keep cooking toward the goals of conviction that will bring good to our families, organizations, companies or churches. One more relational dynamic is unavoidable, completely understandable and terribly discouraging.

4. Expect sabotage. Which is where we turn next.

13

Et Tu, Church?

Sabotage and Staying the Course

*Of courage undaunted, possessing a firmness & perseverance
of purpose which nothing but impossibilities could
divert from its direction . . .*

**THOMAS JEFFERSON, DESCRIBING
MERIWETHER LEWIS IN A LETTER, 1813**

*The important thing to remember about
the phenomenon of sabotage is that it is a systemic part
of leadership—part and parcel of the leadership process. Another way
of putting this is that a leader can never assume success because he or
she has brought about a change. It is only after having first brought
about a change and then subsequently endured the resultant
sabotage that the leader can feel truly successful.*

EDWIN FRIEDMAN, *A FAILURE OF NERVE*

A BIG HUG ON A BAD DAY

"You know I love you, right? And you know that I'm in favor of what you are trying to do, right? In my position, I just can't say anything."

I accepted the hug and the gesture. I was good at collecting these kinds of sentiments. They had been coming in droves. But I have to admit that I sat there scratching my head as this most recent encourager walked off to another important meeting and left me standing in the middle of the convention center at our denomination's General Assembly.

In a couple of hours I would be presenting the work of a two-year national commission I had chaired which studied and proposed that our denomination enter into a nine-year experiment in flexibility of governance to engage and energize the church to face the future. The previous General Assembly, at the unprecedented request of the denominational leadership, had called for this commission because of the urgency of mainline decline. The commission was charged with discerning the best organizational structure for our Presbyterian system that would be "responsive both to the Spirit of Christ and the changing opportunities for discipleship." The charge itself asked, "Are the structures of history the best platforms for carrying our mission into the future?" I was asked to chair the commission because I had led a similar process in our presbytery and was seen as being "impartial" and "outside the system."

For two years, in my role as the moderator of the commission, I had personally consulted with every national leader and most every significant person of regional authority in our denomination. Most of these folks were on my speed dial. In addition, we had conducted conference calls, paid for an extensive survey and used social media to get as much input as possible to engage in a nine-month listening process before suggesting any interventions. We had followed the observations-interpretations-interventions process very closely.

In a spirit of complete transparency our commission had published all of our work in process, had engaged a national conversation about the future of the church and sought for agreement and consensus about all of our proposals every step of the way.[1] My fellow commissioners and I had traveled to every corner of the country to meet with and discuss our ideas with all the interest groups and ordinary folks we could. Our report, though considered somewhat radical, was really nothing more than giving *permission* for regional bodies to try some *experiments* for a *limited* time. It was filled with safeguards and supervision that offered belt-and-suspenders oversight. And most of all there were no surprises. Every step we took we had done in public. We brought the General Assembly exactly what we promised, deliberately shaping our report to align with the larger goals, aspirations and hopes of the most visionary and hopeful proposals of the national staff and the most creative regional leaders. There was some significant opposition, without question. We expected that.

But over and over we had been told, "This is exactly what we need. You all have delivered exactly what we hoped."

So, when we came to the General Assembly, how many of those same leaders who had affirmed our work all along the way made public statements of support? *Zero.*

How many asked to testify to the oversight committee? *Zero.*

How many of those who had hugged me in the hall did *anything at all* to support its passage? *Zero.*

When I asked for public statements to counter the resistance, one person after another told me that the word had come down from "on high" that they couldn't be seen "taking sides" in what was a controversial debate. The whole proposal was soundly rejected with the most benign part referred to a committee for further study.

After the GA floor vote, the huggers all met me in the hall. "It's really too bad, Tod. But this is our Presbyterian system," I was told. More hugs, more private affirmations of personal love and support. No changes at all. Ed Friedman's searing observation about institutional systems raced through my mind:

> In any type of institution whatsoever, when a self-directed, imaginative, energetic, or creative member is being consistently frustrated and sabotaged rather than encouraged and supported, what will turn out to be true one hundred percent of the time, regardless of whether the disrupters are supervisors, subordinates, or peers, is that the person at the very top of that institution is a peace-monger.[2]

For Friedman the "peace-monger" is the leader whose own high degree of anxiety leads him to prefer harmony to health, to appease complainers just to quiet them, but who will not actually demand that they take responsibility for their own part in the organizational problem.

Throughout this book, we have repeatedly come back to this theme from Ronald Heifetz: "Leadership is disappointing your own people at a rate they can absorb." The perceptive and caring leader will invariably wince at the three words in the center of the quote: *your own people.*

That is the rub, isn't it? It's one thing to disappoint and anger the other side, but another thing entirely to endure friendly fire. We leaders comfort ourselves by believing that our leadership style will continually energize our base, that we will, *Braveheart*-style, be able to rally the troops to charge. We assume that our followers will have our backs. But that is all a comforting fantasy if you are truly trying to bring change to an organizational system. Whether it is a family, a church, a business, a not-for-profit or a government, all the best literature makes it clear: to lead you must be able to disappoint *your own people*. But, even doing so well ("at a rate they can absorb") does *not* preclude them turning on you. In fact, when you disappoint your own people, they *will* turn on you.

Even Lewis and Clark faced their own challenge with sabotage. Miles from St. Louis, facing their first hard winter before they headed off the map, they had to deal with the attitude-poisoning influence of Private Moses Reed on Private John Newton. Reed had already been caught trying to desert and had been removed as an official member of the party. Instead of executing him (as would have been standard practice), the captains demoted him to civilian status, made him give up his rifle and declared that he would be sent back to St. Louis in the spring with the next trapping party they encountered. But now Reed's grumbling was becoming contagious, and Newton had made statements that the other men, in an official court-martial, found treasonous. The captains allowed the men to decide Newton's fate, and he too, after being punished, was demoted from official status in the party.[3]

If the change process is "start with conviction, stay connected, stay calm and stay the course," then when you are focused on "staying the course," expect that it is "your own people" who are going to try to knock you off course. And the key to staying the course is wisely and calmly responding to *sabotage*. Note the verb here: not *reacting*, but *responding*. To be sure, Lewis and Clark as military leaders could not tolerate insubordination in their ranks. But while military law would have given them full right to punish desertion and mutinous activities harshly, in both cases they calmly insisted that the group give due process and function at the highest levels of their corps ideals.

I also want to be very clear that I harbor no ill will or even anger toward the leaders who hugged me in the hall but sat silently as our proposal went down in flames. For me to take their actions personally is both misguided and unhelpful. A number of them are beloved colleagues, even friends. I even imagine that as they read this, not one of them will consider what they did (and didn't do) to be sabotage. But from a systems perspective that is exactly what happened. And it happens all the time. Sometimes we are the ones being sabotaged; other times we are the saboteurs. I have to admit that in my own life I have been both. Not only have I had other endeavors sabotaged, but I have also, in other cases, been the "peace-monger" and the unknowing obstacle protecting the status quo. Only as I am able to see the larger systemic issues at play can I avoid sabotaging others in the future and respond well when I get sabotaged.

UNDERSTANDING SABOTAGE

Friedman informs us that

> sabotage is not merely something to be avoided or wished away; instead, it comes with the territory of leading, whether that "territory" is a family or an organization. And a leader's capacity to recognize sabotage for what it is—that is, a systemic phenomenon connected to the shifting balances in the emotional processes of a relationship system and not to the institution's specific issues, makeup, or goals—is the key to the kingdom.[4]

Sabotage is natural. It's *normal*. It's part and parcel of the *systemic* process of leadership. Saboteurs are usually doing nothing but *unconsciously supporting the status quo.* They are protecting the system and keeping it in place. They are preserving something dear to them. If every system is "perfectly designed for the results we are getting," it became clear to me that *our denominational system exists for institutional self-preservation.* When the proposal created too much controversy in an assembly filled with controversial issues, those in authority defaulted back to familiar terrain and allowed the work they had proposed, supported and affirmed to die rather than risk more institutional upset. This is normal. It's natural.

It's also deadly to change efforts.

Many who sabotage you will even claim that they are doing you a favor by doing so. Friedman describes these "peace-mongers" as "highly anxious risk-avoiders" who are "more concerned with good feelings than progress" and consistently prefer the peaceful status quo over the turbulence of change— even if change is necessary. At our core we pastors really are peace-mongers. Interestingly, William Barclay theorizes that Judas's betrayal of Jesus was an act of trying to "force Jesus' hand" to fulfill the expectations of a first-century messiah.[5] When Jesus challenged the status quo with his notions of what the kingdom would be and what a Messiah should do, one of "his own people" (Judas) turned on him. So, what do we do with sabotage and how do we respond to it so that we can "stay the course" of our convictions for change?

First, *expect sabotage.* Anticipation is a great defense. To be aware that sabotage is coming will at least keep us from being surprised when it comes. Even if everybody is excited in the beginning stages of a new organizational shift, change, initiative or restructuring, be aware that a time will come when

> ### *REORIENTATION*
>
> When on the map, leaders could assume that once an affirmative vote was made, the challenge of bringing change was finished.
>
> In uncharted territory, where changes occur so rapidly, leaders cannot assume success until after they have weathered the sabotage that naturally follows.

they certainly will not be. Remember, all change, even necessary change, brings loss. Loss heightens anxiety, and anxiety can lead people to do things that even hours before they wouldn't have considered. Expecting sabotage enables us to stay calm when it comes.

Second, *embrace sabotage as a normal part of an organizational life.* Even the saboteurs aren't really to blame. Systems like stability. Natural survival skills demand it, in fact. You, by bringing change, have upset the emotional equilibrium of the system. The Israelites wanted to go back to slavery in Egypt once things got rough in the desert. Systems always look for and find comfort in the familiar. (Do you hear the root word of "family" in *familiar*? Every organization has its own family system at work.) The art of leadership is helping the system override the instinct to self-preservation and replace it with a new organizational instinct to be curious about and open to the terrifying discomfort of asking, Could God be up to something here?

When I was standing on the platform of the General Assembly watching two years of work go down in a lopsided loss, I really felt a strange sense of calm. I was able to have a "balcony experience" and see how our entire system resolutely protects the status quo. I sat there kind of bemused as I realized that even though we had had one speaker after another challenge us to bring change, to innovate and to faithfully take risks for the sake of the mission of

God, actually taking them was impossible at that moment. Innovation is very hard for any organizational system (especially one whose core belief includes the total depravity of humanity!). This is the default mechanism for an organizational system that encounters new ideas. Unless the changes and adaptations are brought back into the view of our people persistently and consistently over time does the system have any likelihood of adopting them. Only as individual people in the system change, will the system change.

Third, *don't take it personally*. The people following you may be shooting you in the back, but it's really not *you* that they are sabotaging, it's your role as leader. They are sabotaging the change you are bringing. And to be clear, they would do this to *any* leader. By not taking it personally, we can keep monitoring ourselves and keep from reacting in a way that will make the situation worse. Even when people think they *are* making a personal attack, even *they* don't realize that they are actually attacking what you represent (in them, in the system), not you. Consider Jesus from the cross, "Father forgive them; for they do not know what they are doing" (Luke 23:34). By depersonalizing the attack you are much more likely to stay both calm and connected even to the saboteurs, enabling you to make much better decisions as you stay the course of change.

Fourth, *focus your attention on the emotionally strong, not the saboteurs*. We are so focused on quieting our critics, appeasing or answering our accusers and shielding ourselves from the friendly fire that it often knocks us off course. While we need to stay connected to the saboteurs ("Keep your friends close, but your enemies closer"), what actually keeps the change process going is investing even more time in those committed to growing, adapting and changing for good. Find other calm, courageous people and strengthen and support them. Keep building healthy alliances with those who are emotionally mature and share your convictions, and they will join you in the needed change. As you see them begin to grow and change, even as you witness the tiniest bit of God's transforming power in yourself or in others, it will inspire you to stay on course also.

AFTER THE SABOTAGE

In the months following that General Assembly, I found myself thinking a lot about my dad. Dad has the uncanny ability to fix anything with just a butter knife. In Dad's hands that basic kitchen instrument used daily to make PB&J sandwiches for school lunches, becomes at once a screwdriver, a paint scraper, a pry bar, a file, a lever and even a small hammer. It's a wonder to behold. When I was growing up, if some small home repair was needed, more often than not he wouldn't turn to the big tool chest in the garage, he would summon me to go to the silverware drawer and bring him a butter knife.

After our report was turned down, I began to think that what the church needs even more than new structures, organizations, fellowships and denominations are the kinds of people who, like my dad and his butter knife, can innovate and renovate with whatever tools they have at their disposal.

LEADERS MAKE THE FUTURE

Bob Johansen, who described the "volatile, uncertain, complex and ambiguous" (VUCA) world, says "Leaders *make* the future."[6] For Johansen, leaders are "tinkerers" or, as Steven Johnson, in his study of innovation, writes, those who can "cobble together" the parts and pieces in front of them with the tools at hand for a new discovery.[7] Like the Houston engineers in the film *Apollo 13* who had to make a new air filter with only some small parts or the orbiting astronauts would succumb to their own carbon dioxide, the leaders of the future will need to be creative, persistent, resilient and able to make the future out of the parts and pieces of what we've got.

It has become crystal clear to many that another study, conversation, task force or even commission will not bring change to the church. The church will not change until we get a change in leadership. Either we need new leaders who are ready to make the future or the current leaders of every level of the church must find a courage and creativity that has so far eluded them.

The leadership we have today is indeed "perfectly designed for the results we are getting." This leadership is well-schooled in managing divisive politics through zealously guarding the status quo and then wringing hands and blaming the system when nothing changes. In *Apollo 13* the lead engineer, mindful that not only the mission but the lives of his colleagues are at stake, yells at an excuse-making subordinate, "I don't care about what anything was *designed* to do, I care about what it *can* do."

Since leading that sabotaged commission for my denomination, I have been spending a good deal of time learning from my own mistakes in that process (like, for one, not anticipating the amount of resistance and sabotage that would come!) and investing my life in coaching and collaborating with church leaders who refuse to wring their hands in futility or throw up their hands in frustration. They do not worry so much whether another commission (or another denomination or another job or even job description) can somehow save us from ourselves. They have instead gone back to the core conviction that *mission trumps* and looked to the opportunities in their neighborhoods and the needs in their cities. They keep thinking about what churches, seminaries and organizations *can* do, not necessarily what they were *supposed* to do. Even if they don't have the tools they might have had, they are not going to let that stop them. They are too busy in the basement with their butter knives making the future. And I am investing my life in tinkering with them.

As I was walking out of the General Assembly hall, one of the younger members of our commission came up to me distraught. "Tod, I have given years of work to try to help this denomination, and it's all wasted. What do I do now?"

I looked at him and said, "Go home and build the healthiest, best congregation that you possibly can."

Last, *make it a conviction* to stay calm and connected so you can stay on course. Endure. Stick with it. Be dogged and determined. If you stumble onto the Great Falls of Montana, find a way to go around them, even if it takes you thirty times longer than expected.[8] If you find yourself facing the Rocky Mountains instead of a river running downstream, ditch the canoes and find horses. And if someone starts to sabotage what you have already been doing, consider it confirmation that you are exactly in the right path.

Leading change is a *process* not accomplished quickly, and the moments of sabotage are the most crucial times in the change process. At this moment everyone in the system sees the leader's true colors. Sabotage is not only a test of the leader's resolve but also a test of the system's resilience. If you as a leader can stay calm and connected, you get the opportunity to help others in the system work through their own sabotaging instincts so the system can begin to change, and possibly the saboteurs will become change leaders themselves. Friedman noted that when a leader offers healthy, consistent, clear, convicted presence (what Friedman calls "taking a stand"), the organizational system begins to adapt toward health: "I began to see that the same emotional processes that produced dysfunction in an institution when the leader was anxiously reactive or absent could work in reverse."[9]

BLUE ZONE DECISIONS: STAYING THE COURSE AMIDST SABOTAGE

The key skill for staying the course amidst sabotage is to make Blue Zone decisions—*no matter what.* In chapter twelve we explored Osterhaus, Jurkowski and Hahn's Red Zone–Blue Zone decision making. The Red Zone is "all about me"; the Blue Zone is "all about the mission." Blue Zone decisions are made as an expression of the core values and healthy principles, and further the discerned, shared mission conviction of the group.

When making Blue Zone decisions, a set of questions are being asked and answered by the leadership group. These questions are different from the Red Zone "me" questions around survival, acceptance, competence and control. They are

- What furthers the mission?
- What principles are at stake here?
- What values are we expressing?
- What pain must we endure?
- How will we support those who are experiencing loss?

Notice that while these questions take seriously the personal experience, pain and loss a decision will make, the decision itself is entirely focused on the first question, What furthers the mission? *A healthy system makes decisions that further the mission.* Perhaps the hardest truth to swallow for most Christian leaders trying to lead change is this: *You must choose principles over personal need.*

Whenever I talk about this with groups, the hands shoot up. "This contradicts Jesus. Didn't he always choose people over principles?" Frankly, no, he didn't. At least not the way we think of it.

If we look closely at the ministry of Jesus, everything he did was for one purpose: to proclaim and demonstrate the good news: "The kingdom of

God is at hand" (Mark 1:15 NASB). And as much as he ministered to people as an expression of that mission, he also disappointed people constantly. He left towns while there were still crowds waiting to be healed (Mark 1:38). After a miraculous feeding of one large crowd, he refused to feed another, and some of his disciples left him (John 6:30-66). He disappointed his mother and brothers who wanted him to return home (Mark 3:31-35), he initially refused to heal the Syrophoenician woman because his mission was to the "lost sheep of . . . Israel" (Matthew 15:21-28), and he constantly disappointed ministry leaders because he hung out with the wrong sorts (Mark 2:16-17) and did the wrong things, like healing on the Sabbath (Luke 13:10-17).

Every parable Jesus taught that challenged the status quo (the prodigal son, the woman with the coin, the shepherd who leaves the ninety-nine to get the one sheep) did *not* describe his desire to care for and comfort people but, in effect, "I do this because God is like this" (Luke 15) or "I am doing these things because the kingdom of heaven is like this" (Matthew 13). Jesus' mission was to reveal the presence and nature of God's reign and rule. That was his purpose. That was his principle.

When Jesus challenged the Pharisees, it wasn't that they were concerned with religious principles and he was concerned with people, but that they had the *wrong principles* (Matthew 23:15). They valued human tradition over God's own revelation about his character, his love and what he desires (Micah 6:8). Jesus models Blue Zone decision making all the way to his own death, praying aloud after hours of struggle, "Not my will but yours be done" (Luke 22:42). While the followers of Jesus will demonstrate a deep compassion and care for people, we do so because we represent a compassionate and caring God and his loving and just kingdom. Jesus' own actions challenge any temptation to use biblical rationale to support little more than well-meaning dysfunction, fear and failures of nerve.

THE NEED FOR NERVE

Nobody who starts with a conviction intends to abandon that conviction when the heat is turned up. No couple who pledges "'til death do us part" intends to be sitting in a lawyer's office dividing up the couches and flat screen TVs. No parent who draws a line of expectation in the sand intends to cave when arguing starts with his teenager. No leader who plans to take her people to the Promised Land intends to hightail it back to Egypt. Nobody who declares that they will follow Jesus intends to deny him three times in one day. But we do more often than we want to admit. No matter how strong our convictions, we all know that sooner or later we might suffer from what Edwin Friedman calls "a failure of nerve." Stuck systems, bad government, corrupt organizations, dysfunctional families and hypocritical churches all suffer from it. For Friedman, failure of nerve is the tendency among leaders to "adapt to immaturity," that is, to give in to the most anxious elements within themselves or within the community who are clamoring to preserve the status quo and undermining the adaptations and experiments necessary for moving forward and meeting the challenges in front of them.[10]

To combat this natural tendency, *all the best leadership literature emphasizes the need for courage.* It takes courage to stay calm and connected in the face of friendly fire. And it takes enduring, repeated acts of courage to stay the course and keep others on course when they are disappointed in you in your role as a leader.

A PICTURE OF COURAGE

My favorite old movie is *Casablanca.* It's a classic film with Humphrey Bogart, Ingrid Bergman and Paul Henreid, where Bogie owns Rick's Café Americain restaurant in Casablanca, Morocco. It takes place during World War II. Casablanca was then a French territory under German occupation. In one of my favorite scenes a group of Nazi soldiers drinking in Rick's bar gather at the piano and start singing the German national anthem so loudly and without consideration of the number of French citizens sitting glumly around them.

It is a rude gesture. Here they are, a conquering army, in occupied territory, and they are spitting in the face of the French citizens. The downcast French people sit glumly while Victor Laszlo, a brave Czech resistance fighter (played by Paul Henreid), calmly and deliberately walks over to the band and says, "Play 'La Marseillaise'" (the French National anthem).

The band members are tentative. They fear the German officers. But Bogie nods his approval and Laszlo begins to sing at the top of his lungs. The band comes to their feet, playing their instruments with gusto. The music soars, and the crowd comes to life. They do not protest the Nazis. They do not shout them down in anger. They just sing so loudly this song of their hearts that they overwhelm the German soldiers. With that one strong, positive voice, they drown out the destructive voices for that brief moment.

In many ways, what Victor Laszlo did in the midst of the destructive voices in that nightclub in Casablanca is what I believe we are attempting to do in leadership. *We want the positive passions and aspirations to overwhelm the negative, fearful voices that keep our families, companies, organizations or churches oppressed in the status quo.*

Every Victor Laszlo knows that there are citizens who will collude with the opposition, and every leader must recognize that sabotage is not so much a personal attack as the normal, natural reaction of a system seeking safety, security and maintaining the status quo (even if that means being occupied by the enemy). This failure of nerve is what leaders must resist in themselves and overcome in their followers. Victor Laszlo gives us a good picture of how courage can be calm and contagious.

First, leaders must act. Laszlo doesn't cower at the sound of the German officers singing their songs with such bravado; he stands and heads toward the conflict. He takes decisive action and determines not to let this moment pass by. When the heat is on, leaders head *to* the kitchen.

Second, when sabotage or opposition appears, leaders continue *to calmly stand on conviction in the face of it.* Laszlo doesn't rant. He doesn't rave. He doesn't start a fight or call the manager to complain. He goes to the band (very likely French citizens, all) and calls them to act with him. From the backstory of the movie, we know that Laszlo has already suffered for his convictions. He has already spent time in a prison camp. He is being denied exit visas that would take him and his wife to safety. The authorities have him on a watch list, and he is certainly in danger. But nevertheless, *he continues to act on his convictions.* Even, especially in the face of danger, he lives out his calling: Calmly enlisting others to join the cause for freedom. Once the band begins to play, the crowd comes to its feet and joins the song.

Third, leaders inspire. The root word of "courage" is the Latin word for "heart." The actions of a leader should *give heart* to a people who sometimes, amidst fears and frailties, lose heart (see Deuteronomy 20:3; Hebrews 12:3).

When a leader can maintain calm and demonstrate courage in the midst of opposition or sabotage, others find the strength to act on their own convictions. When one voice is willing to sing out loud, others are far more willing to join in. But let's be clear. That act of inspiration only turns up the heat on Laszlo by further angering the German authorities. By standing against the opposition, the opposition will now resist him even more, so it is crucial not to miss the whole point of the film.

Last, leaders don't act alone. Yes, Laszlo is first to his feet and willing to stand alone. Leadership requires a missional conviction that takes a stand whether anyone follows or not. *But for a leader to become a leader, someone must follow.* And when Laszlo makes his move to stand against the boorish and demoralizing tactics of the German officers, he doesn't just stand on a table and try to sing over the voices of the German soldiers, he enlists others in his cause. The whole film is about how Laszlo slowly wins over the crowd, then Rick himself and finally even Louis, the local French constable who up until then had colluded with the Germans. As a leader, Laszlo's presence and example are a catalyst for others to join the good fight.

Casablanca is about both love *and* war, and how relationships and the good fight are always intertwined. So many scenes are conversations between potential friends, or possible enemies, building trust, working out relationships, discerning character and who can be trusted. What makes the movie so intriguing are the relational dynamics being worked out amid the backdrop of conflict, which is, of course, just like "real life."

Sabotage is indeed the critical issue for lasting change. Friedman calls it "the key to the kingdom."[11] The key capacity: Does the leader have the capacity to hang in there when reactivity is at its highest? If a leader can develop the emotional stamina to stay true to principles when reactivity and sabotage are most evident, the adaptation process reverses itself and the followers begin to adapt to the leader. *The paradox of transformational leaders is that the very conviction that causes the leader to be willing to "disappoint your own followers at a rate they can absorb" is what ultimately—when handled well—wins "your own followers" to join you in your cause.* If we as leaders start with conviction, stay connected, calm and on course in the face of opposition, then others around us have both the time and conditions to take on these very convictions as their own.

NAVIGATIONAL GUIDE FOR ORGANIZATIONS
Pace and Space

For Meritt Sawyer every bit of her life is an expression of mission. "The more we prayed about it, the more we realized that our home needs to be a mission station," she told a small group of marketplace leaders gathered around a table in discussion. For Sawyer and her husband, Steve, this means that they entertain a steady stream of guests, host dinners for various organizations and church gatherings, and offer themselves as mentors for many young leaders who need the wise counsel and caring of a Christian couple.

Sawyer explains, "I learned of the importance of community throughout the developing world, but mostly in African countries. I came home from a trip early on and stated to Steve: 'We need a village.' 'We are not moving to Africa, are we?' he asked me. This became the backdrop to our deep desire that our home become this meeting place."

While this is certainly noteworthy in and of itself, Meritt and Steve maintain this mission of hospitality in the midst of already busy lives. They are both leaders in their church, and board members for organizations that they care about deeply. Steve is a senior executive for a large national insurance brokerage firm based in San Francisco, and Meritt is the executive director of a nonprofit organization combating medical and economic development issues that keep families trapped in poverty in Central Africa, based in Chicago. For Meritt Sawyer, being in leadership in an international development organization not only requires her to travel frequently, but also to continually "wrestle with the issues of pace and space."

"I'm always seeking relationships and community," Sawyer says. Indeed, her relationships are a significant part of what centers her as a leader. Even more, some of the particular challenges for women in leadership, she feels, require continually attending to as many of those people as possible. "Women leaders need relationships and networks beyond geography," explains Sawyer. There are so few women in positions like hers that she intentionally cultivates the network of peers that enables her personal and professional growth.

But at the same time the demands of so many relationships—combined with the pace of her work—can easily knock her off center.

So Sawyer has established for herself a spiritual practice of a "weekly fast from all devices." From Saturday sundown to Sunday sundown, she turns off the cell phone, unplugs the computer, closes the iPad cover and refuses to answer an email, text, Facebook message or Tweet. This technological sabbath is critical to her life, work and ministry. "There is no dividing line on my phone between friends, church, work and ministry. There are just people that God has called into my life and this weekly fast is the only way that I can renew, be refreshed, maintain the depth of spirit and the attention to God that I need to continue my whole life's mission."

To be a centered leader who stays on mission and endures through the challenges of leadership requires a rhythm of both attending to and fasting from technologically connected relationships.

Part Five

TRANSFORMATION

TRANSFORMATION

Everybody Will Be Changed
(Especially the Leader)

- 14 -

How a Nursing Mother
Saved America

*She was not, like Lewis and Clark, charged
with scientific purpose; she was not one of the Americans
who owned this new land; she was not . . . claiming
alien territory; she was . . . coming home.*

ERICA FUNKHAUSER, "FINDING SACAGAWEA"

*The indiun woman . . . has been of great Service
to me as a pilot through this Country.*

WILLIAM CLARK, JULY 13, 1806, JOURNAL ENTRY

The future is already here; it is just on the margins.

DAVE GIBBONS

THE ONLY ONE WHO WASN'T LOST

On February 11, 1805, a sound rang out through the Corps of Discovery that
they had never expected to hear. Not the roar of a grizzly bear, not the thunder
of waterfalls, not the call of an unknown bird.

A baby's cry.

The military corps had a new recruit who would go with them from their
winter home over the Rocky Mountains to the shore of the Pacific and, even-

tually, back to America. His name was Jean Baptiste, and because his mother would become the most famous member of the party next to Lewis and Clark themselves, "Pomp" as William Clark would nickname him, would be the youngest member of the Corps of Discovery.

Pomp's mother, Sacagawea, had been born Shoshone. Kidnapped by the Hidatsa when she was eleven or twelve, she was now at sixteen or seventeen years old, one of the wives of a French Canadian trapper named Toussaint Charbonneau. The captains had hired Charbonneau as a guide through the mountains and very quickly they saw the value of having a Shoshone woman to serve as interpreter. While, by all accounts, Lewis and Clark soon took a dim view of Charbonneau's skills and value to the party, their opinion of—and need for—the teenage mother only grew.

A month after she joined the party, Lewis mentions her "fortitude and resolution." Two months into the journey, they worried about losing their translator when Sacagawea fell ill with a fever. When a canoe capsized, her quick-thinking saved the captains' journals.[1] When the captains needed horses to cross the Rockies, they turned to Sacagawea. She led them to the Shoshone, navigated the tense relationship at the first encounter, and when she dis-covered that she was translating between Lewis and her own long-lost brother (a most remarkable, tearful and near-miraculous reunion), she helped broker the deal that brought the Corps the critical horses they needed. When her tribe begged Sacagawea to stay, she instead insisted on going with the Corps and continuing the journey. Later, Clark would praise her as the "pilot" that took them through the country.

To be sure, aside from these few particular incidents, Lewis and Clark barely mention Sacagawea in their journals. There is nothing about her feelings, not even the slightest reflection on what this experience must have been like for her. We don't know how she thought of her place in this party. Was it any different than being a young abductee sold to a trader (or won in a card game)?[2] Products of their times, the captains saw little *intrinsic* value in a native American wife of a fur trader; she was deemed *useful* to them (indeed, more so than her husband).[3] Even though her baby was two months old when they broke camp, they took her with them.

The journals never mention or comment on what it was like to have a nursing mother on this journey across the continent. She—and her baby—

simply endured everything the Corps faced. When the men rode through rapids in a dugout canoe, endured days of hunger, fought off mosquitoes or walked through harsh mountain passages, so did Sacagawea *and her baby.*

While we don't know if the captains were being calculating when asking Charbonneau and his family to join them, we do know that the sight of a nursing mother in the Corps made potentially aggressive war parties double take. On October 19, 1805, William Clark wrote in his journal, "The sight of this Indian woman, wife to one of our [interpreters], confirmed those people of our friendly intentions, as no woman ever accompanies a war party of Indians in this quarter."[4]

While they didn't take the time to paint a picture of Sacagawea as a person, there is no doubt to her value as a member of the party and to the way her presence—and the challenges of unfamiliar terrain—created a truly unique leadership dynamic. That dynamic provides for any leader the lens to rethink assumptions regarding traditional roles, structures and dynamics. In short, when you go off the map, the rules change.

For Lewis and Clark, spending a winter preparing to head off the map must have provided the opportunity to discuss, strategize and plan for all the contingencies ahead. The reality that they were going into unknown territory with little but a few notes of procured local knowledge from the Mandans must have given them pause. Their journals don't reveal any of their thinking, but this much was sure: the only member of the Corps of Discovery with experience beyond the Lemhi Pass, indeed the only member of the Corps of Discovery who was not in uncharted territory when they crossed the Continental Divide and headed over the Rocky Mountains was the teenage mother with her nursing baby. Sacagawea was not venturing into unexplored territory, she was going home.

> ## *REORIENTATION*
>
> Those who had neither power nor privilege in the Christendom world are the trustworthy guides and necessary leaders when we go off the map.
>
> They are not going into uncharted territory. They are at home.

UNEXPECTED LEADERS IN UNCHARTED TERRITORY

"The future is already here; it is just on the margins." For nearly twenty years, these words have been seared on my brain. Years before he led a multinational

movement with international multisite congregations, social enterprises and
a consulting firm, he was a Korean American church planter who had moved
his family across the country to plant a multiethnic congregation in the
middle of Orange County, California, the home of huge homogeneous megachurches. In the early 1990s Dave Gibbons was a guy with no money, no
denominational backing, no big school credentials, no office, no buildings,
no paid staff, planting a church that literally had to move to a different location every time they met for worship. In the wild consumer-driven, user-
friendly mecca of south Orange County, he was starting a church that required people to go to a website to find the location where the church was
meeting that Sunday! As I listened to him I marveled. I was the pastor of an
established congregation on prime real estate in a very desirable and growing
community. At the time we were dedicated to being as user-friendly and even
seeker-friendly as possible, yet getting people to attend a church as convenient and comfortable, accessible and welcoming as we could make it was
still a daunting challenge. Maybe this voice from the margins had something
to offer my very "centered" church.[5]

In the Christendom world the dominant voices were rich, powerful, educated, mostly male, mostly white and from the "center." They were most at
home in the modern world marked by stability, predictability and order. Juan
Martinez explains:

> Those of us formed and framed by Western late modernity have tended to be-
> lieve we can find our way, with enough study, focus and determination. Be it
> the physical or social sciences, be it politics, economics, theology, or even
> church planting, we have often understood our task as clarifying, defining,
> mapping and doing.[6]

But, Martinez points out, "Clearly we are now in a disorienting world, in
the midst of situations where cause and effective often do not seem connected.
Because most of our churches were framed in a different era, they often seem
unable to even understand, much less respond, to what is happening."[7]

As the church has lost power and influence within the larger culture, there
is a tendency to bemoan and even battle to regain that place of dominance.
Fuller Theological Seminary Dean of Students Steve Yamaguchi makes a comparison between those trained for life in a bishop's palace and those whose

ministry has been in the streets of ordinary life. "A church bred under the protection of the state is not trained to fend for itself on the streets. So when state and society withdraw their special favor towards the palace-trained church, it gets a very rude awakening. Disorienting and painful, it can lead to despair, anger and denial."[8]

But for those who have not been privileged by Christendom, the cultural changes of the day are no more upsetting than a mountaineer being told there are no rivers to run. He was counting on climbing, not rowing; he was prepared for hiking, not floating; and so there is nothing to be upset about. Indeed, as we head into the future, those on the margins are ahead of those who were dominant figures in the older world.

For many Christians throughout the world today, the death of Christendom in the West simply means there are more brothers and sisters joining them at the margins, more shared experience within the greater church, more equality of leadership roles, more valuing of previously ignored voices and more opportunities for shared witness to a world that is profoundly in need of the gospel. In other words, the deep disorientation for those trained in Christendom can be helped by learning to look to and partner with those who have already been living in post-Christendom marginality.

The vast experience of women, persons of color and leaders from majority world contexts is as critical to the transitioning Western church as was Sacagawea's to Lewis and Clark. The problem, of course, is that even the reality of being trained for Christendom means that most of us won't recognize the value of a Sacagawea when she is sitting in front of us. Yamaguchi explains that while we tend to view our immigrant brothers and sisters (to use just one example) as mission projects or as "people who can cook exotic foods and dance and sing for their church programs," we rarely look to them as "trainers for the church's future strength."

"Our non-white brothers and sisters," Yamaguchi reminds us, "lead churches that have generations of experience living on the edges, displaced from the center, as more than survivors."[9]

But do we even know that we need them?

In a TED Talk seen over 1.6 million times, novelist Chimamanda Adichie reminds us that unless we are exposed to the diversity of the world, our default mental models will create a "single story" of the world, a narrative to help us make sense by making simplistic assumptions that make us comfortable and keep us from having to change.[10] The danger, says Adichie, is that with a single story, we make assumptions about people who are different from us that allows us to keep them marginalized.

> The single story creates stereotypes, and the problem with stereotypes is not that they are untrue but that they are incomplete. They make one story become the only story.... [I]t's impossible to engage properly with a place or a person without engaging with all of the stories of that place or that people. The consequence of the single story is this: It robs people of dignity. It makes our recognition of our equal humanity difficult. It emphasizes how we are different, rather than how we are similar.[11]

For Christena Cleveland, associate professor of the practice of reconciliation at Duke Divinity School, this is not just a matter of leadership but discipleship. "People can meet God within their cultural context, but in order to follow God, they must cross into other cultures because that's what Jesus did in the incarnation and on the cross. Discipleship is crosscultural."[12]

But Cleveland doesn't stop there; she argues that in a changing world the very act of crossing cultural differences and dealing with our unspoken (and often even unacknowledged) biases, and the conflict it often creates, is at the heart of Christian leadership today.

> When we're rubbing elbows in Christian fellowship with people who are different from us, we can learn from each other and grow more like Christ. Like iron sharpens iron.
>
> For this reason, I believe that churches and Christian organizations should strive for cultural diversity. Regardless of ethnic demographics, every community is multicultural when one considers the various cultures of age, gender, economic status, education level, political orientation and so on. Further, every church should fully utilize the multifaceted cultural diversity within itself, express the diversity of its local community, expertly welcome the other, embrace all who are members of the body of Christ and intentionally collaborate with different churches or organizations in order to impact the kingdom.[13]

Like the Corps of Discovery captains who figured out that all of their on-the-map education was less valuable than the life experience of a Shoshone teenage girl, many Christian leaders are only now beginning to realize that as

the Christendom narrative is being rejected, they are in great need to collaborate with and learn from leaders who, because of their gender, social status,
ethnicity and less-privileged life, actually are more equipped for the world
today. As Theresa Cho, a second-generation Korean American pastor, told a
group of church leaders in 2012:

> My husband and I have been working in small congregations our whole min-
> istry career. Every day, every week, and every year, we are faced with the chal-
> lenge of how to make church relevant in the community; how to make church
> healthier; and how to move the church to change with the changing demo-
> graphics. This is reality. This is the wilderness. This is ministry. For smaller con-
> gregations, there isn't a sense of perishing because the hey day left over 50 years
> ago. You have to HAVE something to feel like you are LOSING something.[14]

While many of us who can remember when our churches had full pews and
overflowing offering plates feel so disoriented in this new day, Cho reminds
us that there are many church leaders who have known nothing else.

Of course, Cho reminds us, Christians whose churches thrived in Christendom don't like this reality. They have to reframe their assumptions of ministry and learn to think differently. "It doesn't feel good to be told that there is
loss and a lot of times my job (as a pastoral consultant) is really to offer hope,
encouragement, even pastoral care, 'It's ok,' I say, 'the water is fine. It's going
to hurt, you are going to have to get used to the temperature, but it's going to
be fine. Come on in.'"[15]

Indeed, for those of us who were trained for Christendom, these friends
have much to teach us. Yamaguchi is one of the most important mentors for
me in this regard. For over thirty years he served first as a pastor of an urban
congregation and then as the executive presbyter for the Los Ranchos Presbytery in Southern California. Yamaguchi is of Japanese American descent
and is conversant in Japanese and Spanish, as well as his native English. His
grandparents and parents were forced into internment camps during World
War II, and he has attended or received degrees from schools like Westmont
College, Harvard Divinity School, Princeton Theological Seminary, Gordon-
Conwell Seminary and Claremont School of Theology. He has experienced
firsthand racism toward Asian American people in predominantly white
Orange County, California, and the power and privilege that comes from

education and position. Once, in a conversation with Steve where I shared with him how profoundly confused I was when colleagues viewed me with suspicion as a middle-age, educated, white male, I asked Steve, "How can I help racial ethnics understand that I really want to understand their experiences and partner with them?"

Steve listened to me for a long time, gently looked at me and then said, "I have one suggestion for now. It would help if you didn't use *racial ethnic* as a noun. It might be better if you were to refer to your colleagues as racial-ethnic *people*."

Steve's kind rebuke of my language helped me to see a blind spot. If I really wanted to be an effective leader, collaborator and partner in the world as it really is, I needed this kind of feedback. Fortunately for me, I work with respectful, caring and candid colleagues who are willing to do so. Yamaguchi explains the work that needs to be done, "Not only the behaviors but also the worldview must be transformed through training. Moreover, the replacement of deeply imbedded mental models only takes place with deep pain and *at a great transformational cost*."[16]

Yes, the cost is great. To function in new ways that go against our previous life lessons is profoundly, even disturbingly, uncomfortable for most of us. But, and this is critical to realize, the result for replacing those "deeply imbedded mental models" is the transformation we desire for ourselves, our organizations and our congregations. What is discovered from going off the map? What changes about the way we "face our greatest challenges and thrive"? What is both necessary and transformative about uncharted territory? Let's see.

MORE VOICES IN THE CONVERSATION

Leadership professor Scott Cormode teaches his students, "Leadership begins in listening."[17] This resonates with Gibbons: "To effectively carry Jesus' gospel to various places around the globe today—more important, to be Jesus' gospel—listening is required. We need to be sensitive and lead with an eager learner's resolve."[18] Perhaps more than anything else, our location in uncharted territory requires leaders to listen more deeply and broadly than ever before. Just as Sacagawea's voice as both translator and guide was critical to the captains of the Corps of Discovery, Christian leaders in a post-Christendom world need to engage, encourage and even *insist* that discernment and decision making begin with making a broader number of voices heard. But do we? And when we do, to whom do we *really* listen?

In her biography, *Lean In: Women, Work and the Will to Lead*, Facebook COO Sheryl Sandberg tells the story of a small dinner party with business executives where the guest of honor pompously carried on without so much as a breath to allow others to ask questions or enter the discussion. Three or four times in the course of the evening, men interrupted to make a comment or ask a question. The speaker would respond and then continue his remarks. When Sandberg herself and later the only other woman executive did the same, they were each publicly scolded by the speaker for interrupting. After the dinner, writes Sandberg, "One of the male CEOs pulled me aside to say that he had noticed that only the women had been silenced. He told me he empathized, because as a Hispanic, he has been treated like this many times."[19]

In a series of interviews conducted with women ministry leaders, similar stories came out.[20] Martha Greene, one of the first women to hold a senior pastor position in the Presbyterian Church (USA), said, "Women allow for interruptions when we speak. Actually, we *expect* to be interrupted."

For most of the women this inability for traditional leaders to listen well was not only demeaning but an awkward blind spot that kept those leaders from being as effective as possible. Indeed, in a global study of leadership forces in corporations, increasing diversity within leadership structures led to more profitable results. "Encouraging . . . diversity in your leadership pool means greater diversity of thought, which, in turn, leads to improved problem solving."[21]

MORE WISDOM IN DECISION MAKING

It was November. The Corps of Discovery had finally made it to the Pacific Ocean, but now found themselves in an unenviable position. Extremely low on supplies, tired and delayed in their journey, they now had to make camp for a long, wet winter in what today is the Oregon coast. The captains themselves didn't see eye to eye on the best location. Lewis wanted to be closer to the shore, Clark farther upstream. What they did at that moment would have been unthinkable only months before. They gathered the Corps for a vote. *A vote.* In a military unit, no less. They gave no rationale in their journals, but the same captains who had expressly gone against the will of the men in choosing which route to follow at the great fork in the Missouri River allowed the decision on where to make camp to be determined by a straight democratic process.

But not only did each man get to have his say on where they would stay, but York, Clark's slave, and Sacagawea herself each registered and had recorded one vote. Just like everyone else. As Stephen Ambrose reflects, "This was the first vote ever held in the Pacific Northwest. It was the first time in American history that a black slave had voted, the first time a woman had voted."[22] If David Gibbons is correct about the future being present in the margins, then the future of America was sitting on the edge of the continent when a Native American woman and a slave were given a vote.

For those of us who have felt the discouragement of trying to come up with new uncharted mountain strategies while continually defaulting to the thinking that made us good river explorers, finding new, creative ways of thinking and being is critical to organizational survival and thriving. We need the new models of thinking and problem solving that come from those who live on the margins between different social systems or cultures and bring their practices and insights into, as one person said to me, the "dead center." (I don't know if the speaker was intentionally making a pun with a bit of a pinch, but I certainly heard it that way.)

When powerbrokers and long-time stakeholders are open to engaging the ideas, models and possibilities of the restless on the fringe, the lowly voice in the cubicle, the field worker with a clipboard, the disconnected in the back pews or lingering in the narthex of the greater church (or even those heading out the door!) with a desire to learn, new ways of thinking and seeing are possible. When the voices of majority-world leaders who have a lifetime of experience influencing, guiding and serving from positions without power are allowed to be heard, a deeper wisdom and greater resilience, adaptability, and creativity is accessible to the group.

Juan Martinez explains,

> Leaders in the majority-world intuitively do adaptive change. Westerners assume a certain type of order, predictability and stability that is based in modernity. Majority-world leaders are not experts in the modern sense of the world, but have the intuition and experience to continually adapt, to continually experiment and not be surprised when things don't work.[23]

Cho sees this as one of the primary distinctives between what Yamaguchi calls those "trained for the palace" and those who have been "trained in the streets"[24] "So many of my seminary classmates from traditional churches had the attitude of "I answered the call of God, I went to seminary and I have all this debt, so now I'm entitled to a job." But as an Asian American woman Cho had no aspirations that a big church was going to look at her right out of seminary, something she sees as an advantage now: "It kept me open to opportunities outside the box."

Even more so, Cho says that the experience of being an outsider has helped her to be able to lead better.

> As a woman, I can never start from a place of entitlement and never know what the assumptions are. I'm quick to observe what is happening, and I respond to the conditions as they are. It's a secret advantage I have as a woman. I never expected to be treated with deference and privilege, so I can walk into a situation and my very presence starts the conversation in a more open place. Because I didn't spend time trying to establish my own credibility and authority, I could spend much more time observing.[25]

For Christendom-trained leaders, perhaps the most encouraging realization is that uncharted territory does not make our experience, education and expertise irrelevant, just incomplete. If the margins and the not-so-dead center can interact with each other relationally and have discussions respectfully, there is possibility for genuine lasting change. James Davison Hunter describes it as follows:

> Change is often initiated outside of the centermost positions. When change is initiated in the center, then it typically comes from outside of the center's nucleus. Wherever innovation begins, it comes as a challenge to the dominant ideas and moral systems defined by the elites who possess the highest levels of symbolic capital.[26]

The key point here is that for lasting cultural change to occur (even within an institution) those in the center and those outside of the center must be truly engaged and valued in decision-making processes. The *interaction* of the margins and the center creates the new possibilities. The combination of ideas and relationships, the sharing of experiences and especially the valuing of perspective come from a lifetime of living in uncharted territory that is needed for Christendom-trained leaders to move into uncharted territory. When the center engages the insights from the margins, the center comes alive and moves toward the future.

At SCPC we initiated our Hispanic Service with good intentions and lots of misguided notions (like calling it a "Hispanic Service" for starters).[27] We truly wanted to reach out to our Spanish-speaking neighbors and created a pastoral position, a worship service and offered the support to do so. We went out of our way to make our new friends feel *nuestra casa es su casa*. And by all accounts, it was one of the most vibrant and healthy decisions we made. We hoped and expected that this almost entirely white, affluent church could be generous and would offer much to our neighbors. What we didn't expect was that the Spanish-speaking congregation would actually take the lead in local mission, would soon have more youth in discipleship and leadership than the English-speaking congregation and would become a model for the whole con-gregation in lay-led leadership. The pastor of the congregation today is bi-vocational, sharing time between preaching and teaching and running his auto repair business. There are now first-generation immigrants and Spanish-dominant speakers on the church Session, and through their efforts the church preschool is rapidly becoming bicultural.

For Christena Cleveland, even humble attempts at this kind of crosscul-tural partnership begin to change the dominant and fixed mindset that "dif-ferent is wrong" and counteracts the tendency for homogeneous groups to become even more narrow-minded as time goes on.[28] But even more im-portant perhaps, "Cultural differences in the body of Christ enable different types of people to draw near to the heart of Jesus."[29]

MORE CREATIVITY WITH STRUCTURE

In a military unit still a long way from safety, every soldier counts. John Colter was not just a good soldier. He was one of the most trusted in the unit. So it is surprising to read in William Clark's journal that on August 15, 1806, the cap-tains agreed to let John Colter leave the Corps of Discovery and join two trappers who were going to explore the Yellowstone River. Once again, the circumstances, terrain and opportunity inspired Lewis and Clark to a most unorthodox decision, but that decision led to one of the most cherished dis-coveries in the West. In the years that followed, John Colter became the first white man to discover and explore the geysers and thermal hot springs that became the center of Yellowstone National Park.[30]

Without question, Lewis and Clark were unorthodox leaders who creatively combined the structure of military chain of command with the flexibility and adaptability that uncharted territory demands. For those of us trained with the mental models of military, business or organizational life of the twentieth century, it's hard to even think about a different style of leadership. Indeed, reflecting a concept called "institutional isomorphism," most organizations simply mimic the structure and assumptions of other organizations around them.[31]

But when those who have lived in or served through different kinds of structures enter the leadership conversation, then the system's default behaviors are brought into question. A number of women leaders interviewed for this book uniformly agreed that women are more flexible, more able to multitask and more reflexive collaborators.

"It's just natural for us," one woman pastor remarked, leading naturally from the relational frame necessary to create the kinds of teams necessary for uncharted territory. When organizations are talking more and more about the necessity of increasing trust, transparency and authenticity, women leaders take that for granted. "Men talk about building trust, women talk about building community," said Jill Hudson, a recently retired senior leader within the national Presbyterian Church (USA).

For the woman leaders interviewed, the differences they bring are also critical to the changing ministry itself. In the same way that Sacagawea was at home on the west side of the Lemhi Pass, leaders who are trying to encourage the church to "move into the neighborhoods" and be more "missional" only need to look to the women in a congregation for experience.

"As the church moves into the community, *they find that women have already been there*. In the schools, in the parks with their kids, in community organizations, with neighbors," says Kara Powell. "Community life is even more important today and women *are* already the fabric of the community."

MORE TRANSFORMED THAN IF YOU STAYED ON THE MAP

Juan Martinez observes,

> As the church seeks to be faithful to the Gospel in the midst of adaptive challenges we are reminded that following Jesus, and being a faithful church, is a

journey of discovery. Many of the biblical images of a faithful church in mission point us toward the reality of exile or of a people on the way. It is because we are a pilgrim people attentive to where God is leading us that we can discover new things, that we can discern where the Spirit of God is doing new things in new ways.[32]

Entering uncharted territory is like boarding a time machine set for the future. Lewis and Clark made decisions and functioned with a leadership style that was decades, even centuries before their time.

- A true partnership without one clear leader in "command."

- A woman in leadership.

- A native American woman and a slave given a vote.

- A soldier released gladly from his duties in order to further knowledge.

Could it be that God is taking our churches and organizations into uncharted territory in order for the church to become even more of a witness for the future of the world?

Sometime in the 2040s, the United States will become a true ethnic plurality. During that decade white Americans will no longer be the majority but one of several considerably large ethnic groups. Even more surprising is that those trends are actually higher in the church and especially in seminaries that provide the training for Christian leadership. While white, mainline and evangelical churches are in decline, racial-ethnic churches are growing and predicted to increase even more; seminary enrollments show increases *only* among nonwhite students.[33] In other words, what will soon be true of America is already becoming true in our churches and seminaries.[34] As the title of an article declares, "2040 Is Already Here in a Seminary Near You." Could it be that God is thrusting the church to the forefront of a changing world in order to prepare us to lead and to serve? As the dominant white culture in North America gives way to an increasingly pluralistic culture, imagine the impact that the church could have, imagine the witness the church could offer! In a world of fear marked by divisive group politics, imagine the difference the church could make because we have already been out to the frontier and explored the world to come.

Leaders in a post-Christendom world must courageously face the future.

But to do so wisely and well will require first and foremost a commitment to collaborative leadership with unexpected partners. Uncharted leadership survives and thrives by listening to the ignored voice (Sacagawea), by expanding the table of participation beyond what is imaginable (Sacagawea's and York's votes), and by discovering new worlds and seeing what will come (Colter's exploration of Yellowstone), but mostly, the challenges of uncharted leadership challenge us to keep exploring and become someone completely different from when the journey began.

"We focus so much on changing the church," Cho gently chides, "but we really need to focus on the transformation in our own lives."[35]

Which is where we will bring this journey to an end.

- 15 -

The End of Our Exploring

We shall not cease from exploration
And the end of all our exploring
Will be to arrive where we started
And know the place for the first time.

T. S. ELIOT, "LITTLE GIDDING"

Wanderer, there is no road,
the road is made by walking.

ANTONIO MACHADO, "CAMPOS DE CASTILLA"

We proceeded on.

JOURNALS OF THE
LEWIS AND CLARK EXPEDITION

WE PROCEEDED ON

It's not hard to imagine the conversation. In the middle of a long, dark, rainy winter—their second since leaving St. Louis—it's reasonable that the captains were growing weary of the expedition. The journal entries of their Christmas celebration were muted. "We have nothing to eat but poor Elk meat and no Salt to Season that with, but still keep in good Spirits as we expect this to be the last winter that we will pass this way," John Ordway wrote.[1] On New Year's Day 1806, Meriwether Lewis was even more blunt about the homesickness the

Corps was feeling. The real celebration he wrote, "consisted principally in the anticipation of the 1st day of January 1807, when in the bosom of our friends we hope to participate in the mirth and hilarity of the day, and . . . enjoy the repast which the hand of civilization has prepared for us."[2]

Six weeks earlier they had been ecstatic. "Ocian in view! O! the joy," Clark had scrawled in his journal on November 7, 1805. After nineteen months of dangerous and demanding travel the Corps of Discovery had accomplished what many had feared was near impossible. But they had done it and understandably felt the thrill of accomplishment.

But now in the middle of the rainy, cold winter the excitement of seeing the Pacific had ebbed. They were still a long way from home. The continent they had just crossed was multiple times bigger than they had expected it to be. Instead of a water route, they had crossed 340 miles over land, 140 of them through rugged mountains, 60 of those through snow.[3] The journey was longer and harder than they had expected and had led to a most stunning discovery: *all the "maps" were wrong.* All of the assumptions and expectations of generations of explorers and rulers of European ancestry had been debunked. The western front of the continent was a completely different geography. Most significantly there was no water route. Explorers and settlers would not be able to use a single waterway as a convenient route for commerce and expansion. Indeed, the "new world" was filled with even more territory to explore than Jefferson could imagine.

It's understandable that they might have hoped that a passing ship would make contact during that long winter. Jefferson had given them letters of credit that would allow them—if a ship passed by—to book passage back to Washington.[4] If nothing else, they could safely send back those journals and a letter to Jefferson to make sure what they had learned so far would not be lost on the journey home.[5] But they must have at least considered the idea of coming home snug in the bottom of a ship instead of starting the long walk back.

It would seem that after so much exploring, so much learning, so many trials and travails, and so much longing for the familiar comforts of friends and kin, the expected decision would be to return as quickly as possible. Now that they had accomplished their goal, it would have seemed logical to take the most direct, safest route in return.

But they didn't.

206 CANOEING THE MOUNTAINS

After they could be confident of the receding of the winter snows, the Corps set out on the return journey. On July 3, 1806, at a place they called Traveler's Rest, Lewis and Clark separated from each other. The notations in their journals made it clear that they had spent some time talking about this during that long, cold winter. They negotiated with the Nez Pierce to provide guides. They divided up the Corps and took two different routes so they could explore more territory. Lewis would go north, Clark would go south, and they would—hopefully—reunite at the convergence of the Missouri and Yellowstone rivers. For five or six weeks the Corps would be split in two. This already small crew would be even more vulnerable. Why do this? Why take on the extra miles and extra risk? This was, as Stephen Ambrose evaluated it, "an excessively dangerous plan."[6] Why not return the way they had come and use the experience gained on the trip to the Pacific to insure that they and their precious journals, findings and stories arrived home safely?

Because there was more to explore.[7]

That spirit of exploration, the spirit of adventure that sometimes inspires huge risks and other times leads to questionable decisions, according to Edwin Friedman, is the key to breaking the "imaginative gridlock" that keeps a system locked into old mental models and outdated strategies even though the world has changed. Friedman views Columbus's discoveries of the new world as the unconscious liberator of creativity that allowed the renaissance and its world-reorganizing discoveries to bring energy and life to a continent that had been, in the terminology of his field, *depressed*.[8] Friedman describes these depressed, imaginatively gridlocked systems as marked by three common characteristics that are "both symptom and cause of a locked-in perspective": "an unending treadmill of trying harder," "looking for answers rather than reframing questions" and "either/or thinking that creates false dichotomies."[9]

> ***REORIENTATION***
>
> Exploration teaches us to see the familiar through a new frame.
>   Exploration brings differentiation.
>   Exploration requires us to become expert experimenters.
>   Exploration demands our best selves.

But with the discovery of 1492, Friedman asserts, there came an awareness of a world where the reality was far different from what had been supposed;

there was a shaking up of assumptions, a reconsideration of what "everyone just knew"—and with it came a burst of contagious new creativity that led to a rapid reordering of the mental models of Europeans.[10]

For Friedman the true genius of both Columbus and Lewis and Clark is not just in their extraordinary courage and capacities as adventurers who went off the map, but *the inspiration* they offered to others to see beyond the old maps and assumptions of the past. Perhaps this spirit of exploration—this adventure-or-die attitude—is the great gift uncharted leaders can give to the church in a post-Christendom world.

Friedman notes,

> The process of discovery that freed Europe from its imaginative gridlock of a thousand years is in large part about the relationship between risk and reality— which means it is also basically about leadership . . . someone simply must be able to separate himself or herself enough from surrounding emotional processes to go first—whether we are considering a marriage or a corporation.[11]

Yes—it is worth repeating—leadership off the map is inherently risky and frequently lonely. Leaders are those who "separate themselves" from the emotional processes of the group around them and "go first." But even beyond inspiration, exploration is also a profoundly powerful teacher with valuable lessons to bestow. Let's look at a few of those.

SEEING AGAIN FOR THE FIRST TIME

The search for a Northwest Passage started long before Jefferson. Indeed, the frame or mental model that inspired Jefferson to send the Corps of Discovery was the offspring of a three-hundred-year-old fixation of Europe on the Far East. For centuries European rulers had wanted both the riches of the Far East and an escape from the sense of being surrounded and hemmed in by Muslim countries.[12] Even after the "discovery" of the new world, the rulers of Europe didn't much consider what they had stumbled on. They were, in the words of Friedman, focused on trying to "get through the damned thing" so they could find their way to Asia. Friedman continues, "It took European civilization almost three centuries to grasp fully that what it had found—North America— might be more important than what it was looking for."[13]

For Friedman this was the true discovery of exploration: *that we begin to see the world and ourselves differently from we had before.* Discovery and exploration do not so much answer all of our questions as they help us to *raise and consider new questions.* This is critical for leaders in every circumstance.

> [An] attribute of imaginatively gridlocked relationship systems is a continual search for new answers to old questions rather than an *effort to reframe the questions themselves.* In the search for the solution to any problem, questions are always more important than answers because the way one frames the question, or the problem, already predetermines the range of answers one can conceive in response.[14]

This reframing or "an ability to think about things in more than one way" is perhaps the most critical skill for adaptive leadership. According to Lee Bolman and Terrence Deal, reframing is the hallmark of a truly great leader.[15] Reframing allows leaders to see possibilities where others see dead ends; it offers us the tools to break the imaginative gridlock of our situation by considering alternative perspectives.

One recent attempt at structural reframing was raised in an article that challenged the usual metrics of weekly church attendance and church membership as signs of a church's spiritual health. A pastor of a church comprising mostly millennials began to recognize that the wild fluctuations in church attendance and the deep resistance of a generation skeptical about joining anything made the old metrics useless.[16] For example, a traditional church often has Easter and Christmas attendance two to three times that of a regular Sunday morning service. But a church of mostly young adults often has *lower attendance* on holidays because the young adults travel to be with family (thus bolstering the attendance at their parents' churches). In addition, how do the usual metrics of money and attendance help us know whether the members of a church are actually growing in depth of faith and commitment? How do we create common measurement indicators when each congregation has a very different membership makeup?

Reframing sees the problem with a new lens. That reframing, Friedman would remind us, is more of an *emotional* capacity than a function of intelligence. "New alternatives cannot even be imagined, much less accepted or 'heard,' until the *emotional processes* that fix the orientation have changed."[17]

Any renaissance, anywhere, whether in a marriage or a business, depends primarily not only on new data and techniques, but on the capacity of leaders to separate themselves from the surrounding emotional climate so that they can break through the barriers that are keeping everyone from "going the other way."[18]

When InterVarsity Christian Fellowship's campus chapters were "derecognized" on California State University campuses because they insisted that only committed Christians should be allowed in leadership (a stance the university leaders denounced as exclusionary), there was a huge outcry from supporters and Christian culture watchers. Indeed, it is a significant challenge, a "huge impediment" to their ministry, reported IVCF's national training director. But that didn't stop their ministry. While they and other college campus ministries know that changing attitudes to religious groups on college campuses will dramatically affect their strategies for ministering to students, campus staff are in many places displaying a calm strategic thinking that comes from being clear on their values and objectives. Campus leaders all over the country have now begun looking at this trend as an opportunity to partner more with local churches. If college ministry meetings cannot be held on campus, then they'd simply invite students to gather at local churches who opened their doors in hospitality. Immediately after "derecognition," one San Diego State University CRU (formerly Campus Crusade for Christ) leader, Josh Dean, responded, "It's been the most fruitful and exciting fall launch we've had here. God is doing some neat things. Somehow, I don't think he's bound by policies.... [One local church] opens their doors to a different organization, every night of the week for no cost, all their equipment, etc. Awesome kingdom mindset."[19] *Kingdom mindset*, indeed.

Even a frame of being an explorer in uncharted territory allows leaders to consider a different way of seeing the challenges in front of them and ask new questions:

- Is *the church* really in decline, or is it the Western, Christendom, *form of church life* that is now less effective?

- Does dwindling church attendance mean that people are less interested in God or that society and culture have stopped giving preference to Christian traditions and institutions?

- Is the lack of culture support for Christians a threat to Christian witness or an opportunity to work together in ways that we didn't have to do so before?

If, as T. S. Eliot said, the ultimate outcome of exploration is to see our location "for the first time," then taking on an adventure-or-die attitude may be the key to seeing the kingdom of God among us, ahead of us, already going forth and beckoning us to follow.

FINDING THE CENTER IN THE BOUNDARIES

As a pastor I had a key to every room in the church. It was called "the 1 key." With it I could get into the kitchen for a snack, into the library to grab a book, into a colleague's office to borrow a pen and call an impromptu meeting in any church room. As a pastor I had access.

Not only that, I discovered that when I entered a room, people always stopped what they were doing to greet me. Even if it was the middle of a Bible study, a prayer group, even a gathering of friends on the patio, if I ducked my head in or entered into the conversation, I was always welcomed. Indeed, very often the discussion came to a halt and whatever agenda I had took precedence. I could literally change the subject of any conversation to my agenda, and most often the people would *thank me* for doing so. As a pastor I was given deference.

But on July 27, 2014, I left my pastorate to take a new role as a seminary administrator and professor, and I gave up my 1 key. I willingly entered an agreement that I would not come back to the church again unless I am invited by the new pastor and the session for some specific occasion. Indeed, I even wrote a letter explaining to my congregation "I am not your pastor anymore. I will not be doing your baptisms, or weddings, or funerals. I will pray for you as your brother in Christ that God will bless your relationship with your new pastor."

A number of my friends and former congregants have balked. We have a history together. We have shared life together. Beth and I raised our kids in that church, and I have been with many of the congregants through both the anguish and celebrations of life.

"What do you mean you can't be our pastor? You are *my* pastor. You will always be."

"No," I gently tell them, "not anymore."

While I cherish our life together and I will have some relationships with a few people that transcend my pastoral role, I cannot be the personal pastor to those who ask me to do so. It's not healthy for the church, and it doesn't have integrity. I am not in the role of pastor of San Clemente Presbyterian Church anymore.

Fortunately for me, I had a family who helped me prepare for this transition long before I needed it. While I was used to having the access and deference of being a pastor at church, whenever I would enter my teenage daughter's room without permission or try to steer a conversation toward my agenda at the dinner table, Ali would respectfully remind me, "Daddy, I'm sorry, but you're interrupting." (Yes, I was. She could recognize it because of how we had raised her.) I had to remember that "the Pastor," not "Tod," had a 1 key. "The Pastor," not "Tod," was welcome to change the agenda of a conversation or meeting. My role received accessibility and deference that I personally did not deserve.

The confusion of self and role is significant for many Christian leaders. We *are* Christians, we *function* as leaders. But very often we have been told, "You *are* a Christian leader." And after a while, we confuse ourselves with our roles. To make it even harder, since authenticity and transparency are so necessary for functioning as a healthy and trustworthy leader, we are often required to bring ourselves to our roles. That is the delicate balance. I tell my coaching clients, "You must bring yourself to your role, but you *are not* your role." There must be a healthy separation of role and self to be a healthy, functioning leader in a healthy organizational system.

This healthy separation of self and role is part of what psychologists call "differentiation." Differentiation is the ability to have a sense of self that is distinct from one's role, one's relationships and the family or organizational system we are part of without having to disconnect relationally. Differentiation requires a truly challenging stance: How to be separate from the emotional gravity of an organizational system without having to separate from it. Differentiation is about having a distinct identity while maintaining one's relationships. It is marked by the ability to take a clear, calm stand of conviction when the emotional energy of a group is going in a particular way. It is about being clear on one's values, beliefs and goals, and allowing others to have their own.[20] It is about taking responsibility for one's own actions while working for something beyond one's own benefit. And according to a fifteen-year study of spiritual formation among seminarians, differentiation is one of the key markers of personal and spiritual maturity.[21]

Differentiation enables the leader to stay *with* the group in the most difficult moments even when the group is blaming the leader for the difficulties. Exploration so challenges our illusions of competence, so triggers strong reactions of others and so often leads to enough conflict that it *requires* differentiation to psychologically endure as a leader. If every failed experiment, every strong reaction, every attempted act of sabotage and every difficult conversation is a personal attack, then we will grow weary. But if we can maintain a sense of a separate identity without the need to disconnect relationally, then the challenging realities of leadership can be reframed as part of the terrain (like harsh weather), part of the expense (like lodging in a big city) or part of the natural difficulties (like sore feet) of a long adventure.

ESCAPING THE EXPERT EXPECTATION

One of the signs of an organization that is resisting change is what Heifetz calls "the flight to authority."[22] Instead of accepting the adaptive challenge of learning and being transformed, the congregation, company or even family will decide to elect an expert to the do the work for them. The expert becomes the "technical solution," which is actually "work avoidance" that creates the illusion that something is being done ("We brought in an expert to solve it!") when in truth nothing is changing.

For many leaders, however, the authority, respect and security that comes from being considered the expert is just too alluring to refuse. In chapter eleven I introduced Osterhaus, Jurkowski and Hahn's concept of Red Zone (emotionally hot)–Blue Zone (emotionally cool). While we discussed the necessity of making Blue Zone organizational decisions, now we see the constant reality of how often we live in the Red Zone. After working within several organizations and their leaders it is clear that not only do Red Zone issues of survival, control, acceptance and competence affect our organizations, they affect us as leaders!

The internal and psychological stress of leading, exploring, learning and keeping an organization on mission is demanding. The fear of failure weighs heavy on all types of leaders, but perhaps even more so for pastors. When failing can mean losing your job (survival), community (acceptance), reputation (competence), even the possibility of failure can make us feel out of control. We start to pine for the security and stability that would come with being considered experts, being granted some kind of tenure, being considered successful. We long to be seen as the expert and experience the deference that people in our society offer to those of us who have made it.

While there is indeed much to learn from experienced—even expert—leaders, the temptation to live in the expert expectation can be both a seduction to become the silver bullet for the organization, the savior—the technical solution that keeps the organization from the transformational adaptive work, as well as a temptation to personal complacency. One of my clients, a senior pastor of one of the largest churches in his denomination, said to me, "You know, I think most of us pastors have a 'goal church' that we hope to finally attain. And then when we are called to that church or our church hits some 'level' of success, we just settle back and enjoy the ride as long as we can."

My client—a strong leader—is also an insatiable learner. (Why else would he insist on having a leadership coach when his church is so successful?) He recognizes that not only does learning keep leaders relevant but expert expectation is a form of collusion between an organization that doesn't want to change ("Our expert leader will fix the problems!") and a leader who wants the security, in Jim Collins's poignant distinction, of being the "time-teller" instead of a "clock builder."[23]

Exploration challenges the expert expectation and indeed even offers us the escape. To publicly acknowledge that we are now in uncharted territory, where there are no maps and few answers, allows us the freedom to innovate through experimentation, to encourage humility and inquisitiveness, to ask questions, and to invite those with us into an adventure of learning.

"The leaders of the future need to continually cultivate a learning posture," offers Steve Yamaguchi. And for Yamaguchi, this comes through developing the "beginner's mind," which is unafraid to ask "stupid questions."[24] A concept from Zen Buddhism and a staple of Japanese martial arts, "beginner's mind" refers to "having an attitude of openness, eagerness, and lack of preconceptions when studying a subject, even when studying at an advanced level, just as a beginner in that subject would."[25]

I encourage leaders to escape the expert expectation by becoming an expert experimenter, an expert question asker instead of answer giver. I often coach my clients, "Make your goal in every conversation to have someone roll their eyes upward (which indicates that they are thinking differently) and say, 'That's a great question.'" A great question when asked, and attempted to answer, offers more than a solution—a transformation.

THE TRANSFORMATION OF EXPLORATION

Perhaps the most powerful lesson to learn from Lewis and Clark and the Corps of Discovery is not what they discovered about the country but what they discovered about themselves. When the men (and one woman!) of the Corps were exploring uncharted territory, they were clearly their best selves.

Far from the enforcement offered by the rule of law, the captains never faced a serious challenge to their authority. The men never mutinied, even when they strongly disagreed with the captains, or when one erstwhile deserter attempted to poison the attitude of the group.[26] In uncharted territory the captains relied more on relationships than the rule book, more on influence than on courts-marshal or lashings.[27]

Offering Sacagawea and York a vote on where to winter, allowing Colter to leave the expedition, maintaining their commitment to equal partnership in every way—all these are examples of how, when tested, the very best parts of Lewis and Clark were on display while on the adventure.

Sadly, while Clark returned to America more dedicated than ever to being a friend to the tribes (indeed, he later lost an election for being "soft on the Indians," and he did keep his promise to Sacagawea to educate her son), there is a disturbing note in one of his letters to Lewis that he had to give York a "severe trouncing" because he had grown arrogant after being part of the Corps. Indeed, York had asked for his freedom as payment for his service on the expedition. Or at least to be near his wife (who was owned by a different master). Clark refused.[28] While on adventure, Clark could see something different in his old companion, but back in America he became a slave master again.

The most tragic tale of the Corps of Discovery, however, is the suicide of Meriwether Lewis. Today, Meriwether Lewis would be treated for severe depression. Even then, it had been noted by Jefferson that Lewis tended to get melancholy and exacerbated it with alcohol. But during the expedition, neither the depression nor any signs of excessive alcohol abuse were ever noted by Clark or the other men. While the long lapses in his journals likely indicate that there were times when his notable depression offered him a greater burden to carry, the toll of returning home, being under deadlines for his journals, suffering writers' block and eventually having creditors on his back became too hard to carry. As a reward for his leadership, Jefferson had granted Lewis the governorship of the Louisiana Territory, but his personal problems overwhelmed him.

In the early hours of October 11, 1809, while staying in a boarding house en route to Washington, Meriwether Lewis shot himself. In trying to make sense of it later, Thomas Jefferson wrote of the "depressions of mind" that his young friend had suffered for years. But Jefferson surmised,

> During his Western expedition, the constant exertion which that required of all the faculties of body & mind, suspended these distressing affections; but after his establishment in St. Louis in sedentary occupations they returned upon with redoubled vigor.[29]

Without intending to make too strong a case, it is worth noting that most leaders are at their best when facing a challenge, and that the desire for safety and security can lead us into the most insecure, indeed, precarious personal positions.

BACK TO THE QUESTION THAT STARTED IT ALL

"What can we do to keep our churches from dying?"

Let's go back to that seminar room filled with Methodist pastors and Christian educators in Portland, Maine. Let me share with you what I would tell them now ten years later. Looking back, I realized that my answers that afternoon were pretty typical. I offered a few tips, a couple nuggets of what I hope was wisdom, an insight or two from my own experience—all in the hope that something might help. In other words, I "defaulted to my training." I did ask some questions but mostly offered advice. I meant well and wanted to encourage these faithful Christian leaders who labor in one of the most unchurched regions in the country. But if I could meet with that group today, I would say something completely different. "If you want to keep your church from dying," I would say,

> *Focus on your own transformation together, not on your church dying.*
> *Focus on the mountains ahead, not the rivers behind.*
> *Focus on continually learning, not what you have already mastered.*

REORIENTATION

While on-the-map leaders are praised for being experts who have it all together, uncharted transformational leadership is absolutely dependent on the leader's own ongoing exploration, learning and transformation.

THE CENTER OF THE THREE CIRCLES

The advice I would offer those Maine Methodists today goes to the very center of leadership (see fig. 15.1) for entering the uncharted territory of a rapidly changing, "volatile, uncertain, complex *and* ambiguous" world. Since leadership is "energizing a community of people toward their own transformation in order to accomplish a shared mission in the face of a changing world," *then it requires* that leaders are first and foremost committed to their own ongoing transformation. In a changing world, the leader must be continually committed to ongoing personal change, to develop new capacities, to be continually transformed in ways that will enable the organization's larger transformation.

This also goes right to the very center of the Christian faith. Christianity is about the Creator God's mission to transform his world and all his creatures. That transformation is accomplished not through signs of power, shows of force or unavoidable miracles that force us to our knees, but *through the transformed lives of people* who transform communities who transform their spheres of influence (Romans 12:2).

Leaders thrust off the map in a rapidly changing world must trust that God is taking us into uncharted territory to extend the healing, justice and loving

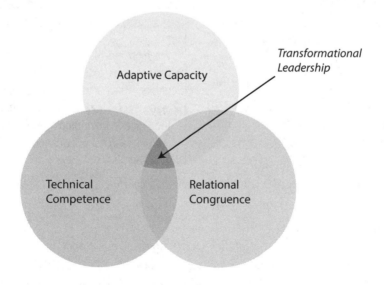

Figure 15.1. Transformational leadership

rule of God to all the world, *and at the same time* to transform *us*. The great discovery in following Christ into his mission is that we find *ourselves being continually formed to be like Jesus*. By doing the work of the kingdom, we become like the King.

Leadership into uncharted territory *requires* and *results* in transformation of the whole organization, starting with the leaders. If we want the organizations and communities we serve to thrive, focus on what God needs to do in *you*, change in *you*, makeover in *you* so he can use you in his mission. Focus on how you need to grow in technical competence, relational congruence and adaptive capacity, and especially focus on what you need to leave behind, let go and even let die so your church can become more and more effective at fulfilling its part in God's mission. Don't focus on whether your church is dying; keep your focus on being transformed into the leader God can use to transform his people for his mission.

Perhaps that is the most important thing to remember: *God is taking us into uncharted territory to transform us*. The great discovery in following Christ into his mission is that we find ourselves. And the beautiful paradox is that the more committed we are to our *own* transformation, the better leader we will be.

REORIENTATION RECAP

- You were trained for a world that is disappearing.
- If you can adapt and adventure, you can thrive.
- But you must let go, learn as you go and keep going no matter what.
- In a Christendom world, speaking *was* leading.
- In a post-Christendom world, leading is multidimensional: apostolic, relational and adaptive.
- Before people will follow you off the map, gain the credibility that comes from demonstrating competence on the map.
- In uncharted territory, trust is as essential as the air we breathe.
- If trust is lost, the journey is over.
- When our old maps fail us, something within us dies.
- Replacing our paradigms is both deeply painful and absolutely critical.

- In a Christendom world, vision was seeing possibilities ahead and communicating excitement.

- In uncharted territory, vision is accurately seeing ourselves and defining reality.

- Leadership in the past meant coming up with solutions.

- Today leadership is learning how to ask new questions we have been too scared, too busy or too proud to ask.

- There is no greater gift that leadership can give a group of people on a mission than to have the clearest, most defined mission possible.

- When dealing with managing the present, win-win solutions are the goal.

- But when leading adaptive change, win-win is usually lose-lose.

- In uncharted territory visionary leadership is more likely going to come from a small Corps of Discovery while the board manages the ongoing health of the organization.

- In uncharted territory, where changes occur so rapidly, leaders cannot assume success until after they have weathered the sabotage that naturally follows.

- Those who had neither power nor privilege in the Christendom world are the trustworthy guides and necessary leaders when we go off the map.

- Those without power or privilege are not going into uncharted territory. They are at home.

- Exploration teaches us to see the familiar through a new frame and demands that we become our best selves.

- Uncharted leadership is absolutely dependent on the leader's own ongoing exploration, learning and transformation.

Epilogue

Taking the Hill with Grandma

GIVEN ALL OF THIS Lewis and Clark imagery, it is probably no surprise that I tend to think of myself as a "take the hill" kind of guy. I like a challenge. I resonate with the idea of being a leader of a mission.

One of my colleagues is rather different than I am. Maybe he's seen enough pain in lives and congregations to be skeptical of the kinds of "charges" leaders like me seem to relish. My colleague has been called to minister to a church in the middle of a retirement home. He tells me with a sigh of great satisfaction that he spends his days "hugging and kissing, teaching and ministering to some of the greatest saints you'll ever meet." Sometimes I am jealous of him, and I get the sense that sometimes he thinks he's supposed to be more like me.

I take the hill; he cares for grandma. And I think most of us assume that these are two different types of callings. It is common to hear talk about the differences between *missional* ministry and *chaplaincy*, between *leading* and *caretaking*. But I think those distinctions reveal both our own projections about ourselves and a convenient way to avoid what is true about all Christian organizations, especially churches: We *all* have hills to take, and all of our organizations are filled with grandmas.

None of us in church leadership get the luxury of a single-focused call, no matter how important we think it is. None of us get to handpick our own Corps of Discovery with nothing but the best, bravest, faithful, loyal and mature. Every church and Christian organization I know is filled with people of varying degrees of competence, courage and capacity to embrace change. As leaders, our calling is to further the mission of the kingdom of heaven, to expand the proclamation and demonstration of the gospel, *with the very people whom God has given us.*

It's one thing to imagine being the leader of a mission if you get to personally select, train and deploy the most able and eager. It's another thing to accomplish the same mission with whoever happens to be given to you regardless of ability (or even interest) in the task. It's one thing to lead a school where everyone is committed to delivering a good education; it's another to rally people to change the whole institutional structure to better fit a rapidly changing world. It's one thing to create a church family who loves each person just as they are; it's another to inspire and equip those people to take on a challenge that will require them to change, grow and expend resources they may not even have.

We have to love the kindly grandmas and grandpas, cute little children, cranky aunts and uncles, overcommitted brothers and sisters, and sometimes irascible and often inspiring teenagers with whom God has called us to be spiritual family. Then we have to try to motivate that group to work, sacrifice, give and take on the responsibilities of furthering the mission of the kingdom as we are called to do it. We are a family that wants to sit together cozy by the campfire, but we have to get up and charge the hill (at potentially great cost).

To me this is the most demanding aspect of being a Christian leader: *The complexity of it all.* The real complexity of any Christian leadership (something that has only been reaffirmed after leaving the pastorate to become a seminary administrator) is due to what Ed Friedman calls "the emotional field" that is the Christian organization system itself.[1] Building on a metaphor from physics, Friedman views all relational systems like planets caught in the gravitational pull of another planet. Once the emotional field (gravity) comes into existence through forming a relationship, the gravitational pull of the relationship is more powerful than that of each planet itself. *In the same way, relationships are more powerful than any one person in the system.*

Christian leaders, especially, live in an emotional field filled with competing values.[2] Remember our earlier discussion about the nature of a family business (chap. 12)? We love, care and value each other with a kind of unconditional love and, at the same time, we need to make decisions based on the conditions of what will further the spiritual "bottom line" of furthering our mission.

We are all called to take the hill—with grandma.

Christian work is a "family" and a "business" at the same time. To be a Christian is to find identity and mutual commitment in relationships constituted by God that make us into brothers and sisters; these relationships are *inherently* and *intrinsically* important. And at the same time we are a business with a mission to fulfill, services to offer, constituencies to support and regulations, demands, and obligations required of us. The organization that has *inherently* valuable relationships also has an *instrumentally* critical purpose. And holding that tension, leading a Christian organization that is faithful to both mission and family, is indeed the challenge for most of us.

This means that Christian leaders function almost constantly in dual relationships. For the pastor, the church that pays the salary (and in most cases, not all that well) also asks the pastor's family for tithes and offerings to contribute to the budget (with the expectation that we will be role models of faithfulness and generosity).[3] The staff they hire also ministers to their families and friends. The youth director under review and facing dismissal for not meeting expectations is the beloved mentor to the pastor's own teenage son (and is bringing his new fiancé to dinner, too!). The choir member upset about the change in worship direction is the biggest giver to the church. The beloved Sunday School teacher who is like a grandmother to a whole generation of children is showing signs of dementia and poses a potential risk to the children she loves. The church wants us to be both professional and personal. As a pastor, I knew that many people expected me to know everything there is to know about the mystery of God and every person's name in our congregation when I ran into them at the grocery store. We are expected to perfectly exegete and translate the Scriptures, and perfectly understand, translate and oversee the financials. Our board is both our customer and our client, and our partners and our bosses at the same time. Again, this is not to say that the Christian leader's work is harder than other leaders', but that the unique challenge of leadership includes managing emotional complexity amid all the demands.[4] And for most of us this is difficult. We feel inadequate most of the time. We never feel as if we can get the mastery needed. We are always in uncharted territory of the mountains and start pining for the rivers again. We need friends and companions, mentors and teachers, indeed we all need a corps if we are going to go on discovery. But the corps we are given is the one that God has chosen, not us. The adventure set before us is God's own expedition, not our own. And the resources God offers us are far more than what he has put within us, but also with *whom* he has put around us. For Lewis and Clark not only had each other and their handpicked troops, but they had people (including a baby!) they picked up along the way, the friendship and favor that they were granted as strangers in a strange land.

From the overwhelming success and incredible amount of safety (imagine only losing one man—and that from appendicitis) to the world-changing discoveries and the inspiring leadership lessons, the story of Lewis and Clark provides a wealth of wisdom for learning to lead in a changing world. But perhaps the most intriguing character of all is the one who didn't go on the expedition but who imagined it in the first place.

THE SENIOR CITIZEN WHO REORIENTED THE WHOLE WORLD

Thomas Jefferson was sixty when he enlisted Meriwether Lewis for his grand expedition. And make no mistake, it was Jefferson's idea. He had lived in France and was the young nation's true Renaissance man. He would be the founder of the country's first public university and as a young man had written most of the Declaration of Independence himself. But he had never traveled more than fifty miles west of the Shenandoah Valley. That lack of personal experience or the physical attributes necessary for such a journey did not slake his curiosity. His personal library contained more books about the region than any other library in the world. Monticello even faced west.[5]

Without question Jefferson's passion for discovery led to the Corps of Discovery even though he never saw the majesty of Great Falls or the view from Lemhi Pass. Jefferson was the patron and protector, the instructor and inspiring initiator who gave Meriwether Lewis the vision and the captains both their charge.

For all his own ambivalence about Christian faith, Jefferson can serve as a model for those of us who are in leadership today as Christendom is fading away. We can and must inspire the next generation to go where we have not. We can create the kinds of communities and organizations that encourage risk, humility, learning and experimentation.[6] We can read, study, encourage and embolden emerging leaders by offering them prayers, support and opportunity. We can remind them that maps change, that mental models are always incomplete, that the leaders of the future are the learners, not the experts, of today. We can call them to experiment, and we can create the conditions for a church that is always, always, always focused on continually being transformed into the very likeness of Jesus. And—if nothing else—we can sound the call to the Lewises, Clarks *and* Sacagaweas of the church, who will be the true adventurers for the mission of God in a rapidly changing world.

Acknowledgments

IN CELEBRATION OF THE LEADERSHIP of what Stephen Ambrose calls "Lewisandclark," this book is a commendation to a different kind of collaborative, missional leadership in a changing world. So the irony is not lost on me that I am the sole author of this work. As such the responsibilities for any errors are completely mine.

But I would be remiss and dishonest if I didn't acknowledge here what I trust is completely apparent throughout this book: I absolutely did not write this book (nor do I ever lead) alone. Leadership, even writing about leadership, is always about partnership. It is a product of teams, relationships and companions with whom I have been privileged to lead and learn. (Indeed, the very title of the book came from a coffee shop conversation with Steve Johnson, who was then a member of my church. Thanks, Steve. You may not even remember it, but "Canoeing the Mountains" was your idea, not mine!)

During the almost ten years that this book was being researched, written and revised, I have been privileged to be part of three different leadership teams and engaged as a consultant or project leader with over fifty churches, organizations and denominational bodies and their leaders. I was asked to speak or offer workshops in over two dozen settings, and was able to implement everything I was learning in all of my roles.

The pastors, elders and staff at San Clemente Presbyterian from 2006 to 2014 were eager collaborators and colearners with me as we determined to become "adaptive leaders" for the mission Christ had given us. During that time I was granted two sabbaticals (the first of which was generously funded by the Lilly Endowment), first to explore the concepts and then later to write the first draft of a manuscript. Being the pastor of SCPC was a gift to my family and me. It is no coincidence that the story of my "learning to lead (them) all over again" is woven through this narrative. While there are so many that I served with who were critical to this conversation, three people stand out as true partners: Jim Toole and Charlie Campbell were more than just colleagues, they were thought-partners, letting me talk out loud for hours at a time. Elder Bill Rice was perhaps the single person most committed to learning along with me as a lay leader in our congregation.

From 2009 to 2014 I was part of the consultant team of TAG Consulting. Kevin Graham Ford and Jim Osterhaus were coaches, supervisors and genuine partners. They allowed me to not only learn from them but also collaborate with them as they sought to serve clients in churches, businesses and nonprofit organizations. I will be forever grateful to them for introducing me to the work of Ronald Heifetz (whom I hope someday to meet!) and for allowing me to work out these concepts in real time with candid feedback. Kevin also read early drafts of the book and his feedback gave me some well-needed encouragement at a critical time.

In 2014, I joined the administration and faculty at Fuller Theological Seminary. There I was welcomed and engaged by a truly respected leadership scholar in Scott Cormode, and the most generous, visionary and humble senior leader I have ever served in president Mark Labberton. That they have encouraged me to bring everything I have learned about adaptive leadership to the work that we are doing to re-engineer Christian leadership formation and theological education has been a gift greater than I could have imagined. Mark Roberts joined our team in 2015, but was involved in exploring with me the issues of leadership at the heart of this book long before he became the executive director of the De Pree Leadership Center. And without the incredible skill, creativity and hard work of Ryan Gutierrez and Amy Drennan working alongside me, I could not even imagine having the time to write and think about larger leadership issues.

First at Los Ranchos Presbytery and then for the PC(USA) denomination, I was invited to lead teams considering large-scale missional reorganization. The members of those teams, and especially my partners, Steve Yamaguchi and Jill Hudson, allowed me to learn and experiment (and often fail!) on a scale that tested every principle in this book. I am deeply indebted to the governing bodies that gave me the opportunities and to my colleagues in the Los

Ranchos Presbytery Odyssey Group and the PCUSA Mid-Council Commission for the joy of working on truly "big, hairy, audacious goals."

Many colleagues and friends listened to presentations, responded to blog posts, read drafts of the book and engaged me in conversation, but I must thank especially Mark Labberton, Steve Yamaguchi, Kevin Graham Ford, Jim Singleton, Mark Roberts, Steve Wright, Daniel White and Shane Berg.

My brother Scot Bolsinger, who is by far the most gifted writer in the family, brought his great skill for good prose to bear on the manuscript, becoming a personal trainer prodding me to write better. Cara Miller brought the expertise of a PhD in leadership to the earliest drafts. Scot and Cara read every word of this book and it is undoubtedly more readable and more credible because they did.

To my agent, Kathryn Helmers, for believing in this project and making it better; to the good folks at InterVarsity Press, especially publisher Bob Fryling and my incredible editor, Helen Lee—you are a dream team that embodies collaboration and partnership. I love being part of the IVP family.

To my wife, Beth, who has not only been my best friend and partner in life, but through her own executive coaching and consulting is my most trusted and favorite conversation partner: thank you for spending your life listening to me ramble and for spending a day driving to the top of the Lemhi Pass. This is all so, so much sweeter because of you.

One final word to the one who has been my biggest cheerleader and collaborator in this process: if there was any steady "Clark" to my crazy "Lewis," it was Steve Yamaguchi. First as my pastor in the Los Ranchos Presbytery, and my partner in holy mischief with the Odyssey Group, and now as my colleague at Fuller Theological Seminary, Steve has been the constant companion through my own transformational journey. I am deeply indebted to you, Steve, and overjoyed that we continue to adventure together.

To all the leaders I have met along the way who are already heading into uncharted territory—thank you for letting me join you in the journey. It is an honor.

STUDY GUIDE

*Leadership is energizing a community of people toward
their own transformation in order to accomplish a
shared mission in the face of a changing world.*

WELCOME TO THIS "TRAIL MAP" of *Canoeing the Mountains: Christian
Leadership in Uncharted Territory.* This guide is meant to help you learn the
main lessons and begin to develop the capacities to lead your community,
church, organization, or company "off the map" and into uncharted territory.

The following six lessons are intended to be used both individually and
in small groups—ideally in both! There are concepts for you to reflect on
that are intended to help you honestly consider your own leadership capacity in a rapidly changing world. I believe that growth and development
as a leader begins in honest self-reflection. But it doesn't end there! In the
same way that Meriwether Lewis recognized his need for a true partner—
"equal in every way"—we need leadership formation partners. We need
friends, trusted coworkers, mentors or teammates to learn, hash-out, and
grow with.

But there is one more aspect of leadership formation that enables you to
become an adaptive leader who can go off the map and into uncharted territory: putting your leadership lessons into practice. You have to embody the
lesson. You have to act!

So these lessons are formatted in a four-part process: *learn, reflect, relate,
practice.* Here is an overview of each section before we get started.

LEARNING: KEY LEADERSHIP LESSONS

In the Learning section we review some of the most critical material. You are
free (even encouraged!) to reflect on the passages that are most relevant to
your experience and context. I will offer passages that focus on understanding
the challenge of uncharted territory and the shift of thinking and acting necessary to becoming an adaptive leader.

Adaptive challenges are the true tests of leadership. They are challenges that go beyond the technical solutions of resident experts or best practices, or even the organization's current knowledge. They arise when the world around us has changed but we continue to live on the successes of the past. They are challenges that cannot be solved through compromise or win-win scenarios, or by adding another ministry or staff person to the team. They demand that leaders make hard choices about what to preserve and to let go. They are challenges that require people to learn and to *change*, that require leaders to experience and navigate profound *loss*. (19)

To develop the adaptive capacity needed for leading in uncharted territory, this study guide focuses on helping leaders learn, including

- learning a new way of leading

- learning by listening to the margins

- learning through honest conversations with trusted confidants

- learning through facing loss

- learning to help followers navigate loss

REFLECT: PERSONAL AND GROUP PONDERINGS

Leadership is learned in the doing and by reflecting on the doing.... (John Dewey reportedly wrote: "We don't learn from experience, we learn by reflecting on experience.") (22)

The Reflect section of the study guide can be done either individually or as part of a group discussion. The purpose of the reflection questions is to prod each participant to think more deeply about the lessons learned and to engage in some self-examination and personal assessment about one's current leadership practices, beliefs and implicit biases.

In his journal, Meriwether Lewis used the occasion of his thirty-first birthday to pause amid the demands of leading the Corps of Discovery to think about his own life to that point:

I reflected that I had yet done but little, very little indeed, to further the happiness of the human race, or to advance the information of the succeeding generation ... and resolved in the future ... to live for mankind, as I have heretofore lived for myself. (95)

While there will be some specific questions for each section, the basic format is to take you to a deeper self-understanding of your leadership practice and to recognize the underlying beliefs that result in those leadership practices.

- What part of the reading from this section inspires you?

- What raises questions that need to be clarified?

- What do you find yourself resisting?

- What changes are you considering in your own leadership because of reading this section?

RELATE: GOING DEEPER WITH A TRUSTED COMPANION

> Lewis and Clark were partners, co-commanders and "equals in all respects." . . .
> This partnership forged out of friendship and Meriwether Lewis's keeping of
> his word to Clark created the context for building much more than a military
> unit—the very Corps of Discovery. From their first conversation to every
> action on the expedition (and indeed, until Meriwether Lewis's tragic death),
> they remained solid friends. (62, 64)

The Relate section is for those leaders who are willing to engage in even deeper, more personal reflection with a trusted mentor or companion. In the book, we make the distinction between "allies" and "confidants." This section is meant for a leader to discuss with a confidant—someone who is usually outside your organizational system and is more loyal to you than they are to your leadership mission. (Note: the example of Lewis and Clark themselves demonstrates that sometimes a confidant can be an ally, but for most of us, keeping these relationships more distinct is better.)

In this section the suggested questions are not asked *of* the leader, but instead the questions are asked of a trusted adviser or friend *by* the leader in order to gain honest feedback.

The goal of this section is to listen deeply and to gain a better sense of one's own impact on other people. It is to ask questions of someone who knows you well enough to hold up a mirror so you can see your own leadership practices and values more clearly. You will need the internal posture of being open to feedback, allowing your trusted confidant to speak candidly, and taking personal responsibility for your own growth as a leader.

PRACTICE: EMBODYING LEADERSHIP TRANSFORMATION

Leadership is itself a practice. Leaders act. Leaders create an organizational culture and move people toward transformation by their own actions embodying their ongoing transformation. In this section, I will offer you two or three specific leadership formation practices to integrate into your own practice of leadership in order to keep developing your capacity to be transformed and to lead others into the life transforming challenge of uncharted territory.

- Study 1 -
The Landscape, the Challenge, *Your* Leadership Adventure

Read chapter one of *Canoeing in the Mountains*.

This study focuses on the big picture—the overall challenge of leading in uncharted territory and the kind of transformation required of you as a leader. In this first study, we look at all five core leadership lessons of the book in overview and then each subsequent lesson will look more deeply at each of the lessons.

LEARNING: KEY LEADERSHIP LESSONS

Traditional churches will only become missionary churches as those in authority (and even those without formal authority) develop capacity to lead their congregations through a long, truly transformational process that starts with the transformation of the leaders and requires a thoroughgoing change in leadership functioning. (39)

At the heart of adaptive leadership for the church is this conviction: The church is the body of Christ. It is a living organism, a vibrant *system*. And just like human bodies, human organizations thrive when they are cooperating with the wisdom of God for how that system is designed, how it grows and how it adapts to changing external environments.

You know your body has to adjust to a new time zone after a plane flight, or to new foods when you arrive in a new culture. And you know you have to learn a new language or develop the skills for navigating an outdoor market in a foreign land. That is what adaptive leadership is all about: *the way that*

> *living human systems learn and adapt to a changing environment so they can fulfill their purpose for being.* (100)

The challenge of a changing world requires organizational transformation. Organizational transformation requires ongoing transformation in leaders, including a different way of leading. In this book, we are introduced to adaptive leadership, a concept taken from biology. It is based on the idea that when an environment changes, biological creatures and living systems are required to make critical decisions that will enable them to survive, thrive and face the challenge of the changing environment. In *Canoeing the Mountains*, we examine the demands of leadership for Christian leaders in a rapidly changing environment. Those key leadership lessons for this uncharted territory define the structure for the five sections of the book.

1. The world in front of you is nothing like the world behind you.

2. No one is going to follow you off the map unless they trust you on the map.

3. In uncharted territory, adaptation is everything.

4. You can't go alone, but you haven't succeeded until you've survived the sabotage.

5. Everybody will be changed (especially the leader).

REFLECT: PERSONAL AND GROUP PONDERINGS

Take a moment and look again at those five lessons.

- What evokes a strong reaction from you?
- What resonates with your experience?
- What reaffirms what you have already learned?
- What challenges your assumptions?

Meriwether Lewis and several of the members of the Corps of Discovery kept journals during their adventure into uncharted territory. Consider journaling your reflections to these questions. In the book, I shared a critical insight borne of personal reflection that led me to a whole new season of leadership.

> For me it all began . . . with understanding that *for our church mission to win I had to lose.* The changing world around us and even the success we had experienced had brought us to a new place where we would need a new strategy. To

paraphrase Marshall Goldsmith, "What got us here wouldn't take us *there*." So, I had to lose some of my status, power and control. I had to lose "say" over certain aspects of the mission, and mostly I had to lose my identity as the resident expert and *learn to lead all over again*. (19)

- What is your leadership challenge?
- What is the leadership adventure before your community, church, organization or company?
- What learning will it require of you?
- What losses do you anticipate that you should be prepared to face?

RELATE: GOING DEEPER WITH A TRUSTED COMPANION

The following questions are for you to use in a conversation with a trusted adviser, confidant or honest friend in order to better understand your own leadership in light of this section.

- In what ways have you observed my openness to learning?
- In what ways do you think I can improve as a learner?
- When have you observed me dealing with loss in an appropriate and healthy way?
- In what ways can I grow as a leader in order to better deal with my own losses and help my followers in front of their losses?

PRACTICE: EMBODYING LEADERSHIP TRANSFORMATION

The primary practice of transformational and adaptive leadership is to "get up on the balcony" (see chap. 9 for a longer description). Getting up on the balcony is about regularly putting yourself in a position to see the larger dynamics of an organizational system at work, make observations, and get enough distance from the challenges facing you to consider different options for leading—including your own default actions.

Some leaders create a "balcony meeting" or a "balcony team" that helps them to see the larger leadership dynamics of their organization or church and the way that they as leaders interact in the system. Others take time alone to get some distance and perspective. Whichever is best for you, your first practice of leadership is to *reflect* on your *current* practice of leading—to take a few steps onto the balcony and ask yourself some questions about what you are actually already doing as a leader:

- What are the current components of the way I actually lead?

- What are the underlying beliefs and assumptions about people and my church or organization that shape the way I lead?

- What has shaped my leadership practice? Where did I learn it?

- What aspects of my leadership behavior do I need to consider changing in order to lead in uncharted territory?

- Study 2 -

The World in Front of You Is Nothing Like the World Behind You

Read chapters two and three of *Canoeing in the Mountains*.

LEARNING: KEY LEADERSHIP LESSONS

The key leadership lessons for this study is the way the rapidly changing world is being played out even more profoundly in the church. This movement from Christendom (where Christianity had cultural privilege and support in society) to a post-Christendom world (where Christianity is one of many different belief systems in a pluralistic society) requires leaders to reconsider the ways they have been trained and the new learning needed. The first reality to face is that being trained for Christendom doesn't automatically prepare us to lead well in the "uncharted territory" of a post-Christendom world.

> The story of the Corps of Discovery is the driving metaphor for our present moment in history. In every field, in every business, every organization, leaders are rapidly coming to the awareness that the world in front of us is radically different from everything behind us. (27)

> Like Meriwether Lewis sitting on the crest of Lemhi Pass and looking at a landscape he couldn't have imagined, Christian leaders today are sitting in meetings, reading reports and conversing with colleagues about a brutal truth: *All that we*

have assumed about leading Christian organizations, all that we have been trained for, is out of date. We have left the map, we are in uncharted territory, and it is different than we expected. We are experienced river rafters who must learn to be mountaineers. And some of us face "the most terrible mountain we have ever beheld." (27-28)

In the moment of crisis, you will not rise to the occasion; you will default to your training. (32)

REFLECT: PERSONAL AND GROUP PONDERINGS

Spend some time thinking about the ways the world and the church have changed in your lifetime.

Brainstorm a list of as many of those changes that you can. Then, while thinking about that list and reviewing chapters two and three of the book, consider these questions:

- What evokes a strong reaction from you? What are the emotions of those reactions?

- What resonates with your experience? What reaffirms what you have already learned?

- What challenges your assumptions?

- In what ways have you been prepared to lead in this changing world, and in what ways do you feel ill-equipped?

RELATE: GOING DEEPER WITH A TRUSTED COMPANION

The following questions are for you to use in a conversation with a trusted adviser, confidant or honest friend in order to better understand your own leadership in light of this section.

- In what ways have you seen me defaulting to my training when I should be looking for other solutions?

- What one characteristic could I better develop in order to be a leader into uncharted territory?

- How well do I respond to people who insist on living in the past and resist changing?

PRACTICE: EMBODYING LEADERSHIP TRANSFORMATION

Two practices for living and leading in a post-Christendom context:

1. Seek out voices or opinions dramatically different from your own on issues that are important to you. Seek out and add friends to your Facebook page, or follow the Twitter feed of people (especially Christians) who have both *deeply held* and *different* convictions from your own. Do not engage them in dialogue or debate; just try to listen to these different voices with empathy and understanding.

2. Take up a new hobby activity or subject matter completely different from what you have previously mastered or enjoyed. Make it as fun and challenging as possible. Note how you experience being a learner as well as your own internal dialogue about learning and something new.

- Study 3 -

No One Is Going to Follow You Off the Map Unless They Trust You On the Map

Read chapters four through six in *Canoeing in the Mountains*.

LEARNING: KEY LEADERSHIP LESSONS

> In uncharted territory, trust is as essential as the air we breathe. If trust is lost, the journey is over. (65)

The great temptation when a leader is energized to bring change or sees the necessity for change is to embark on the change process too soon. The process of leading a church or organization into uncharted territory is to build up the necessary credibility, trust, and healthy organizational culture to face the looming challenge of a changing environment. In this study we examine the combination of competency that leads to credibility and congruence that leads to trust—and how both credibility and trust enable the healthy organizational culture needed to leave the rivers, drop the canoes and head over the uncharted mountains.

Before people will follow you off the map, gain the credibility that comes from demonstrating competence on the map. (53)

According to Osterhaus, "Trust is gained like a thermostat and lost like a light switch." A leader builds trust slowly over time by constantly monitoring the conditions and actions that create the climate of trust in the room. But even one action, if perceived as incongruent, can make the levels of trust plummet into darkness. (67)

Relational congruence is the ability to be fundamentally the same person with the same values in every relationship, in every circumstance and especially amidst every crisis. (67)

JR Woodward writes, "While management acts within culture, leadership *creates* culture." Creating a healthy culture with the capacity to experiment, innovate, take risks and adapt is one of the primary preparatory tasks of a leader. (75)

REFLECT: PERSONAL AND GROUP PONDERINGS

What do you consider the characteristics of a trustworthy person?

If you were embarking on a difficult or potentially dangerous journey, what would you want in the trip leader?

In the book, an executive coach is quoted saying, "Trust is gained like a thermostat and lost like a light switch" (67). It takes time for a leader to build trust and requires persistence. But one wrong move—even a simple act—can have significant consequences. How have you experienced this in your own life? What does a leader need to do to restore broken trust?

How would you define the characteristics of a healthy organizational culture? What does a leader or team of leaders need to do to foster a healthy organizational culture? From your experience what hinders healthy organizational cultures?

RELATE: GOING DEEPER WITH A TRUSTED COMPANION

The following questions are for you to use in a conversation with a trusted adviser, confidant, or honest friend in order to better understand your own leadership in light of this section.

- What things have you observed me doing or not doing that build trust in other people, especially my followers?

- What things have you observed me doing or not doing that diminish trust in my leadership?

- In what ways do I demonstrate relational congruence? In what ways have I undermined people's trust in me by being relationally incongruent?

PRACTICE: EMBODYING LEADERSHIP TRANSFORMATION

The following are two practices for building credibility and trust:

1. Credibility is built through the practice of regular self-assessment. Review the section on technical competence in chapter four and review the descriptions about the technical skills needed to build credibility (Scriptures and tradition, souls and communities, and teams and tasks). How well do you think you do in each of these areas? Where do you need to grow? Are there three to five people you could ask to give you honest assessment of these critical technical competencies?

2. Trust is built through authenticity. Practice honestly saying "I don't know" out loud (whenever you really don't know) and learning to ask good questions in conversations. (Leadership expert Jim Collins counsels trying to ask two questions for every statement you make in a conversation.)

- Study 4 -

In Uncharted Territory, Adaptation Is Everything

Read chapters seven through eleven in *Canoeing the Mountains*.

LEARNING: KEY LEADERSHIP LESSONS

These five chapters are the heart of the book, and this study is a sweeping overview. While you may want to go back and study each of them in detail, the core concepts of adaptive leadership are best understood by reading through all five chapters during a shorter span.

Adaptive leadership focuses on three realities: The challenge you are facing (1) requires *learning*, (2) results in *loss* and (3) results in navigating *competing values*. In the next two studies we will look at what is needed to wisely navigate the necessary losses that will come, but in this study the focus is on the learning—both the mindset of learning "as you go" and the actual learning necessary to lead people to "mind the gap" of internal and organizational competing values that are revealed in uncharted territory. Review the following sections and look over what you have highlighted in your own reading.

> Adaptive leadership is about "letting go, learning as we go, and keeping going." It's about loss, learning and gaps. (88)

> At the core of adaptive work is clarifying what is precious, elemental—even essential—to the identity of an organization. The core ideology of any group functions as both a charter and an identity statement. *This is who we are*, we say. If we stop being about *this*, we stop being. (94)

> [Lewis and Clark] *relied* on new learning. At the heart of adaptive leadership is *learning*. To put it bluntly, *if you are not learning anything new, it is not adaptive work*. It might be a good, necessary, wise, even vital strategy. But if your group is addressing a new challenge with an old solution, relying on a best practice or implementing the plan of a resident expert, then the solution is a technical one, not adaptive. (97)

> In adaptive leadership, reframing is another way of talking about the shift in *values, expectations, attitudes* or *habits of behavior* necessary to face our most difficult challenges. It is a way of looking at the challenge before us through a different lens and in seeing it differently finding the possibilities for a new way of being and leading. (96)

REFLECT: PERSONAL AND GROUP PONDERINGS

If possible, review these chapters with a small group of people, looking closer at the parts of the book each of you underlined or highlighted. Ask yourself some reflective questions about the content, noticing where you or the group have the most amount of energy (feelings, reactions, questions, concerns).

- What evokes a strong reaction from you?
- What resonates with your experience?
- What reaffirms what you have already learned?
- What challenges your assumptions?

Then take a deep breath, pause as a group, let the conversation or inner conversation settle for a moment and ask: *What do I need to do differently or not do any more in order to better lead the people God has entrusted to me into uncharted territory?*

RELATE: GOING DEEPER WITH A TRUSTED COMPANION

The key to leading people into learning, through loss and into the midst of their own competing values, is to develop "adaptive capacity." In the book adaptive capacity is described as being marked by the capacity to:

- calmly face the unknown
- refuse quick fixes
- engage others in the learning and transformation necessary to take on the challenge that is before them
- seek new perspectives
- ask questions that reveal competing values and gaps in values and actions
- raise up the deeper issues at work in a community
- explore and confront resistance and sabotage
- learn and change without sacrificing personal or organizational fidelity
- act politically and stay connected relationally
- help the congregation make hard, often painful decisions
- effectively fulfill their mission in a changing context (90-91)

Take an hour by yourself and do an honest self-evaluation. When was the last time you demonstrated this capacity? What do you need to learn in order to exercise greater adaptive capacity in leadership? Then ask a trusted companion to listen to you and give you feedback about your self-evaluation.

PRACTICE: EMBODYING LEADERSHIP TRANSFORMATION

One of the most important practices of adaptive leadership is learning to discern the difference between what should *never change* because it is core to an organization or congregation's identity, purpose or mission, and what must change in order for that mission to continue in a new environment. To teach empathy and be clear on what will never change, an exercise to do with a group of people is called "Tell me a story."

Consider the stories of your church or organization. What stories are told over and over again? What stories represent the best moments of the organization, the heroes of the community? What are the stories that capture "This is who we really are"? And what values do those stories represent?

Before you attempt to lead change, make sure you know all the most important stories. Adaptive change that lasts is always a healthy, missional adaptation of the core DNA revealed in these stories and these values.

- Study 5 -

You Can't Go Alone, but You Haven't Succeeded Until You've Survived the Sabotage

Read chapters twelve and thirteen in *Canoeing the Mountains*.

LEARNING: KEY LEADERSHIP LESSONS

There is a noble but deeply misguided belief that leadership requires broad shoulders and an ability to stand under pressures *alone*. Most of us give lip service to needing colleagues and being collaborative, but when the buck stops, we really do believe that it stops on one desk only. Sadly, this is far removed from the New Testament witness where, short of Jesus' own work on the cross, virtually every other expression of the ministry of the Spirit was revealed to the world in pairs or trios (or more). (155-56)

Perhaps the most important lesson found in the story of Lewis and Clark is that they are known mostly as "Lewisandclark"—partners who were "equal in everyway." Together, with the assistance of Sacagawea and the entire Corps of Discovery, they did indeed chart uncharted territory. But they also faced resistance both in the people they encountered and the men within the Corps itself. By far, the most painful part of leading a people into uncharted territory is the resistance that comes from the very people who are on the journey. But that pain becomes almost unbearable when faced with *sabotage*.

Friedman informs us that

> sabotage is not merely something to be avoided or wished away; instead, it comes with the territory of leading, whether that "territory" is a family or an organization. And a leader's capacity to recognize sabotage for what it is—that is, a systemic phenomenon connected to the shifting balances in the emotional processes of a relationship system and not to the institution's specific issues, makeup, or goals—is the key to the kingdom.

Sabotage is natural. It's *normal*. It's part and parcel of the *systemic* process of leadership. Saboteurs are usually doing nothing but *unconsciously supporting the status quo.* They are protecting the system and keeping it in place. They are preserving something dear to them. (173-74)

REFLECT: PERSONAL AND GROUP PONDERINGS

This section teaches us the necessity of relationships in exercising adaptive leadership.

1. What are the messages or myths of our culture about "lone" leaders? What have you learned in your own life about the tasks of leadership and managing the demands of relationship?

2. Review the story of Gus and Hal. What does this little real-life parable teach us about different ways of approaching leadership?

3. What do we learn from Lewis and Clark about relational leadership both on and off the map? What are some of the possible pitfalls with this relational view of leadership?

4. Reflect on the whole concept of sabotage. What is your response to Friedman's assertion that sabotage is "normal," "natural," to be expected? How does thinking about sabotage as part of a human system help you prepare for it?

RELATE: GOING DEEPER WITH A TRUSTED COMPANION

In the book, the path of adaptive change in the face of every challenge is the same: "start with conviction, stay calm, stay connected and stay the course" (15). With a trusted adviser, recount a time that you experienced sabotage or challenge to your leadership. Thinking about what you have learned regarding the strategy for facing sabotage, reflect on the following questions about that particular experience with your trusted companion.

1. What conviction was at stake for you? What was your deepest commitment in that confrontation or challenge?

2. What was your emotional response to the challenge? What happened to you internally? How did you express your emotions? What do you need in order to be the "less anxious presence" in the situation?

3. What was your relational response to those who challenged you, sabotaged you or abandoned you? What were you able to do to maintain connection, or what kept you from being connected to these challengers? What do you need to communicate to those who oppose the idea?

4. What did you do in the face of opposition? What would you do differently? What does it mean to you to "stay the course"?

PRACTICE: EMBODYING LEADERSHIP TRANSFORMATION

1. In chapter twelve, the book cites the six types of relationships that a leader must navigate and attend to in order be effective in leading adaptive change: allies, confidants, opponents, senior authorities, dissenters and casualties. Review the section of the book and try to name one person in each category. What can you do this week to strengthen your relationship with a person in each category?

2. Look closely at the difference between allies and confidants.

Allies	Confidants
Within organization	Usually outside of organization
See your goals	See your heart
Have other (even competing) loyalties	Loyal only to you
Give you perspective	Give you encouragement
Can build alliances	Can build you up
Not friends	*Not* partners

Identify at least one ally and one confidant in your life who can be with you in a leadership journey.

3. What do you need from your allies? What do you need from confidants? Have a conversation this week with each person (without necessarily telling them what category they are in!) and ask them to help you become a better leader.

- Study 6 -
Everybody Will Be Changed
(Especially the Leader)

Read chapters fourteen and fifteen in *Canoeing the Mountains*.

LEARNING: KEY LEADERSHIP LESSONS

Perhaps the most powerful lesson and greatest opportunity in uncharted territory is that uncharted territory is the location of transformation. A central conviction of *Canoeing in the Mountains* is that God is taking the church from the Christendom world and into uncharted territory to change us.

At the heart of those changes is the learning (and, for some, the sense of loss) that comes from listening to and giving space and even privilege to those on the margins. As Dave Gibbons said, "The future is already here; it is just on the margins" (191).

> Those who had neither power nor privilege in the Christendom world are the trustworthy guides and necessary leaders when we go off the map.
>
> They are not going into uncharted territory. They are at home. (191)

> For Christendom-trained leaders, perhaps the most encouraging realization is that uncharted territory does not make our experience, education and expertise irrelevant, just incomplete. If the margins and the not-so-dead center can interact with each other relationally and have discussions respectfully, there is possibility for genuine lasting change. (199)

REFLECT: PERSONAL AND GROUP PONDERINGS

> No one is going to change as a result of our desires. In fact, they will resist our efforts to change them simply due to the coercive aspect of the interaction. People resist coercion much more strenuously than they resist change. Each of us has a free will at our core, so like it or not, others will choose to change more readily from the example set by our own transformation than by any demand we make of them. To move away from the spirit of coercion, we replace the question "How do you get them to change?" with "What is the transformation in me that is required?" Or, "What courage is required of me right now?"[1]

As you consider this final section and contemplate the changes that are necessary in your own life, look back over these chapters and reflect also on the larger themes of the book.

1. What have you learned that encourages, motivates or inspires you to learn a new way of leading?

2. What still doesn't make sense or could use greater clarification? What concepts do you need to go back and review?

3. What is rubbing you wrong or creating resistance in you? What piece of this whole paradigm makes you want to discard the whole, or what about this whole paradigm frustrates you?

4. What do you need to begin to do differently if you are going to learn to lead all over again?

RELATE: GOING DEEPER WITH A TRUSTED COMPANION

For this last Relate section, take your answers to questions 3 and 4 above and discuss them in greater depth. Since leading into adaptive change is about leading through resistance for the sake of a greater mission, spend some time considering your own resistance.

Apply the adaptive leadership principles to yourself by discussing with a trusted companion your answers to the following questions:

1. What do I need to learn in order to lead in uncharted territory?

2. What losses do I need to face or prepare myself to face in order to keep going?

3. What are the competing values or gaps between my aspirations and actual behaviors that I need to face?

PRACTICE: EMBODYING LEADERSHIP TRANSFORMATION

1. *Find your balcony.* Adaptive leadership requires being able to find a place regularly that offers you a sense of perspective. Heifetz and Linsky write that to lead adaptive change you have to "look from the balcony and listen on the floor." A balcony can be a meeting with a group of colleagues where you keep talking about the big picture and looking to the horizon. It can

be a regular time away unplugged from the demands of technology or the urgency of to-do lists. As best you can, have a regular practice of getting a God's-eye view and trying to see the challenge in front of you as the big adventure that it is.

2. ***Be a mentee.*** I often say that if I were in charge of the world, I would make it illegal for anyone to be in leadership who does not have a spiritual director, a therapist, a coach or a mentor. No one would ever try to lead or learn to lead without someone who they can go to for counsel. But even more important than having a mentor is for a leader to always be a "mentee."

In this study guide, I have encouraged you to discuss every lesson with a trusted companion. That companion can be a peer, an adviser, or even a younger leader. If you are an established leader, find a Sacagawea. Engage in reverse mentoring by asking them to teach you about the world that you find yourself in. Remember for younger leaders, this changing world is all they have ever known. If you are a younger leader, find a Jefferson. Someone to sponsor you, to mentor you, to give you advice, to give you feedback. It doesn't have to be a formal relationship; you just need to be with someone you trust and respect who you can ask on occasion, "Can I buy you a cup of coffee?" and then you show up with the questions, with the agenda, with an open heart and open mind. Listen well, pay for the coffee, thank them for their time and ask if you can call them again.

As long as you are leading, be a learner.

Notes

1 SEMINARY DIDN'T PREPARE ME FOR THIS

[1]See Ryan K. Bolger, *The Gospel After Christendom: New Voices, New Cultures, New Expressions*, Kindle ed. (Grand Rapids: Baker, 2012), loc. 419-20; and Lloyd Pietersen, *Reading the Bible After Christendom*, Kindle ed. (Milton Keynes, UK: Paternoster, 2011), loc. 170-71.

[2]See, for example, "Cottonwood Christian Center v. City of Cypress," *Becket Fund for Religious Liberty*, accessed May 22, 2015, www.becketfund.org/cottonwoodchristian; Ed Stetzer, "InterVarsity 'Derecognized' at California State University's 23 Campuses: Some Analysis and Reflections," *Christianity Today*, September 6, 2014, www.christianitytoday .com/edstetzer/2014/september/intervarsity-now-derecognized-in-california-state -universit.html; and "'Nones' on the Rise," *Pew Research Center*, October 9, 2012, www .pewforum.org/2012/10/09/nones-on-the-rise.

[3]"What Pastors Face Today," *Barnabas Ministries*, accessed May 22, 2015, www.barnabas ministriesinc.org/86-front-page-articles/8-what-pastors-face-today; Richard J. Krejcir, "What Is Going On with Pastors in America?" *Schaeffer Institute*, 2007, www.intothyword .org/apps/articles/?articleid=36562; and Bo Lane, "Why Do So Many Pastors Leave the Ministry? The Facts Will Shock You," *Expastors*, accessed May 22, 2015, www.expastors .com/why-do-so-many-pastors-leave-the-ministry-the-facts-will-shock-you.

[4]The quote, taken from Guder's unpublished manuscript "The Missiological Context," was Guder's own summation of Lesslie Newbigin's description of the challenge facing western churches in a post-Christendom context. For example: "[Most thoughtful Christians] recognize that, with the radical secularization of Western culture, the churches are in a missionary situation in what was once Christendom" (Lesslie Newbigin, *The Open Secret* [Grand Rapids: Eerdmans, 1995], 3). With thanks to Professor Guder for providing me a personal copy of the manuscript. Used by permission.

[5]Edwin H. Friedman, *A Failure of Nerve: Leadership in the Age of the Quick Fix*, Kindle ed. (New York: Church Publishing, 1999), loc. 4493-96.

[6]T. S. Eliot, "Little Gidding" (1942).

[7]Ronald A. Heifetz and Marty Linsky, *Leadership on the Line: Staying Alive Through the Dangers of Leading* (Boston: Harvard Business School Press, 2002), 13.

[8]"Our previous success often prevents us from achieving more success." Marshall Goldsmith and Mark Reiter, *What Got You Here Won't Get You There: How Successful People Become Even More Successful*, Kindle ed. (New York: Hyperion, 2007), loc. 168-69.

[9]Ronald A. Heifetz, Marty Linsky and Alexander Grashow, *The Practice of Adaptive Leadership: Tools and Tactics for Changing Your Organization and the World*, Kindle ed. (Boston: Harvard Business School Press, 2009), loc. 4894-97.

[10]Edwin Friedman, "A Failure of Nerve: Leadership in the Age of the Quick Fix," lecture given in 1996 in Michigan; available from www.leadershipinministry.org/resources/audio-and-video-resources.

[11]"Leadership for today's world requires *enlarging one's capacity* to see the whole board, as in a chess match—to see the complex, often volatile interdependence among the multiple systems that constitute the new commons." Sharon Daloz Parks, *Leadership Can Be Taught: A Bold Approach for a Complex World*, Kindle ed. (Boston: Harvard Business School Press, 2005), loc. 103-4; emphasis mine.

[12]"Experience, one often hears, is the best teacher, but that is true only if you reflect on it and extract its real lessons." Lee G. Bolman and Terrence E. Deal, *How Great Leaders Think: The Art of Reframing* (San Francisco: Jossey-Bass, 2014), 12.

[13]Richard Blackburn, "Healthy Congregations" (workshop sponsored by Lombard Mennonite Peace Center, Lombard, IL, hosted by Trinity Presbyterian Church, Santa Ana, CA, 2006).

2 ADVENTURE OR DIE

[1]Thomas Jefferson to Meriwether Lewis, cited in Stephenie Ambrose Tubbs and Clay Jenkinson, *The Lewis and Clark Companion: An Encyclopedic Guide to the Voyage of Discovery* (New York: Henry Holt, 2003), 193.

[2]Meriwether Lewis, journal entry, August 12, 1805; The Journals of the Lewis and Clark Expedition, http://lewisandclarkjournals.unl.edu/read/?_xmlsrc=1805-08-12.xml&_xslsrc=LCstyles.xsl.

[3]Clay Jenkinson, "The Relevance of the Lewis and Clark Expedition to Modern Travelers," *Chronicle* (Lewis and Clark College), Winter 2003, http://legacy.lclark.edu/dept/chron/relevancew03.html.

[4]John Ordway, journal entry, September 18, 1805; The Journals of the Lewis and Clark Expedition, http://lewisandclarkjournals.unl.edu/read/?_xmlsrc=1805-09-18.xml&_xslsrc=LCstyles.xsl.

[5]Patrick Gass, journal entry; cited in Stephen E. Ambrose, *Undaunted Courage: Meriwether Lewis, Thomas Jefferson and the Opening of the American West*, Kindle ed. (New York: Simon & Schuster, 2013), loc. 5988.

Like Lewis and Clark and their mission, General Stanley McChrystal and his colleagues describe a similar reality as the heart of the challenge for the US armed forces who battled Al-Qaeda in Iraq. "The Task Force hadn't chosen to change; we were driven by necessity. Although lavishly resourced and exquisitely trained, we found ourselves losing to an enemy that, by traditional calculus, we should have dominated. Over time we came to realize that more than our foe, we were actually struggling to cope with an environment that was fundamentally different from anything we'd planned or trained for." General Stanley McChrystal with Tantum Collins, David Silverman and Chris Fussell, *Team of Teams: New Rules of Engagement for a Complex World*, Kindle ed. (New York: Penguin, 2015), loc. 2.

[6]Bob Johansen, *Leaders Make the Future: Ten New Leadership Skills for an Uncertain World*, 2nd ed. (San Francisco: Berrett-Koehler, 2009), 2.

[7]"Trends Continue in Church Membership Growth or Decline Reports 2011 Yearbook of American & Canadian Churches," *National Council of Churches USA*, February 14, 2011, www.ncccusa.org/news/110210yearbook2011.html; and David A. Roozen, "A Decade of Change in American Congregations: 2000-2010," *Faith Communities Today*, accessed May 26, 2015, http://faithcommunitiestoday.org/decade-change. These trends are clear for churches regardless of theological orientation or geographical location.

[8]In my own presbytery (Presbytery of Los Ranchos in Orange County, California) in 1968 there were twenty-two congregations with one thousand members or more. In 2012 there were four.

[9]"The number of Americans who do not identify with any religion continues to grow at a rapid pace. One-fifth of the U.S. public—and a third of adults under 30—are religiously unaffiliated today, the highest percentages ever in Pew Research Center polling. In the last five years alone, the unaffiliated have increased from just over 15% to just under 20% of all U.S. adults." "'Nones' on the Rise," Pew Forum on Religion and Public Life, October 9, 2012, www.pewforum.org/2012/10/09/nones-on-the-rise.

[10]Lesslie Newbigin, *Unfinished Agenda*, 2nd ed. (Somerset, UK: St. Andrews Press, 1993), 236. Newbigin's thought is documented especially in his *The Other Side of 1984: Questions for the Churches* (Geneva: World Council of Churches, 1983); *Foolishness to the Greeks: The Gospel and Western Culture* (Grand Rapids: Eerdmans, 1986); and *The Gospel in a Pluralist Society* (Grand Rapids: Eerdmans, 1987).

[11]Darrell Guder, "Walking Worthily: Missional Leadership after Christendom," *Princeton Seminary Bulletin* 28, no. 3 (2007), 252. Cf. Darrell Guder, ed., *Missional Church: A Vision for the Sending of the Church in North America* (Grand Rapids: Eerdmans, 1998). The early missional church discussion has been shaped by the publications of the Gospel and Our Culture Network: Guder, *Missional Church*; Darrell Guder, *The Continuing Conversion of the Church* (Grand Rapids: Eerdmans, 2000); Lois Barrett, ed., *Treasure in Clay Jars: Patterns in Missional Faithfulness* (Grand Rapids: Eerdmans, 2002); Craig van Gelder, ed., *Confident Witness–Changing World: Rediscovering the Gospel in North America* (Grand Rapids: Eerdmans, 1999); Craig van Gelder, *The Ministry of the Missional Church: A Community Led by the Spirit* (Grand Rapids: Baker, 2007); George Hunsberger, ed., *The Church Between Gospel and Culture: The Emerging Mission in North America* (Grand

Rapids: Eerdmans, 1996); George R. Hunsberger, *Bearing the Witness of the Spirit: Lesslie Newbigin's Theology of Cultural Plurality* (Grand Rapids: Eerdmans, 1998); James Brownson, *Speaking the Truth in Love: New Testament Resources for a Missional Hermeneutic* (Harrisburg, PA: Trinity Press International, 1998); and James Brownson, ed., *StormFront: The Good News of God* (Grand Rapids: Eerdmans, 2003).

[12]Guder, "Walking Worthily," 256.

[13]Christopher Wright, *The Mission of God: Unlocking the Bible's Grand Narrative* (Downers Grove, IL: IVP Academic, 2006), 62.

[14]Alan Hirsch, *The Forgotten Ways* (Grand Rapids: Brazos, 2007), 82.

[15]For a very helpful discussion of these shifts and the dislocation they cause, see JR Woodward, *Creating a Missional Culture: Equipping the Church for the Sake of the World* (Downers Grove, IL: InterVarsity Press, 2012), 65-76.

[16]Tony Jones, *The New Christians: Dispatches from the Emergent Frontier* (San Francisco: Jossey-Bass, 2008), 8; Phyllis Tickle, *The Great Emergence: How Christianity Is Changing and Why* (Grand Rapids: Baker, 2008); Thomas L. Friedman, *The World Is Flat: A Brief History of the Twenty-First Century*, 3rd ed. (New York: Straus & Giroux, 2007); Joshua Cooper Ramo, *The Age of the Unthinkable: Why the New World Disorder Constantly Surprises Us and What We Can Do About It* (New York: Back Bay Books, 2010); Don Tapscott and Anthony D. Williams, *Wikinomics: How Mass Collaboration Changes Everything* (New York: Portfolio, 2006); Ori Brafman and Rod A. Beckstrom, *The Starfish and the Spider: The Unstoppable Power of Leaderless Organizations* (New York: Portfolio, 2007); Steven Johnson, *Where Good Ideas Come From: The Natural History of Innovation* (New York: Riverhead, 2010); and John Seely Brown, *A New Culture of Learning: Cultivating the Imagination for a World of Constant Change* (Lexington: n.p., 2011).

[17]Guder, "Walking Worthily," 254.

[18]As General McChrystal explains about the struggles of the US Army in combating Al-Qaeda, "We're not lazier or less intelligent than our parents or grandparents, but what worked for them simply won't do the trick for us now." McChrystal et al., *Team of Teams*, loc. 4.

[19]Used by permission.

[20]Edwin H. Friedman, *A Failure of Nerve: Leadership in the Age of the Quick Fix*, Kindle ed. (New York: Church Publishing, 1999), loc. 658-63.

[21]Ibid.

3 A LEADERSHIP MODEL FOR UNCHARTED TERRITORY

[1]Abraham Joshua Heschel, "The Holy Dimension," in *Moral Grandeur and Spiritual Audacity: Essays* (New York: Farrar, Straus & Giroux, 1997), 334, cited in "Abraham Joshua Heschel Quote," *iz quotes*, accessed July 18, 2013, http://izquotes.com/quote/237136.

[2]"Ecclesia is a movement or, more technically, an apostolic movement." Alan Hirsch and Tim Catchim, *The Permanent Revolution: Apostolic Imagination and Practice for the 21st Century Church*, Kindle ed. (San Francisco: Jossey-Bass, 2012), loc. 874.

[3]Darrell Guder, "Walking Worthily: Missional Leadership after Christendom," *Princeton Seminary Bulletin* 28, no. 3 (2007), 256. Guder sees in the modern textual variant of Mark 1:14 the model, "And he appointed twelve, whom he also named apostles, to be with him and to be sent out."

[4]Guder, "Walking Worthily," 261.

[5]Ronald A. Heifetz and Marty Linsky, *Leadership on the Line: Staying Alive Through the Dangers of Leading* (Boston: Harvard Business School Press, 2002), 18 (emphasis mine).

[6]Peter Coutts, review of Ronald A. Heifetz, *Leadership Without Easy Answers* (Cambridge, MA: Belknap Press of Harvard Press, 1994); Leadership: A Resource for The Presbyterian Church in Canada, accessed July 3, 2015, www.telusplanet.net/public/pdcoutts /leadership/Heifetz.htm.

[7]Ronald Heifetz and Donald Laurie, "The Work of Leadership," *Harvard Business Review*, January 1997, reprinted December 2001, 6.

[8]John Kotter says, "The central issue is never strategy, structure, culture, or systems. All those elements, and others, are important. But the core of the matter is always about changing the behavior of people, and behavior change happens in highly successful situations mostly by speaking to people's feelings." John P. Kotter and Dan S. Cohen, *The Heart of Change: Real-Life Stories of How People Change Their Organizations*, Kindle ed. (Boston: Harvard Business Review Press, 2012), loc. 140-42.

4 COMPETENCE AND CREDIBILITY

[1]Thomas Jefferson, cited in Stephenie Ambrose Tubbs and Clay Jenkinson, *The Lewis and Clark Companion: An Encyclopedic Guide to the Voyage of Discovery* (New York: Henry Holt, 2003), 188.

[2]Ibid., 193.

[3]Ibid., 191.

[4]I first became familiar with this term from Scott Cormode, Hugh De Pree Professor of Leadership Development at Fuller Seminary, in a personal conversation in May 3, 2012. Used by permission. For more information, see the paper Cormode commissioned by Lisa Berlinger called "The Behavioral Competency Approach to Ecclesial Leadership," *Journal of Religious Leadership* 2, no. 2 (Spring 2003), arl-jrl.org/Volumes/BerlingerFA03. pdf. See also Daniel Goleman, "What Makes a Leader?," in *Harvard Business Review's 10 Must Reads on Leadership* (Boston: Harvard Business School Press, 2011). Goleman refers to the "threshold capabilities" needed to even be considered for executive leadership.

[5]"Code is the defining essence of a church. Healthy growth is the result of a church's congruence with its code; poor health is caused by incongruence." Kevin G. Ford, *Transforming Church: Bringing Out the Good to Get to Great*, Kindle ed. (Wheaton, IL: SaltRiver, 2007), loc. 915-16.

[6]Rule 8 of Ori Brafman and Rod A. Beckstrom, *The Starfish and the Spider: The Unstoppable Power of Leaderless Organizations* (New York: Portfolio, 2007).

[7]Ronald A. Heifetz, "Leadership, Adaptability, Thriving," *Faith & Leadership*, November 18, 2009, www.youtube.com/watch?v=CSZId1VlYxc.

[8]The original motto, *ecclesia reformata, semper reformanda,* is attributed to Dutch theologian Gisbert Voetius (1589–1676), a strict high Calvinist.

[9]See 1 Corinthians 6:15; 12:12-27; Romans 12:4-15; Colossians 1:18, 24; 2:19; 3:15; Ephesians 2:15-16; 3:6; 4:4; 4:12-16; 4:25.

5 PREPARING FOR THE UNKNOWN

[1]Jefferson knew full well that Lewis also struggled with "depressions of the mind" and, at times, excessive drinking.

[2]Meriwether Lewis, cited in Stephen E. Ambrose, *Undaunted Courage: Meriwether Lewis, Thomas Jefferson and the Opening of the American West* (New York: Simon & Schuster, 2013), 99.

[3]Ibid., 135.

[4]There is some speculation that Jefferson himself opposed the idea of a co-captaincy and wanted Lewis in sole command—or at the very least he neglected or overlooked something that was clearly within his power to influence (Ambrose, *Undaunted Courage*, 135).

[5]See Stephen Ambrose, "Friends," in Dayton Duncan and Ken Burns, *Lewis and Clark: An Illustrated History* (New York: Knopf, 2012), 119.

[6]Ronald A. Heifetz, "Leadership, Adaptability, Thriving," *Faith & Leadership*, November 18, 2009, www.youtube.com/watch?v=CSZId1VlYxc.

[7]See Alan Deutschman, *Change or Die* (New York: HarperCollins, 2009), 4.

[8]Ronald A. Heifetz, "The Nature of Adaptive Leadership," *Faith & Leadership*, video interview, February 4, 2009, www.youtube.com/watch?v=QfLLDvnopI8.

[9]Ronald A. Heifetz and Marty Linsky, *Leadership on the Line: Staying Alive Through the Dangers of Leading* (Boston: Harvard Business School Press, 2002), 13.

[10]Heifetz, "Leadership, Adaptability, Thriving."

[11]Ronald A. Heifetz, Marty Linsky and Alexander Grashow, *The Practice of Adaptive Leadership: Tools and Tactics for Changing Your Organization and the World*, Kindle ed. (Boston: Harvard Business School Press, 2009), loc. 2567-70.

[12]"In communal transformation, leadership is about intention, convening, valuing relatedness, and presenting choices." Peter Block, *Community: The Structure of Belonging*, Kindle ed. (San Francisco: Berrett-Koehler, 2009), loc. 977-78.

[13]Sharon Daloz Parks, *Leadership Can Be Taught: A Bold Approach for a Complex World*, Kindle ed. (Boston: Harvard Business School Press, 2005), loc. 607-8.

[14]Margaret Wheatley, "When Change Is Out of Our Control," *Margaret Wheatley*, "Writings," www.margaretwheatley.com/articles/whenchangeisoutofcontrol.html. A version of this essay was published in *Human Resources for the 21st Century*, ed. Marc Effron, Robert Gandossy and Marshall Goldsmith (Hoboken, NJ: Wiley & Sons, 2003).

[15]"Honesty/Ethics in Professions," *Gallup*, December 8-11, 2014, www.gallup.com/poll/1654/honesty-ethics-professions.aspx.

[16]Dennis Rea and Michelle Rea, "The HR Executive's Role in Rebuilding Trust," from *The Human Resource Executive Online*, May 2, 2007, www.hreonline.com/HRE/view/story .jhtml?id=12160414. See also Stephen M. R. Covey, "How the Best Leaders Build Trust," *Leadership Now*, accessed May 25, 2015, www.leadershipnow.com/CoveyOnTrust.html.

[17]From a phone interview conducted by the author with Jim Osterhaus, June 2011.

[18]See Amy J. C. Cuddy, Matthew Kohut and John Neffinger, "Connect Then Lead," *Harvard Business Review*, July–August 2013, http://hbr.org/2013/07/connect-then-lead/ar/1.

[19]Edwin H. Friedman, *A Failure of Nerve: Leadership in the Age of the Quick Fix*, Kindle ed. (New York: Seabury Books, 2007), loc. 339-44.

[20]Wheatley, "When Change Is Out of Our Control." Emphasis added.

[21]While they certainly faced expected morale issues, with one erstwhile deserter and one trial for mutiny, what is most significant is that the overall attitude of the Corps was such that these malcontents were tried and judged by a tribunal of the men, not the captains themselves. Even the convicted mutineer, Private John Newton, asked to be forgiven and reinstated, but he was not and was sent back. Ambrose, *Undaunted Courage*, loc. 4300.

[22]See Ambrose, "Friends," in Duncan and Burns, *Lewis and Clark*, 124.

[23]Ibid.

[24]According to General Stanley McChrystal, the rediscovery of the power of building trusting relationships within and between cohesive teams was the critical lesson that the Joint Task Force learned when faced with defeating Al-Qaeda in Iraq. "Our operators' most useful preparation lay in the trust they had built, shared hardship by shared hardship, over years of service. It is often said that trust is learned on the battlefield. But for groups like the SEALs, *the oneness imbued by trust and purpose is a prerequisite to deployment.* Entering the battlefield as a group of individuals without those characteristics would be like walking into a firefight without wearing body armor." General Stanley McChrystal with Tantum Collins, David Silverman and Chris Fussell, *Team of Teams: New Rules of Engagement for a Complex World*, Kindle ed. (New York: Penguin, 2015), loc. 103 (emphasis mine).

6 EATING STRATEGY FOR BREAKFAST

[1]Ford Motor Company CEO Mark Fields popularized the attribution of this phrase to Drucker by posting the quote in his executive board room in 2006; see Jeffrey Mc-Cracken, "'Way Forward' Requires Culture Shift at Ford," *The Wall Street Journal*, January 23, 2006, www.wsj.com/articles/SB113797951796853248. Compare: "Culture matters because it is a powerful, tacit, and often unconscious set of forces that determine both our individual and collective behavior, ways of perceiving, thought patterns, and values. Organizational culture in particular matters because cultural elements determine strategy, goals, and modes of operating"; Edgar H. Schein, *The Corporate Culture Survival Guide* (Hoboken, NJ: Wiley & Sons, 2009), 19. See also Nilofer Merchant, "Culture Trumps Strategy, Every Time," *Harvard Business Review*, March 22, 2011, https://hbr.org/2011/03 /culture-trumps-strategy-every.

[2]"Culture is, first of all, the name for our relentless, restless human effort to take the world as it's given to us and make something else." Andy Crouch, *Culture Making: Recovering Our Creative Calling*, Kindle ed. (Downers Grove, IL: InterVarsity Press, 2013), loc. 191-92.

[3]JR Woodward, *Creating a Missional Culture: Equipping the Church for the Sake of the World* (Downers Grove, IL: InterVarsity Press, 2012), 20.

[4]John Kotter, "The Key to Changing Organizational Culture," *Forbes*, September 27, 2012, www.forbes.com/sites/johnkotter/2012/09/27/the-key-to-changing-organizational-culture.

[5]Ibid.

[6]"Willard Words," *Dallas Willard*, accessed August 13, 2013, www.dwillard.org/resources /WillardWords.asp.

[7]Woodward, *Creating a Missional Culture*, 19.

[8]See Peter Senge, *The Fifth Discipline: The Art and Practice of the Learning Organization*, Kindle ed. (New York: Doubleday, 2006), loc. 1105.

[9]Nilofer Merchant, "Culture Trumps Strategy Every Time," *Harvard Business Review*, accessed July 15, 2013, http://blogs.hbr.org/cs/2011/03/culture_trumps_strategy_every .html.

[10]Woodward, *Creating a Missional Culture*, 20 (emphasis added).

[11]John Kotter, "What Leaders Really Do," *Harvard Business Review*, December 2001, 29 (emphasis added).

[12]Patrick M. Lencioni, *The Advantage: Why Organizational Health Trumps Everything Else in Business* (Hoboken, NJ: John Wiley, 2012), 5.

[13]Ibid.

[14]"After two decades of working with CEOs and their teams of senior executives, I've become absolutely convinced that the seminal difference between successful companies and mediocre or unsuccessful ones . . . has everything to do with how healthy they are" (ibid., 8-9).

[15]Tod Bolsinger, "Starfish and the Spider #10: Really, Really Important Rule #8," *Tod Bolsinger* (blog), January 5, 2009, http://bolsinger.blogs.com/weblog/2009/01/starfish -and-the-spider-10-really-really-important-rule-8.html.

[16]Ori Brafman and Rod A. Beckstrom, *Starfish and the Spider: The Unstoppable Power of Leaderless Organizations* (New York: Portfolio, 2008), 207.

[17]As Collins and Porras have written in *Built to Last*, the first task of leadership is determining "what will *never* change" and then being willing to change *everything* else. James C. Collins and Jerry I. Porras, *Built to Last: Successful Habits of Visionary Companies* (New York: HarperBusiness, 2004), xiv.

[18]David Burkus, "A Tale of Two Cultures: Why Culture Trumps Core Values in Building Ethical Organizations," *Journal of Values Based Leadership* 4, no. 1 (Winter–Spring 2011), www.valuesbasedleadershipjournal.com/issues/vol4issue1/tale_2culture.php.

[19]Peter L. Steinke, *Healthy Congregations: A Systems Approach* (Herndon, VA: The Alban Institute), Kindle loc. 56-60.

[20]Which is why on the alignment work that I do with churches and organizations we talk about infrastructure only *after* we have clarity on core ideology and culture.

[21]Kotter, "Key to Changing Organizational Culture."

[22]Compare: "For a soldier trained at West Point as an engineer, the idea that a problem has different solutions on different days was fundamentally disturbing." McChrystal et al., *Team of Teams*, loc. 3.

[23]While I don't recommend that other churches use another church's simple rules, I am often asked to share San Clemente Presbyterian Church's with them. (1) Commit to the whole. (Every ministry must be committed to the overall health and well-being of the church first and foremost.) (2) Connect to the core. (Every ministry must be an expression of and consistent with our core values, and the leaders must have representation at the monthly leadership core meetings.) (3) Collaborate with every circle. (Every ministry must be willing to collaborate with every other ministry that is related to it.) (4) Clean up your mess. (Every ministry must take responsibility to help solve any problems that arise because of their ministry.)

[24]Ronald A. Heifetz, "Leadership, Adaptability, Thriving," *Faith & Leadership*, November 18, 2009, www.youtube.com/watch?v=CSZId1VlYxc.

7 NAVIGATING THE "GEOGRAPHY OF REALITY"

[1]Dayton Duncan and Ken Burns, *Lewis and Clark: An Illustrated History* (New York: Knopf, 2012), 118.

[2]John Logan Allen, "Summer of Decision: Lewis and Clark in Montana, 1805," *We Proceeded On* 8, no. 4 (Fall 1976), cited in Stephen E. Ambrose, *Undaunted Courage: Meriwether Lewis, Thomas Jefferson and the Opening of the American West* (New York: Simon & Schuster, 2013), 266. See also John Logan Allen, *Lewis and Clark and the Image of the American Northwest* (Mineola, NY: Dover, 2012).

[3]Patrick Gass, cited in "The Journals of the Lewis and Clark Expedition," *University of Nebraska Lincoln*, accessed August 16, 2013, http://lewisandclarkjournals.unl.edu /read/?_xmlsrc=1805-09-16&_xslsrc=LCstyles.xsl.

[4]Ronald Heifetz, *Leadership Without Easy Answers* (Cambridge, MA: Belknap Press of Harvard University Press, 1994), 22.

[5]Ronald A. Heifetz, Marty Linsky and Alexander Grashow, *The Practice of Adaptive Leadership: Tools and Tactics for Changing Your Organization and the World*, Kindle ed. (Boston: Harvard Business School Press, 2009), loc. 4888-89.

[6]Meriwether Lewis's May 26, 1805, journal entry, cited in *The Lewis and Clark Journals: An American Epic of Discovery*, ed. Gary Moulton (Lincoln: University of Nebraska Press, 2003).

[7]Jim Collins refers often to the necessity of leaders to be able to live in what he calls "the Stockdale Paradox." Named for Admiral James Stockdale, the highest ranking POW of the Vietnam War, who described how leaders survive terrible ordeals: "You must never confuse faith that you will prevail in the end—which you can never afford to lose—with

the discipline to confront the most brutal facts of your current reality, whatever they might be." James Stockdale, cited in Jim Collins, *Good to Great: Why Some Companies Make the Leap . . . and Others Don't* (New York: HarperBusiness, 2001), 85.

[8]After his return to St. Louis, Lewis wrote Jefferson with accurate precision. See Stephen E. Ambrose, *Undaunted Courage: Meriwether Lewis, Thomas Jefferson and the Opening of the American West*, Kindle ed. (New York: Simon & Schuster, 2013), loc. 8412-14.

[9]Thomas Jefferson in a letter to Meriwether Lewis, cited in Ambrose, *Undaunted Courage*, 116.

[10]Jack Uldrich, *Into the Unknown: Leadership Lessons from Lewis and Clark's Daring Westward Expedition*, Kindle ed. (New York: AMACOM, 2004), loc. 309-14.

[11]Lewis's August 18, 1805, journal entry, cited in Moulton, *Lewis and Clark Journals*, 224.

[12]Uldrich, *Into the Unknown*, loc. 332-33. Uldrich also notes, "Lewis and Clark were willing to forge ahead during their brutal thirty-two-day portage around the Great Falls and their nearly fatal eleven-day ordeal in the Bitterroot Range because the stakes were higher than just commercial interests" (ibid., loc. 416-17).

[13]"Reframing requires an ability to understand and use multiple perspectives, to think about the same thing in more than one way" (Lee G. Bolman and Terrence E. Deal, *Reframing Organizations: Artistry, Choice, and Leadership*, Kindle ed. [San Francisco: Jossey-Bass, 2013], loc. 231-32).

[14]See Rodney Stark, *The Rise of Christianity: How the Obscure, Marginal Jesus Movement Became the Dominant Religious Force in the Western World in a Few Centuries* (New York: HarperCollins, 1997).

[15]I will say more in a later chapter about the power of reframing as a most necessary leadership skill. According to Lee Bolman and Terrence Deal, when great leaders develop the ability to reframe it "sets them free, and [helps them] avoid getting trapped in cognitive ruts." Lee G. Bolman and Terrence E. Deal, *How Great Leaders Think: The Art of Reframing*, Kindle ed. (San Francisco: Jossey-Bass, 2014), loc. 448.

8 MY ITALIAN GRANDFATHER WAS KILLING ME

[1]Max De Pree, *Leadership Is an Art* (New York: Doubleday, 2004), 9.

[2]Lee G. Bolman and Terrence E. Deal, *How Great Leaders Think: The Art of Reframing*, Kindle ed. (San Francisco: Jossey-Bass, 2014), loc. 89-90.

[3]Wendell Berry, "Health Is Membership," *BT Connect*, October 17, 1994, http://home2 .btconnect.com/tipiglen/berryhealth.html.

[4]For more on this see my book *It Takes a Church to Raise a Christian: How the Community of God Transforms Lives* (Grand Rapids: Brazos, 2004).

[5]Edwin H. Friedman, *A Failure of Nerve: Leadership in the Age of the Quick Fix*, Kindle ed. (New York: Seabury Books, 2007), loc. 3609-10. Compare "A system is more than the sum of its parts. It may exhibit adaptive, dynamic, goal-seeking, self-preserving, and sometimes evolutionary behavior" (Donella H. Meadows, *Thinking in Systems: A Primer*, Kindle ed. [White River Junction, VT: Chelsea Green, 2008], loc. 173-74).

⁶Ibid., loc. 180-81.

⁷"DNA," *Wikipedia,* accessed May 25, 2015, http://en.wikipedia.org/wiki/DNA.

⁸Kevin G. Ford, *Transforming Church: Bringing Out the Good to Get to Great,* Kindle ed. (Colorado Springs: David C. Cook, 2008), loc. 915-16.

⁹Ibid.

¹⁰Ibid., loc. 919-20.

¹¹Ibid., loc. 944-47.

¹²Ronald A. Heifetz, "Leadership, Adaptability, Thriving," *Faith & Leadership,* November 18, 2009, www.youtube.com/watch?v=CSZId1VlYxc.

¹³Ronald A. Heifetz and Marty Linsky, *Leadership on the Line: Staying Alive Through the Dangers of Leading* (Boston: Harvard Business School Press, 2002), 11.

9 DON'T JUST DO SOMETHING, STAND THERE . . . THEN DO SOMETHING

¹Quoted by permission.

²Laurence Gonzales, *Everyday Survival: Why Smart People Do Stupid Things* (New York: Norton, 2009), 30.

³Ruth Moon, "Game Changer: Pastors Blame Kids' Sports for Attendance Dips," *Christianity Today,* August 27, 2013, www.christianitytoday.com/ct/2013/september/game -changer.html?utm_source=ctdirect-html&utm_medium=Newsletter&utm_ term=9829118&utm_content=203661422&utm_campaign=2013.

⁴Ronald A. Heifetz, Marty Linsky and Alexander Grashow, *The Practice of Adaptive Leadership: Tools and Tactics for Changing Your Organization and the World,* Kindle ed. (Boston: Harvard Business School Press, 2009), loc. 679-82.

⁵Ibid.

⁶"This is a critical point: When you observe from the balcony you must see yourself as well as the other participants. Perhaps this is the hardest task of all—to see yourself objectively." Ronald A. Heifetz and Marty Linsky, *Leadership on the Line: Staying Alive Through the Dangers of Leading* (Boston: Harvard Business School Press, 2002), 54.

⁷Michael Lombardi, "NFL Opens Pandora's Box by Offering All-22 Tape to Public," June 22, 2012, *NFL.com,* www.nfl.com/news/story/09000d5d82a0b2d8/article/nfl-opens -pandoras-box-by-offering-all22-tape-to-public.

⁸Heifetz and Linsky, *Leadership on the Line,* 53.

⁹These three questions are themselves adaptations of the Appreciative Inquiry questions at the heart of Mark Lau Branson's book, *Memories, Hopes, and Conversations: Appreciative Inquiry and Congregational Change* (Lanham, MD: Rowman & Littlefield, 2004).

¹⁰Heifetz, Linsky and Grashow, *Practice of Adaptive Leadership,* loc. 720-23.

¹¹Peter Senge, *The Fifth Discipline: The Art and Practice of the Learning Organization* (New York: Doubleday, 2006), 62.

¹²This was later validated when we repeated the Transforming Church Index with TAG Consulting a few months later. While a decentralized and collaborative leadership style

meant that our lay leadership was healthier and more engaged than ever, the transition to a different culture of participation was taking longer than we hoped and the people in the pew reported an enduring need to be more connected to each other.

[13]Quoted in William C. Taylor, "The Leader of the Future: Harvard's Ronald Heifetz offers a Short Course on the Future of Leadership," *Fast Company*, May 31, 1999, www.fast company.com/37229/leader-future.

[14]David McRaney, "Survivorship Bias," *You Are Not So Smart* (blog), May 23, 2013, http://youarenotsosmart.com/2013/05/23/survivorship-bias.

10 THE MISSION TRUMPS!

[1]Ronald Heifetz and Marty Linsky, "Leadership on the Line: Staying Alive Through the Dangers of Leading," *Working Knowledge* (Harvard Business School blog), May 28, 2002, http://hbswk.hbs.edu/archive/2952.html.

[2]Peter M. Senge, "The Leader's New Work: Building Learning Organizations," *MIT: Sloan Management Review* 32, no. 1 (Fall 1990); and Ronald A. Heifetz, "Leadership, Adaptability, Thriving," *Faith & Leadership*, November 18, 2009, www.youtube.com/watch?v=CSZId1VlYxc. Describing the difference between the strategies in which he was trained and what he had to execute as commander in Iraq against Al-Qaeda, Stanley McChrystal writes, "This was not a war of planning and discipline; it was one of agility and innovation." McChrystal et al., *Team of Teams*, loc. 14.

[3]"This phrase is borrowed from biology, which tries to understand the uncanny self-organizing ability of some embryos that duplicate themselves even after some of their parts have been rearranged or cut away." Edwin H. Friedman, *A Failure of Nerve: Leadership in the Age of the Quick Fix*, Kindle ed. (New York: Seabury Books, 2007), loc. 307-9.

[4]Thanks to Richard Blackburn of the Lombard Mennonite Peace Center for this powerful and pithy phrase.

[5]Lawrence G. Shattuck, "Communicating Intent and Imparting Presence," *Military Review*, March–April, 2000, 66.

[6]Jim Collins, *Good to Great and the Social Sectors: A Monograph to Accompany "Good to Great,"* Kindle ed. (New York: HarperCollins, 2011), loc. 241-43. See also Jimcollins.com, "The Hedgehog Concept," www.jimcollins.com/lab/hedgehog/p2.html and www.jimcollins.com/media_topics/hedgehog-concept.html#audio=79.

[7]Eric Hellweg, "The Eight-Word Mission Statement," *Harvard Business Review*, October 22, 2010, http://blogs.hbr.org/hbr/hbreditors/2010/10/the_eight-word_mission_stateme.html.

[8]Parker Palmer, *Let Your Life Speak: Listening for the Voice of Vocation* (San Francisco: Jossey-Bass, 1999), 46.

11 TAKE A GOOD LOOK INTO THE COFFIN

[1]Edwin H. Friedman, *A Failure of Nerve: Leadership in the Age of the Quick Fix*, Kindle ed. (New York: Seabury Books, 2007), loc. 386.

[2]Ronald A. Heifetz and Marty Linsky, *Leadership on the Line: Staying Alive Through the Dangers of Leading* (Boston: Harvard Business School Press, 2002), 11-12.

[3]Peter Senge, *The Fifth Discipline: The Art and Practice of the Learning Organization* (New York: Doubleday, 2006), 57.

[4]John Kotter, "The 8-Step Process for Leading Change," *Kotter International*, accessed May 27, 2015, www.kotterinternational.com/our-principles/changesteps/step-1.

[5]Heifetz and Linsky, *Leadership on the Line*, 146.

[6]See John Kotter, "A Sense of Urgency," *Kotter International*, accessed May 27, 2015, www.kotterinternational.com/our-principles/urgency/falseurgency.

[7]One excellent tool is TAG Consulting's Transforming Church Insight and Discovery process. See "What We Use," *TAG*, May 27, 2015, http://transformingchurch.net/what-we-use.

[8]This suggestion came from Friedman, *A Failure of Nerve*, loc. 459-60.

[9]Jeffrey Miller, *The Anxious Organization: Why Smart Companies Do Dumb Things* (Blairsville, GA: Facts on Demand, 2002), 14.

[10]This is what Daniel Goleman calls "Amygdala Hijack." For a great book on how an emotionally flooded brain keeps us from listening well and working together, see Mark Goulston, *Just Listen: Discover the Secret to Getting Through to Absolutely Anyone* (New York: AMACOM, 2009).

[11]James P. Osterhaus, Joseph M Jurkowski and Todd A. Hahn, *Thriving Through Ministry Conflict*, Kindle ed. (Grand Rapids: Zondervan, 2009), loc. 26-33, 104.

[12]"Move yourself from OH F#@& TO OK," in Goulston, *Just Listen*, loc. 577-78.

[13]Figure 11.1 is adapted from Osterhaus, Jurkowski and Hahn, *Thriving Through Ministry Conflict*, loc. 103.

[14]Peter L. Steinke, *Congregational Leadership in Anxious Times: Being Calm and Courageous No Matter What*, Kindle ed. (Lanham, MD: Rowman & Littlefield, 2014), loc. 60.

[15]Ibid., loc. 107.

12 GUS AND HAL GO TO CHURCH

[1]Jim Collins and Jerry I. Porras, *Built to Last: Successful Habits of Visionary Companies* (New York: HarperBusiness 1994), 113.

[2]McChrystal quotes Alan Mullaly, CEO of Ford Motor Company during their remarkable turnaround from 2005 to 2009: "Working together always works. It always works. Everybody has to be on the team. They have to be interdependent with one another." General Stanley McChrystal with Tantum Collins, David Silverman and Chris Fussell, *Team of Teams: New Rules of Engagement for a Complex World*, Kindle ed. (New York: Penguin, 2015), loc. 195.

[3]From the ordination vows of Presbyterian Church (USA) ruling and teaching elders.

[4]Ronald A. Heifetz, Marty Linsky and Alexander Grashow, *The Practice of Adaptive Leadership: Tools and Tactics for Changing Your Organization and the World*, Kindle ed. (Boston: Harvard Business School Press, 2009), loc. 1576-79.

[5]Patrick M. Lencioni, *The Advantage: Why Organizational Health Trumps Everything Else in Business*, Kindle ed. (Hoboken, NJ: John Wiley, 2012), loc. 1389.

[6]Heifetz, Linsky and Grashow, *Practice of Adaptive Leadership*, chap. 10.

[7]"Potential allies have interests and perspectives of the adaptive challenge closely aligned with yours and will gain the most if your intervention succeeds." Ibid., loc. 2289-90.

[8]Edwin H. Friedman, *A Failure of Nerve: Leadership in the Age of the Quick Fix*, Kindle ed. (New York: Seabury Books, 2007), loc. 421-23.

[9]See Tod Bolsinger, "The Whisper That Made Me Leave My Church," *Tod Bolsinger* (blog), May 16, 2014, http://bolsinger.blogs.com/weblog/2014/05/it-was-the-whisper-that-made-me-leave-my-church-it-was-the-one-line-that-i-heard-over-and-over-again-in-the-five-years-that.html.

[10]John P. Kotter, *Buy-In: Saving Your Good Idea from Getting Shot Down* (New York: Perseus Books, 2010), 88.

[11]John P. Kotter, *Leading Change*, Kindle ed. (Boston: Harvard Business School Press, 2012), loc. 477 (chap. 4).

[12]Heifetz, Linsky and Grashow, *Practice of Adaptive Leadership*, loc. 383.

[13]Margaret Wheatley, "Writings," *Margaret Wheatley*, accessed July 23, 2013, www.margaretwheatley.com/articles/whenchangeisoutofcontrol.html.

13 ET TU, CHURCH?

[1]While transparency is universally considered admirable and necessary for building trust, there is still significant resistance to the actual practice of transparent communication in many leadership arenas. However, even within the military where top-secret information is a life or death issue, McChrystal insists on transparency. "Our standing guidance was 'Share information until you're afraid it's illegal.'" General Stanley McChrystal with Tantum Collins, David Silverman and Chris Fussell, *Team of Teams: New Rules of Engagement for a Complex World*, Kindle ed. (New York: Penguin, 2015), loc. 164.

[2]Edwin H. Friedman, *A Failure of Nerve: Leadership in the Age of the Quick Fix*, Kindle ed. (New York: Seabury Books, 2007), loc. 326-27.

[3]Stephen E. Ambrose, *Undaunted Courage: Meriwether Lewis, Thomas Jefferson and the Opening of the American West*, Kindle ed. (New York: Simon & Schuster, 2013), locs. 3210, 3685.

[4]Friedman, *Failure of Nerve*, loc. 278-79.

[5]William Barclay, quoted in James Martin, "Why Did Judas Do It?," *America*, April 20, 2011, http://americamagazine.org/content/all-things/why-did-judas-do-it.

[6]Bob Johansen, *Leaders Make the Future: Ten New Leadership Skills for an Uncertain World* (San Francisco: Berrett-Koehler, 2009).

[7]Steven Johnson, *Where Good Ideas Come From: The Natural History of Innovation* (New York: Riverhead, 2010), 28-29.

[8]Lewis and Clark assumed that portaging the Great Falls would take them about a day of carrying the canoes. In actuality it took them over thirty days.

[9]Friedman, *Failure of Nerve*, loc. 3363-78; 407-8.

[10]Ibid., loc. 121-24.

[11]Ibid., loc. 4480-84.

14 HOW A NURSING MOTHER SAVED AMERICA

[1]Stephen E. Ambrose, *Undaunted Courage: Meriwether Lewis, Thomas Jefferson and the Opening of the American West* (New York: Simon & Schuster, 2013), 225.

[2]Ibid., 187.

[3]Ibid. The captains hired Charbonneau and *one* wife. Nothing is known about the fate of the other wife.

[4]William Clark, quoted in *The Lewis and Clark Journals: An American Epic of Discovery*, ed. Gary Moulton (Lincoln: University of Nebraska Press, 2003), 267.

[5]Twenty years later, Newsong Church (newsong.net) now worships in seven locations internationally and is considered a model for what churches of the future could be. Dave Gibbons is the author of *The Monkey and the Fish: Liquid Leadership for a Third-Culture Church*, Leadership Network Innovation Series (Grand Rapids: Zondervan, 2009). Cf. "Dave Gibbons is a Church Misfit," *Orange County Weekly*, September 8, 2011, www.oc weekly.com/2011-09-08/news/newsong-dave-gibbons.

[6]Juan Martinez, interview by the author at Fuller Theological Seminary, August 28, 2014.

[7]Juan Francisco Martinez, "Discovering God's Initiative in the Midst of Adaptive Challenge," *Journal of Missional Practice*, no. 1 (Autumn 2012), http://journalofmissional practice.com/discovering-gods-initiatives-in-the-midst-of-adaptive-challenge.

[8]Steve Yamaguchi, "From the Palace to the Streets," *Fuller* 1, no. 1, accessed April 23, 2015, http://fullermag.com/from-the-palace-to-the-streets.

[9]Steve Yamaguchi, interview by the author at Fuller Theological Seminary, August 28, 2014.

[10]Chimamanda Adichie, "The Danger of a Single Story," *TED Talk*, October 7, 2009, www youtube.com/watch?v=D9Ihs2417eg.

[11]Ibid.

[12]Christena Cleveland, *Disunity in Christ: Uncovering the Hidden Forces That Keep Us Apart* (Downers Grove, IL: InterVarsity Press, 2013), 21.

[13]Ibid.

[14]Theresa E. Cho, "What's Next PCUSA: Living in the Wilderness," *Still Waters*, February 29, 2012, http://theresaecho.com/2012/02/29/whats-next-pcusa-living-in-the-wilderness.

[15]Theresa Cho, phone interview with the author, September 3, 2014.

[16]Yamaguchi, "From the Palace to the Streets."

[17]Scott Cormode, personal conversation with the author at Fuller Theological Seminary, September 9, 2014.

[18]Dave Gibbons, *The Monkey and the Fish: Liquid Leadership for a Third-Culture Church*, Leadership Network Innovation Series, Kindle ed. (Grand Rapids: Zondervan, 2009), loc. 201-5.

[19]Sheryl Sandberg, *Lean In: Women, Work, and the Will to Lead,* Kindle ed. (New York: Doubleday, 2013), loc. 311-13.

[20]I want to thank my wife, Beth Bolsinger, who conducted interviews with women in ministry leadership in May-July 2013. I also want to thank the following women for generously sharing their expertise and experience: Susan Andrews, Wendy Bailey, Amy Fowler, Robin Garvin, Martha Greene, Liza Hendricks, Jill Hudson, Amy McNelly, Sarah Moore-Nokes, Jane Odell, Kara Powell, Lucy Rupe and Sara Singleton.

[21]Samantha Cole, "Why the Most Successful Organizations Have Women and Millennials in Charge," *Fast Company,* accessed May 27, 2015, www.fastcompany.com/3033950/the -future-of-work/why-the-most-successful-organizations-have-women-and-millennials -in-charg.

[22]Ambrose, *Undaunted Courage,* loc. 6489-92.

[23]Juan Martinez, interview with the author at Fuller Theological Seminary, August 28, 2014.

[24]"Today the palace church suffers because of its palatial instincts. It needs to be trained by people without these palace instincts, most likely people who have never lived in the palace. Where better to find such people than among the immigrants in our midst or those who have long been systematically excluded from the palace?" (Yamaguchi, "Palace to the Streets").

[25]Theresa Cho, interview with the author.

[26]James Davison Hunter, *To Change the World: The Irony, Tragedy, and Possibility of Christianity in the Late Modern World,* Kindle ed. (New York: Oxford University Press, 2010), loc. 598-600.

[27]David Gonzalez, "What's Wrong with 'Hispanic'? Just Ask a Latino," *New York Times,* November 15, 1992, www.nytimes.com/1992/11/15/weekinreview/ideas-trends-what-s -the-problem-with-hispanic-just-ask-a-latino.html.

[28]"In the absence of diverse influences, homogenous group members tend to adopt more extreme and narrow-minded thinking as time passes" (Cleveland, *Disunity in Christ,* 27).

[29]Ibid., 20.

[30]Stephenie Ambrose Tubbs and Clay Jenkinson, *The Lewis and Clark Companion: An Encyclopedic Guide to the Voyage of Discovery* (New York: Henry Holt, 2003), 73-76.

[31]Paul J. DiMaggio and Walter W. Powell, "The Iron Cage Revisited," *American Sociological Review* 48 (April 1983).

[32]Juan Martinez, "Discovering God's Initiative in the Midst of Adaptive Challenge."

[33]Barbara G. Wheeler and Anthony T. Ruger, "Sobering Figures Point to Overall Enrollment Decline," *In Trust,* Spring 2013, www.intrust.org/Portals/39/docs/IT413wheeler .pdf.

[34]Juan Martinez, "It's Already 2040 at a Seminary Near You," *Center for Religion and Civic Culture,* April 2, 2014, http://crcc.usc.edu/blog/news/its-already-2040-at-a-seminary -near-you.

[35]Theresa Cho, interview with the author.

15 THE END OF OUR EXPLORING

[1]John Ordway, cited in Dayton Duncan and Ken Burns, *Lewis and Clark: An Illustrated History* (New York: Knopf, 2012), 166-67.

[2]Meriwether Lewis, cited in Duncan and Burns, *Lewis and Clark*, 166-67.

[3]Stephen E. Ambrose, *Undaunted Courage: Meriwether Lewis, Thomas Jefferson and the Opening of the American West*, Kindle ed. (New York: Simon & Schuster, 2013), loc. 8412-14.

[4]Ibid., loc. 82-86.

[5]Ibid., loc. 6285-88.

[6]Ibid., loc. 7774-79.

[7]Ambrose points out that Lewis was also thinking of the possibilities for engaging the Blackfeet and the Sioux as peaceful allies in what he could see would be a bustling fur-trade endeavor that would only benefit the new nation (ibid., 375-77).

[8]Edwin H. Friedman, *A Failure of Nerve: Leadership in the Age of the Quick Fix*, Kindle ed. (New York: Seabury Books, 2007), loc. 610-11.

[9]Ibid., loc. 690-95.

[10]Ibid., loc. 613-15.

[11]Ibid., loc. 795-800.

[12]Friedman, *Failure of Nerve*, loc. 764-67.

[13]Ibid., loc. 714-15.

[14]Ibid., loc. 740-42 (emphasis added).

[15]Lee G. Bolman and Terrence E. Deal, *How Great Leaders Think: The Art of Reframing* (San Francisco: Jossey-Bass, 2014), 9.

[16]James Emery White, "A Metric That Matters," *Leadership Journal*, July 29, 2014, www .christianitytoday.com/le/2014/august/metric-that-matters.html?start=3&utm_ content=buffer31629&utm_medium=social&utm_source=twitter.com&utm_ campaign=buffer. See also Thom S. Rainer, "#1 Reason for the Decline in Church Atten-dance," *Tom S. Rainer* (blog), August 19, 2013, http://thomrainer.com/2013/08/19 /the-number-one-reason-for-the-decline-in-church-attendance-and-five-ways-to-ad dress-it.

[17]Friedman, *Failure of Nerve*, loc. 769-71 (emphasis added).

[18]Ibid., loc. 664-67.

[19]Ed Stetzer, "InterVarsity 'Derecognized' at California State University's 23 Campuses: Some Analysis and Reflections," *Christianity Today*, September 6, 2014, www.christianity today.com/edstetzer/2014/september/intervarsity-now-derecognized-in-california -state-universit.html. Thanks to Josh Dean and others who responded to a post on my Facebook page on September 6, 2014.

[20]Friedman, *Failure of Nerve*, loc. 3363-78.

[21]Stephen Sandage and Mary Jensen, "Relational Spiritual Formation," *Simon Fraser University Library*, accessed May 27, 2015, http://journals.sfu.ca/rpfs/index.php/rpfs/article/viewFile /268/267.

[22]Ronald Heifetz, *Leadership Without Easy Answers* (Cambridge, MA: Belknap Press of Harvard University Press, 1994), 73.

[23]Jim Collins, "Building Companies to Last," *Jim Collins* (blog), 1995, www.jimcollins.com /article_topics/articles/building-companies.html.

[24]Steve Yamaguchi, interview by the author at Fuller Theological Seminary, August 28, 2014.

[25]"Shoshin," *Wikipedia*, accessed May 27, 2015, http://en.wikipedia.org/wiki/Shoshin. "In the beginner's mind there are many possibilities, in the expert's mind there are few" (Shunryu Suzuki, cited in ibid.).

[26]Ambrose, *Undaunted Courage*, loc. 3685-95.

[27]Jack Uldrich, *Into the Unknown: Leadership Lessons from Lewis and Clark's Daring Westward Expedition*, Kindle ed. (New York: AMACOM, 2004), loc. 1114-16.

[28]Ambrose, *Undaunted Courage*, 458. At least ten years later, Clark gave York his freedom (Duncan and Burns, *Lewis and Clark*, 213).

[29]Thomas Jefferson, in Ambrose, *Undaunted Courage*, 477.

EPILOGUE: TAKING THE HILL WITH GRANDMA

[1]Edwin H. Friedman, *A Failure of Nerve: Leadership in the Age of the Quick Fix*, Kindle ed. (New York: Seabury Books, 2007), loc. 3634.

[2]See "A Profile of Protestant Pastors in Anticipation of 'Pastor Appreciation Month,'" *Barna Group*, September 25, 2001, www.barna.org/barna-update/article/5-barna -update/59-a-profile-of-protestant-pastors-in-anticipation-of-qpastor-appreciation -monthq; and Thom S. Rainer, "How Many Hours Must a Pastor Work to Satisfy a Congregation?" *Thom S. Rainer* (blog), July 24, 2013, http://thomrainer.com/2013/07/24 /how-many-hours-must-a-pastor-work-to-satisfy-the-congregation.

[3]This is true, of course, for all nonprofit leaders. And mostly to the equal detriment of the organizations and the leaders. See Dan Pallotta, *Uncharitable: How Restraints on Nonprofits Undermine Their Potential* (Lebanon, NH: Tufts University Press, 2010).

[4]For a discussion of how even church budgeting needs to be reconsidered in a changing world, see "The Shocking Un-Truth About Church Budgets," *Baptist News Global*, September 5, 2013, www.abpnews.com/opinion/item/8824-the-shocking-un-truth-about -church-budgets?fb_action_ids=10151922777714880&fb_action_types=og.likes&fb_ ref=.UinjiQvqosc.like&fb_source=aggregation&fb_aggregation_id=288381481237582# .UjtAmIakpip. See also Dan Pallotta, "The Way We Think of Charity Is Dead Wrong." *TED Talks*, March 2013, www.ted.com/talks/dan_pallotta_the_way_we_think_about_ charity_is_dead_wrong.html.

[5]Dayton Duncan and Ken Burns, *Lewis and Clark: An Illustrated History* (New York: Knopf, 2012), 6; and Stephenie Ambrose Tubbs and Clay Jenkinson, *The Lewis and Clark Companion: An Encyclopedic Guide to the Voyage of Discovery* (New York: Henry Holt, 2003), 162.

6"Leaders must immerse themselves in the future and practice their skills in a low-risk environment." Bob Johansen, *Leaders Make the Future: Ten New Leadership Skills for an Uncertain World*, Kindle ed. (San Francisco: Berrett-Koehler, 2012), loc. 367.

STUDY GUIDE

1Peter Block, *The Answer to How Is Yes* (San Francisco: Berrett-Koehler, 2003), 21.

IVP PRAXIS

EQUIPPING LEADERS FOR MINISTRY

God has called us to ministry. But it's not enough to have a vision for ministry if you don't have the practical skills for it. Nor is it enough to do the work of ministry if what you do is headed in the wrong direction. We need both vision *and* expertise for effective ministry. We need *praxis*.

Praxis puts theory into practice. It brings cutting-edge ministry expertise from visionary practitioners. You'll find sound biblical and theological foundations for ministry in the real world, with concrete examples for effective action and pastoral ministry. Praxis books are more than the "how to"—they're also the "why to." And because *being* is every bit as important as *doing*, Praxis attends to the inner life of the leader as well as the outer work of ministry. Feed your soul, and feed your ministry.

If you are called to ministry, you know you can't do it on your own. Let Praxis provide the companions you need to equip God's people for life in the kingdom.

www.ivpress.com/praxis